The Magician's Library Volume I

The Magician's Library Volume I
Hermes Trismegistus

COVENSTEAD PRESS
Buffalo, New York

ISBN 978-0-6151-4835-9

Contents:

The Kybalion

By Three Initiates

The Kybalion

A Study of the Hermetic Philosophy of Ancient Egypt and Greece

By Three Initiates

"The Lips of Wisdom are closed, except to the Ears of Understanding."

Originally published by: *The Yogi Publication Society Masonic Temple, Chicago, Illinois, 1912*

To Hermes Trismegistus,
Known by the ancient Egyptians as "The Great Great"
and "Master of Masters," this little volume of Hermetic
Teaching is reverently dedicated.

Contents:

Introduction

We take great pleasure in presenting to the attention of students and investigators of the Secret Doctrines this little work based upon the world-old Hermetic Teachings. There has been so little written upon this subject, not withstanding the countless references to the Teachings in the many works upon occultism, that the many earnest searchers after the Arcane Truths will doubtless welcome the appearance of this present volume.

The purpose of this work is not the enunciation of any special philosophy or doctrine, but rather is to give to the students a statement of the Truth that will serve to reconcile the many bits of occult knowledge that they may have acquired, but which are apparently opposed to each other and which often serve to discourage and disgust the beginner in the study. Our intent is not to erect a new Temple of Knowledge, but rather to place in the hands of the student a Master Key with which he may open the many inner doors in the Temple of Mystery through the main portals he has already entered.

There is no portion of the occult teachings possessed by the world which have been so closely guarded as the fragments of the Hermetic Teachings which have come down to us over the tens of centuries which have elapsed since the lifetime of its great founder, Hermes Trismegistus, the "scribe of the gods," who dwelt in old Egypt in the days when the present race of men was in its infancy. Contemporary with Abraham, and, if the legends be true, an instructor of that venerable sage, Hermes was, and is, the Great Central Sun of Occultism, whose rays have served to illumine the countless teachings which have been promulgated since his time. All the fundamental and basic teachings embedded in the esoteric teachings of every race may be traced back to Hermes. Even the most ancient teachings of India undoubtedly have their roots in the original Hermetic Teachings.

From the land of the Ganges many advanced occultists wandered to the land of Egypt, and sat at the feet of the Master. From him they obtained the Master Key which explained and reconciled their divergent views, and thus the Secret Doctrine was firmly established. From other lands also came the learned ones, all of whom regarded Hermes as the Master of Masters, and his influence was so great that in spite of the many wanderings from the path on the part of the centuries of teachers in these different lands, there may still be found a certain basic resemblance and correspondence which underlies the many and often quite divergent theories entertained and taught by the occultists of these different lands today. The student of Comparative Religions will be able to perceive the influence of the Hermetic Teachings in every religion worthy of the name, now known to man, whether it be a dead religion or one in full vigor in our own times. There is always certain correspondence in spite of the contradictory features, and the Hermetic Teachings act as the Great Reconciler.

The lifework of Hermes Trismegistus seems to have been in the direction of planting the great Seed-Truth which has grown and blossomed in so many strange forms, rather than to establish a school of philosophy which would dominate, the world's thought. But, nevertheless, the original truths taught by him have been kept intact in their original purity by a few men of each age, who, refusing great numbers of half-developed students and followers, followed the Hermetic custom and reserved their truth for the few who were ready to comprehend and master it. From lip to ear the truth has been handed down among the few. There have always been a few Initiates in each generation, in the various lands of the earth, who kept alive the sacred flame of the Hermetic Teachings, and such have always been willing to use their lamps to re-light the lesser lamps of the outside world, when the light of truth grew dim, and clouded by reason of neglect, and when the wicks became clogged with foreign matter. There were always a few to tend faithfully the altar of the Truth, upon which was kept alight the Perpetual Lamp of Wisdom. These men devoted their lives to the labor of love which the poet has so well stated in his lines:

"O, let not the flame die out! Cherished age after age in its dark cavern-in its holy temples cherished. Fed by pure ministers of love-let not the flame die out!"

These men have never sought popular approval, nor numbers of followers. They are indifferent to these things, for they know how few there are in each generation who are ready for the truth, or who would recognize it if it were presented to them. They reserve the "strong meat for men," while others furnish the "milk for babes." They reserve their pearls of wisdom for the few elect, who recognize their value and who wear them in their crowns, instead of casting them before the materialistic vulgar swine, who would trample them in the mud and mix them with their disgusting mental food. But still these men have never forgotten or overlooked the original teachings of Hermes, regarding the passing on of the words of truth to those ready to receive it, which teaching is stated in The Kybalion as follows: *"Where fall the footsteps of the Master, the ears of those ready for his Teaching open wide."* And again: *"When the ears of the student are ready to hear, then cometh the lips to fill them with wisdom."* But their customary attitude has always been strictly in accordance with the other Hermetic aphorism, also in The Kybalion: *"The lips of Wisdom are closed, except to the ears of Understanding."*

There are those who have criticized this attitude of the Hermetists, and who have claimed that they did not manifest the proper spirit in their policy of seclusion and reticence. But a moment's glance back over the pages of history will show the wisdom of the Masters, who knew the folly of attempting to teach to the world that which it was neither ready nor willing to receive. The Hermetists have never sought to be martyrs, and have, instead, sat silently aside with a pitying smile on their closed lips, while the "heathen raged noisily about them" in their customary amusement of putting to death and torture the honest but misguided enthusiasts who imagined that they could force upon a race of barbarians the truth capable of being understood only by the elect who had advanced along The Path.

And the spirit of persecution has not as yet died out in the land. There are certain Hermetic Teachings, which, if publicly promulgated, would bring down upon the teachers a great cry of scorn and revilement from the multitude, who would again raise the cry of "Crucify! Crucify."

In this little work we have endeavored to give you an idea of the fundamental teachings of The Kybalion, striving to give you the working Principles, leaving you to apply them yourselves, rather than attempting to work out the teaching in detail. If you are a true student, you will be able to work out and apply these Principles-if not, then you must develop yourself into one, for otherwise the Hermetic Teachings will be as "words, words, words" to you.

The Three Initiates.

i. The Hermetic Philosophy

"The lips of wisdom are closed, except to the ears of Understanding"
-The Kybalion.

From old Egypt have come the fundamental esoteric and occult teachings which have so strongly influenced the philosophies of all races, nations and peoples, for several thousand years. Egypt, the home of the Pyramids and the Sphinx, was the birthplace of the Hidden Wisdom and Mystic Teachings. From her Secret Doctrine all nations have borrowed. India, Persia, Chaldea, Medea, China, Japan, Assyria, ancient Greece and Rome, and other ancient countries partook liberally at the feast of knowledge which the Hierophants and Masters of the Land of Isis so freely provided for those who came prepared to partake of the great store of Mystic and Occult Lore which the masterminds of that ancient land had gathered together.

In ancient Egypt dwelt the great Adepts and Masters who have never been surpassed, and who seldom have been equaled, during the centuries that have taken their processional flight since the days of the Great Hermes. In Egypt was located the Great Lodge of Lodges of the Mystics. At the doors of her Temples entered the Neophytes who afterward, as Hierophants, Adepts, and Masters, traveled to the four corners of the earth, carrying with them the precious knowledge which they were ready, anxious, and willing to pass on to those who were ready to receive the same. All students of the Occult recognize the debt that they owe to these venerable Masters of that ancient land.

But among these great Masters of Ancient Egypt there once dwelt one of whom Masters hailed as "The Master of Masters." This man, if "man" indeed he was, dwelt in Egypt in the earliest days. He was known as Hermes Trismegistus. He was the father of the Occult

Wisdom; the founder of Astrology; the discoverer of Alchemy. The details of his life story are lost to history, owing to the lapse of the years, though several of the ancient countries disputed with each other in their claims to the honor of having furnished his birthplace- and this thousands of years ago. The date of his sojourn in Egypt, in that his last incarnation on this planet, is not now known, but it has been fixed at the early days of the oldest dynasties of Egypt-long before the days of Moses. The best authorities regard him as a contemporary of Abraham, and some of the Jewish traditions go so far as to claim that Abraham acquired a portion of his mystic knowledge from Hermes himself.

As the years rolled by after his passing from this plane of life (tradition recording that he lived three hundred years in the flesh), the Egyptians deified Hermes, and made him one of their gods, under the name of Thoth. Years after, the people of Ancient Greece also made him one of their many gods -calling him "Hermes, the god of Wisdom." The Egyptians revered his memory for many centuries - yes, tens of centuries- calling him "the Scribe of the Gods," and bestowing upon him, distinctively, his ancient title, "Trismegistus," which means "the thrice-great"; "the great-great"; "the greatest-great"; etc. In all the ancient lands, the name of Hermes Trismegistus was revered, the name being synonymous with the "Fount of Wisdom."

Even to this day, we use the term "hermetic" in the sense of "secret"; "sealed so that nothing can escape"; etc., and this by reason of the fact that the followers of Hermes always observed the principle of secrecy in their teachings. They did not believe in "casting pearls before swine," but rather held to the teaching "milk for babes"; "meat for strong men," both of which maxims are familiar to readers of the Christian scriptures, but both of which had been used by the Egyptians for centuries before the Christian era.

And this policy of careful dissemination of the truth has always characterized the Hermetics, even unto the present day. The Hermetic Teachings are to be found in all lands, among all religions, but never identified with any particular country, nor with any particular religious sect. This because of the warning of the ancient teachers against allowing the Secret Doctrine to become crystallized into a creed. The wisdom of this caution is apparent to all students of history. The ancient occultism of India and Persia degenerated, and was largely lost, owing to the fact that the teachers became priests, and so mixed theology with the philosophy, the result being that the occultism of India and Persia has been gradually lost amidst the mass of religious superstition, cults, creeds and "gods." So it was with Ancient Greece and Rome. So it was with the Hermetic Teachings of the Gnostics and Early Christians, which were lost at the time of Constantine, whose iron hand smothered philosophy with the blanket of theology, losing to the Christian Church that which was its very essence and spirit, and causing it to grope throughout several centuries before it found the way back to its ancient faith, the indications apparent to all careful observers in this Twentieth Century being that the Church is now struggling to get back to its ancient mystic teachings.

But there were always a few faithful souls who kept alive the Flame, tending it carefully, and not allowing its light to become extinguished. And thanks to these staunch hearts, and fearless minds, we have the truth still with us. But it is not found in books, to any great extent. It has been passed along from Master to Student; from Initiate to Hierophant; from lip to ear. When it was written down at all, its meaning was veiled in terms of alchemy and astrology so that only those possessing the key could read it aright. This was made necessary in order to avoid the persecutions of the theologians of the Middle Ages, who fought the Secret Doctrine with fire and sword; stake, gibbet and cross. Even to this day there will be found but few reliable books on the Hermetic Philosophy, although there are countless references to it in many books written on various phases of Occultism. And yet, the Hermetic Philosophy is the only Master Key which will open all the doors of the Occult Teachings!

In the early days, there was a compilation of certain Basic Hermetic Doctrines, passed on from teacher to student, which was known as "**The Kybalion**," the exact significance and meaning of the term having been lost for several centuries. This teaching, however, is known to many to whom it has descended, from mouth to ear, on and on throughout the centuries. Its precepts have never been written down, or printed, so far as we know. It was merely a collection of maxims, axioms, and precepts, which were non-understandable to outsiders, but which were readily understood by students, after the axioms, maxims, and precepts had been explained and exemplified by the Hermetic Initiates to their Neophytes. These teachings really constituted the basic principles of "The Art of Hermetic Alchemy," which, contrary to the general belief, dealt in the mastery of Mental Forces, rather than Material Elements-the Transmutation of one kind of Mental Vibrations into others, instead of the changing of one kind of metal into another. The legends of the "Philosopher's Stone" which would turn base metal into Gold, was an allegory relating to Hermetic Philosophy, readily understood by all students of true Hermeticism.

In this little book, of which this is the First Lesson, we invite our students to examine into the Hermetic Teachings, as set forth in **The Kybalion**, and as explained by ourselves, humble students of the Teachings, who, while bearing the title of Initiates, are still students at the feet of **Hermes,** the Master. We herein give you many of the maxims, axioms and precepts of **The Kybalion**, accompanied by explanations and illustrations which we deem likely to render the teachings more easily comprehended by the modern student, particularly as the original text is purposely veiled in obscure terms.

The original maxims, axioms, and precepts of **The Kybalion** are printed herein, in italics, the proper credit being given. Our own work is printed in the regular way, in the body of the work. We trust that the many students to whom we now offer this little work will derive as much benefit from the study of its pages as have the many who have gone on before, treading the same Path to Mastery throughout the centuries that have passed since the times of **Hermes Trismegistus** -the Master of Masters-the Great-Great. In the words of **The Kybalion**:

"Where fall the footsteps of the Master, the ears of those ready for his Teaching open wide."-The Kybalion.

"When the ears of the student are ready to hear, then cometh the lips to fill them with Wisdom."-The Kybalion.

So that according to the Teachings, the passage of this book to those ready for the instruction will attract the attention of such as are prepared to receive the Teaching. And, likewise, when the pupil is ready to receive the truth, then will this little book come to him, or her. Such is The Law. The Hermetic Principle of Cause and Effect, in its aspect of The Law of Attraction, will bring lips and ear together-pupil and book in company. So mote it be!

ii. The Hermetic Philosophy

The Seven Hermetic Principles

"The Principles of Truth are Seven; he who knows these, understandingly, possesses the Magic Key before whose touch all the Doors of the Temple fly open."-The Kybalion.

The Seven Hermetic Principles, upon which the entire Hermetic Philosophy is based, are as follows:

1. The Principle of Mentalism
2. The Principle of Correspondence
3. The Principle of Vibration
4. The Principle of Polarity
5. The Principle of Rhythm
6. The Principle of Cause and Effect
7. The Principle of Gender

These Seven Principles will be discussed and explained as we proceed with these lessons. A short explanation of each, however, may as well be given at this point.

1. The Principle of Mentalism

*"**The All is Mind**; The Universe is Mental."*-The Kybalion.

This Principle embodies the truth that "All is Mind." It explains that **The All** (which is the Substantial Reality underlying all the outward manifestations and appearances which we know under the terms of "The Material Universe"; the "Phenomena of Life";

"Matter"; "Energy"; and, in short, all that is apparent to our material senses) is **Spirit** which in itself is _Unknowable_ and _Undefinable_, but which may be considered and thought of as **a Universal, Infinite, Living Mind.** It also explains that all the phenomenal world or universe is simply a Mental Creation of **The All**, subject to the Laws of Created Things, and that the universe, as a whole, and in its parts or units, has its existence in the Mind of **The All**, in which Mind we "live and move and have our being." This Principle, by establishing the Mental Nature of the Universe, easily explains all of the varied mental and psychic phenomena that occupy such a large portion of the public attention, and which, without such explanation, are non-understandable and defy scientific treatment. An understanding of this great Hermetic Principle of Mentalism enables the individual to readily grasp the laws of the Mental Universe, and to apply the same to his well-being and advancement. The Hermetic Student is enabled to apply intelligently the great Mental Laws, instead of using them in a haphazard manner. With the Master Key in his possession, the student may unlock the many doors of the mental and psychic temple of knowledge, and enter the same freely and intelligently. This Principle explains the true nature of "Energy," "Power," and "Matter," and why and how all these are subordinate to the Mastery of Mind. One of the old Hermetic Masters wrote, long ages ago: "He who grasps the truth of the Mental Nature of the Universe is well advanced on The Path to Mastery." And these words are as true today as at the time they were first written. Without this Master Key, Mastery is impossible, and the student knocks in vain at the many doors of The Temple.

2. The Principle of Correspondence

  "As above, so below; as below, so above."-The Kybalion.

  This Principle embodies the truth that there is always a Correspondence between the laws and phenomena of the various planes of Being and Life. The old Hermetic axiom ran in these words: "*As above, so below; as below, so above.*" And the grasping of this Principle gives one the means of solving many a dark paradox, and hidden secret of Nature. There are planes beyond our knowing, but when we apply the Principle of Correspondence to them we are able to understand much that would otherwise be unknowable to us. This Principle is of universal application and manifestation, on the various planes of the material, mental, and spiritual universe-it is a Universal Law. The ancient Hermetists considered this Principle as one of the most important mental instruments by which man was able to pry aside the obstacles which hid from view the Unknown. Its use even tore aside the Veil of Isis to the extent that a glimpse of the face of the goddess might be caught. Just as a knowledge of the Principles of Geometry enables man to measure distant suns and their movements, while seated in his observatory, so a knowledge of the Principle of Correspondence enables Man to reason intelligently from the Known to the Unknown. Studying the monad, he understands the archangel.

3. The Principle of Vibration

"*Nothing rests; everything moves; everything vibrates.*"

-The Kybalion.

This Principle embodies the truth that "everything is in motion"; "everything vibrates"; "nothing is at rest"; facts which Modern Science endorses, and which each new scientific discovery tends to verify. And yet this Hermetic Principle was enunciated thousands of years ago, by the Masters of Ancient Egypt. This Principle explains that the differences between different manifestations of Matter, Energy, Mind, and even Spirit, result largely from varying rates of Vibration. From **the** All, which is Pure Spirit, down to the grossest form of Matter, all is in vibration-the higher the vibration, the higher the position in the scale. The vibration of Spirit is at such an infinite rate of intensity and rapidity that it is practically at rest-just as a rapidly moving wheel seems to be motionless. And at the other end of the scale, there are gross forms of matter whose vibrations are so low as to seem at rest. Between these poles, there are millions upon millions of varying degrees of vibration. From corpuscle and electron, atom and molecule, to worlds and universes, everything is in vibratory motion. This is also true on the planes of energy and force (which are but varying degrees of vibration); and also on the mental planes (whose states depend upon vibrations); and even on to the spiritual planes. An understanding of this Principle, with the appropriate formulas, enables Hermetic students to control their own mental vibrations as well as those of others. The Masters also apply this Principle to the conquering of Natural phenomena, in various ways. *"He who understands the Principle of Vibration, has grasped the scepter of power,"* says one of the old writers.

4. The Principle of Polarity

"Everything is Dual; everything has poles; everything has its pair of opposites; like and unlike are the same; opposites are identical in nature, but different in degree; extremes meet; all truths are but half-truths; all paradoxes may be reconciled." -The Kybalion.

This Principle embodies the truth that "everything is dual"; "everything has two poles"; "everything has its pair of opposites," all of which were old Hermetic axioms. It explains the old paradoxes, that have perplexed so many, which have been stated as follows: "Thesis and antithesis are identical in nature, but different in degree"; "opposites are the same, differing only in degree"; "the pairs of opposites may be reconciled"; "extremes meet"; "everything is and isn't, at the same time"; "all truths are but half-truths"; "every truth is half-false"; "there are two sides to everything," etc., etc., etc. It explains that in everything there are two poles, or opposite aspects, and that "opposites" are really only the two extremes of the same thing, with many varying degrees between them. To illustrate: Heat and Cold, although "opposites," are really the same thing, the differences consisting merely of degrees of the same thing. Look at your thermometer and see if you can discover where "heat" terminates and "cold" begins! There is no such thing as "absolute heat" or "absolute cold"-the two terms "heat" and "cold" simply indicate varying degrees of the same thing, and that "same thing" which manifests as "heat" and "cold" is merely a form, variety, and rate of Vibration. So "heat" and "cold" are simply the "two poles" of that which we call "Heat"-and the phenomena attendant thereupon are manifestations of the Principle of Polarity. The same Principle manifests in the case of "Light and Darkness," which are the same thing, the difference consisting of varying degrees between the two poles of the phenomena. Where does "darkness" leave off, and "light" begin? What is the difference between "Large and Small"? Between "Hard and Soft"? Between "Black and White"? Between "Sharp and Dull"? Between "Noise and Quiet"? Between "High and Low"? Between "Positive and Negative"? The Principle of Polarity explains these paradoxes, and no other Principle can supersede it. The same Principle operates on the Mental Plane. Let us take a radical and extreme example-that of "Love and Hate," two mental states apparently totally different. And yet there are degrees of Hate and degrees of Love, and a middle point in which we use the terms "Like or Dislike," which shade into each other so gradually that sometimes we are at a loss to know whether we "like" or "dislike" or "neither." And all are simply degrees of the same thing, as you will see if you will but think a moment. And, more than this (and considered of more importance by the Hermetists), it is possible to change the vibrations of Hate to the vibrations of Love, in one's own mind, and in the minds of others. Many of you, who read these lines, have had personal experiences of the involuntary rapid transition from Love to Hate, and the reverse, in your own case and that of others. And you will therefore realize the possibility of this being accomplished by the use of the Will, by means of the Hermetic formulas. "Good and Evil" are but the poles of the same thing, and the Hermetist understands the art of transmuting Evil into Good, by means of an application of the Principle of Polarity. In short, the "Art of Polarization" becomes a phase of "Mental Alchemy" known and practiced by the ancient and modern Hermetic Masters. An understanding of the Principle will enable one to change his own Polarity, as well as that of others, if he will devote the time and study necessary to master the art.

5. The Principle of Rhythm

"Everything flows, out and in; everything has its tides; all things rise and fall; the pendulum-swing manifests in everything; the measure of the swing to the right is the measure of the swing to the left; rhythm compensates."-The Kybalion.

This Principle embodies the truth that in everything there is manifested a measured motion, to and fro; a flow and inflow; a swing backward and forward; a pendulum-like movement; a tide-like ebb and flow; a high-tide and low-tide; between the two poles which exist in accordance with the Principle of Polarity described a moment ago. There is always an action and a reaction; an advance and a retreat; a rising and a sinking. This is in the affairs of the Universe, suns, worlds, men, animals, mind, energy, and matter. This law is manifest in the creation and destruction of worlds; in the rise and fall of nations; in the life of all things; and finally in the mental states of Man (and it is with this latter that the Hermetists find the understanding of the Principle most important). The Hermetists have grasped this Principle, finding its universal application, and have also discovered certain means to overcome its effects in themselves by the use of the appropriate formulas and methods. They apply the Mental Law of Neutralization. They cannot annul the Principle, or cause it to cease its operation, but they have learned how to escape its effects upon themselves to a certain degree depending upon the Mastery of the Principle. They have learned how to **use** it, instead of being **used by** it. In this and similar methods, consist the Art of the Hermetists. The Master of Hermetics polarizes himself at the point at which he desires to rest, and then neutralizes the Rhythmic swing of the pendulum which would tend to carry him to the other pole. All individuals who have attained any degree of Self-Mastery do this to a certain degree, more or less unconsciously, but the Master does this consciously, and by the use of his Will, and attains a degree of Poise and Mental Firmness almost impossible of belief on the part of the masses who are swung backward and forward like a pendulum. This Principle and that of Polarity have been closely studied by the Hermetists, and the methods of counteracting, neutralizing, and *using* them form an important part of the Hermetic Mental Alchemy.

6. The Principle of Cause and Effect

"Every Cause has its Effect; every Effect has its Cause; everything happens according to Law; Chance is but a name for Law not recognized; there are many planes of causation, but nothing escapes the Law."-The Kybalion.

This Principle embodies the fact that there is a Cause for every Effect; an Effect from every Cause. It explains that: "Everything Happens according to Law"; that nothing ever "merely happens"; that there is no such thing as Chance; that while there are various planes of Cause and Effect, the higher dominating the lower planes, still nothing ever entirely escapes the Law. The Hermetists understand the art and methods of rising above the ordinary plane of Cause and Effect, to a certain degree, and by mentally rising to a higher plane they become Causers instead of Effects. The masses of people are carried along, obedient to environment; the wills and desires of others stronger than themselves; heredity; suggestion; and other outward causes moving them about like pawns on the Chessboard of Life. But the Masters, rising to the plane above, dominate their moods, characters, qualities, and powers, as well as the environment surrounding them, and become Movers instead of pawns. They help to *play the game of life*, instead of being played and moved about by other wills and environment. They *use* the Principle instead of being its tools. The Masters obey the Causation of the higher planes, but they help to *rule* on their own plane. In this statement there is condensed a wealth of Hermetic knowledge-let him read who can.

7. The Principle of Gender

"Gender is in everything; everything has its Masculine and Feminine Principles; Gender manifests on all planes. -The Kybalion.

This Principle embodies the truth that there is **gender** manifested in everything-the Masculine and Feminine Principles ever at work. This is true not only of the Physical Plane, but of the Mental and even the Spiritual Planes. On the Physical Plane, the Principle manifests as SEX, on the higher planes it takes higher forms, but the Principle is ever the same. No creation, physical, mental or spiritual, is possible without this Principle. An understanding of its laws will throw light on many a subject that has perplexed the minds of men. The Principle of Gender works ever in the direction of generation, regeneration, and creation. Everything, and every person, contains the two Elements or Principles, or this great Principle, within it, him or her. Every Male thing has the Female Element also; every Female contains also the Male Principle. If you would understand the philosophy of Mental and Spiritual Creation, Generation, and Re-generation, you must understand and study this Hermetic Principle. It contains the solution of many mysteries of Life. We caution you that this Principle has no reference to the many base, pernicious and degrading lustful theories, teachings and practices, which are taught under fanciful titles, and which are a prostitution of the great natural principle of Gender. Such base revivals of the ancient infamous forms of Phallicism tend to ruin mind, body and soul, and the Hermetic Philosophy has ever sounded the warning note against these degraded teachings which tend toward lust, licentiousness, and perversion of Nature's principles. If you seek such teachings, you must go elsewhere for them-Hermeticism contains nothing for you along these lines. To the pure, all things are pure; to the base, all things are base.

iii. Mental Transmutation

"Mind (as well as metals and elements) may be transmuted from state to state; degree to degree; condition to condition; pole to pole; vibration to vibration. True Hermetic Transmutation is a Mental Art."

-The Kybalion.

As we have stated, the Hermetists were the original alchemists, astrologers, and psychologists, Hermes having been the founder of these schools of thought. From astrology has grown modern astronomy; from alchemy has grown modern chemistry; from the mystic psychology has grown the modern psychology of the schools. But it must not be supposed that the ancients were ignorant of that which the modern schools suppose to be their exclusive and special property. The records engraved on the stones of Ancient Egypt show conclusively that the ancients had a full comprehensive knowledge of astronomy, the very building of the Pyramids showing the connection between their design and the study of astronomical science. Nor were they ignorant of Chemistry, for the fragments of the ancient writings show that they were acquainted with the chemical properties of things; in fact, the ancient theories regarding physics are being slowly verified by the latest discoveries of modern science, notably those relating to the constitution of matter. Nor must it be supposed that they were ignorant of the so-called modern discoveries in psychology-on the contrary, the Egyptians were especially skilled in the science of Psychology, particularly in the branches that the modern schools ignore, but which, nevertheless, are being uncovered under the name of "psychic science" which is perplexing the psychologists of to-day, and making them reluctantly admit that "there may be something in it after all."

The truth is, that beneath the material chemistry, astronomy and psychology (that is, the psychology in its phase of "brain-action") the ancients possessed a knowledge of transcendental astronomy, called astrology; of transcendental chemistry, called alchemy; of transcendental psychology, called mystic psychology. They possessed the Inner Knowledge as well as the Outer Knowledge, the latter alone being possessed by modern scientists. Among the many secret branches of knowledge possessed by the Hermetists, was that known as Mental Transmutation, which forms the subject matter of this lesson.

"Transmutation" is a term usually employed to designate the ancient art of the transmutation of metals-particularly of the base metals into gold. The word "Transmute" means "to change from one nature, form, or substance, into another; to transform" (Webster). And accordingly, "Mental Transmutation" means the art of changing and transforming mental states, forms, and conditions, into others. So you may see that Mental Transmutation is the "Art of Mental Chemistry," if you like the term-a form of practical Mystic Psychology.

But this means far more than appears on the surface. Transmutation, Alchemy, or Chemistry on the Mental Plane is important enough in its effects, to be sure, and if the art stopped there it would still be one of the most important branches of study known to man. But this is only the beginning. Let us see why!

The first of the Seven Hermetic Principles is the Principle of Mentalism, the axiom of which is "**The All** is Mind; the Universe is Mental," which means that the Underlying Reality of the Universe is Mind; and the Universe itself is Mental-that is, "existing in the Mind of **The All**." We shall consider this Principle in succeeding lessons, but let us see the effect of the principle if it be assumed to be true.

If the Universe is Mental in its nature, then Mental Transmutation must be the art of _**changing the conditions of the universe**_, along the lines of Matter, Force and mind. So you see, therefore, that Mental Transmutation is really the "Magic" of which the ancient; writers had so much to say in their mystical works, and about which they gave so few practical instructions. If All be Mental, then the art which enables one to transmute mental conditions must render the Master the controller of material conditions as well as those ordinarily called "mental."

As a matter of fact, none but advanced Mental Alchemists have been able to attain the degree of power necessary to control the grosser physical conditions, such as the control of the elements of Nature; the production or cessation of tempests; the production and cessation of earthquakes and other great physical phenomena. But that such men have existed, and do exist today, is a matter of earnest belief to all advanced occultists of all schools. That the Masters exist, and have these powers, the best teachers assure their students, having had experiences which justify them in such belief and statements. These Masters do not make public exhibitions of their powers, but seek seclusion from the crowds of men, in order to better work their may along the Path of Attainment. We mention their existence, at this point, merely to call your attention to the fact that their power is entirely Mental, and operates along the lines of the higher Mental Transmutation, under the Hermetic Principle of Mentalism.

"The Universe is Mental"-The Kybalion.

But students and Hermetists of lesser degree than Masters-the Initiates and Teachers-are able to freely work along the Mental Plane, in Mental Transmutation. In fact all that we call "psychic phenomena,"; "mental influence"; "mental science"; "new-thought phenomena," etc., operates along the same general lines, for there is but one principle involved, no matter by what name the phenomena be called.

The student and practitioner of Mental Transmutation works among the Mental Plane, transmuting mental conditions, states, etc., into others, according to various formulas, more or less efficacious.

The various "treatments," "affirmations," "denials" etc., of the schools of mental science are but formulas, often quite imperfect and unscientific, of The Hermetic Art. The majority of modern practitioners are quite ignorant compared to the ancient masters, for they lack the fundamental knowledge upon which the work is based.

Not only may the mental states, etc., of one's self be changed or transmuted by Hermetic Methods; but also the states of others may be, and are, constantly transmuted in the same way, usually unconsciously, but often consciously by some understanding the laws and principles, in cases where the people affected are not informed of the principles of self-protection. And more than this, as many students and practitioners of modern mental science know, every material condition depending upon the minds of other people may be changed or transmuted in accordance with the earnest desire, will, and "treatments" of person desiring changed conditions of life. The public are so generally informed regarding these things at present, that we do not deem it necessary to mention the same at length, our purpose at this point being merely to show the Hermetic Principle and Art underlying all of these various forms of practice, good and evil, for the force can be used in opposite directions according to the Hermetic Principles of Polarity.

In this little book we shall state the basic principles of Mental Transmutation, that all who read may grasp the Underlying Principles, and thus possess the Master Key that will unlock the many doors of the Principle of Polarity.

We shall now proceed to a consideration of the first of the Hermetic Seven Principles -the Principle of Mentalism, in which is explained the truth that "**The All** is Mind; the Universe is Mental," in the words of The Kybalion. We ask the close attention, and careful study of this great Principle, on the part of our students, for it is really the Basic Principle of the whole Hermetic Philosophy, and of the Hermetic Art of Mental Transmutation.

iv. The All

"Under, and back of, the Universe of Time, Space and Change, is ever to be found The Substantial Reality-the Fundamental Truth." -The Kybalion.

"Substance" means: "that which underlies all outward manifestations; the essence; the essential reality; the thing in itself," etc. "Substantial" means: "actually existing; being the essential element; being real," etc. "Reality" means: "the state of being real; true, enduring; valid; fixed; permanent; actual," etc.

Under and behind all outward appearances or manifestations, there must always be a Substantial Reality. This is the Law. Man considering the Universe, of which he is a unit, sees nothing but change in matter, forces, and mental states. He sees that nothing really *Is*, but that everything *Is Becoming* and *Changing*. Nothing stands still -everything is being born, growing, dying- the very instant a thing reaches its height, it begins to decline -the law of rhythm is in constant operation-there is no reality, enduring quality, fixity, or substantiality in anything- nothing is permanent but Change. He sees all things evolving from other things, and resolving into other things-constant action and reaction; inflow and outflow; building up and tearing down; creation and destruction; birth, growth and death. Nothing endures but Change. And if he be a thinking man, he realizes that all of these changing things must be but outward appearances or manifestations of some Underlying Power-some Substantial Reality.

All thinkers, in all lands and in all times, have assumed the necessity for postulating the existence of this Substantial Reality. All philosophies worthy of the name have been based upon this thought. Men have given to this Substantial Reality many names-some have called it by the term of Deity (under many titles). Others have called it "The Infinite and Eternal Energy" others have tried to call it "Matter"-but all have acknowledged its existence. It is self-evident. It needs no argument.

In these lessons we have followed the example of some of the world's greatest thinkers, both ancient and modern- the Hermetic. Masters- and have called this Underlying Power-this Substantial Reality-by the Hermetic name of *"The All,"* which term we consider the most comprehensive of the many terms applied by Man to *That* which transcends names and terms.

We accept and teach the view of the great Hermetic thinkers of all times, as well as of those illumined souls who have reached higher planes of being, both of whom assert that the inner nature of **The All** is *unknowable*. This must be so, for naught but **The All** itself can comprehend its own nature and being.

The Hermetists believe and teach that **The All**, "in itself," is and must ever be *unknowable*. They regard all the theories, guesses and speculations of the theologians and metaphysicians regarding the inner nature of **The All**, as but the childish efforts of mortal minds to grasp the secret of the Infinite. Such efforts have always failed and will always fail, from the very nature of the task. One pursuing such inquiries travels around and around in the labyrinth of thought, until he is lost to all sane reasoning, action or conduct, and is utterly unfitted for the work of life. He is like the squirrel which frantically runs around and around the circling treadmill wheel of his cage, traveling ever and yet reaching nowhere-at the end a prisoner still, and standing just where he started.

And still more presumptuous are those who attempt to ascribe to **The All** the personality, qualities, properties, characteristics and attributes of themselves, ascribing to **The All** the human emotions, feelings, and characteristics, even down to the pettiest qualities of mankind, such as jealousy, susceptibility to flattery and praise, desire for offerings and worship, and all the other survivals from the days of the childhood of the race. Such ideas are not worthy of grown men and women, and are rapidly being discarded.

(At this point, it may be proper for me to state that we make a distinction between Religion and Theology-between Philosophy and Metaphysics. Religion, to us, means that intuitional realization of the existence of **The All**, and one's relationship to it; while Theology means the attempts of men to ascribe personality, qualities, and characteristics to it; their theories regarding its affairs, will, desires, plans, and designs, and their assumption of the office of '' middlemen'' between **The All** and the people. Philosophy, to us, means the inquiry after knowledge of things knowable and thinkable; while Metaphysics means the attempt to carry the inquiry over and beyond the boundaries and into regions unknowable and unthinkable, and with the same tendency as that of Theology. And consequently, both Religion and Philosophy mean to us things having roots in Reality, while Theology and Metaphysics seem like broken reeds, rooted in the quicksand of ignorance, and affording naught but the most insecure support for the mind or soul of Man. we do not insist upon our students accepting these definitions-we mention them merely to show our position. At any rate, you shall hear very little about Theology and Metaphysics in these lessons.)

But while the essential nature of **The All** is Unknowable, there are certain truths connected with its existence which the human mind finds itself compelled to accept. An examination of these reports form a proper subject of inquiry, particularly as they agree with the reports of the Illumined on higher planes. And to this inquiry we now invite you.

*"**That** which is the Fundamental Truth-the Substantial Reality-is beyond true naming, but the Wise Men call it **The All**."*

-The Kybalion.

"In its Essence, THE ALL is UNKNOWABLE."-The Kybalion.

"But, the report of Reason must be hospitably received, and treated with respect."-The Kybalion.

The human reason, whose reports we must accept so long as we think at all, informs us as follows regarding **The All**, and that without attempting to remove the veil of the Unknowable:

1. **The All** must be **All** that *Really Is*. There can be nothing existing outside of **The All**, else **The All** would not be **The All**

2. **The All** must be *infinite*, for there is nothing else to define, confine, bound, limit; or restrict **The All**. It must be Infinite in Time, or *eternal*,-it must have always continuously existed, for there is nothing else to have ever created it, and something can never evolve from nothing, and if it had ever "not been," even for a moment, it would not "be" now,-it must continuously exist forever, for there is nothing to destroy it, and it can never "not-be," even for a moment, because something can never become nothing. It must be Infinite in Space-it must be Everywhere, for there is no place outside of **The All** –it cannot be otherwise than continuous in Space, without break, cessation, separation, or interruption, for there is nothing to break, separate, or interrupt its continuity, and nothing with which to "fill in the gaps." It must be Infinite in Power, or Absolute, for there is nothing to limit, restrict, restrain, confine, disturb or condition it-it is subject to no other Power, for there is no other Power.

3. **The All** must be *immutable*, or not subject to change in its real nature, for there is nothing to work changes upon it nothing into which it could change, nor from which it could have changed. It cannot be added to nor subtracted from; increased nor diminished; nor become greater or lesser in any respect whatsoever. It must have **The All** -there has never been, is not now, and never will be, anything else into which it can change.

The All being Infinite, Absolute, Eternal and Unchangeable it must follow that anything finite, changeable, fleeting, and conditioned cannot be **The All**. And as there is Nothing outside of

The All, in Reality, then any and all such finite things must be as Nothing in Reality. Now do not become befogged, nor frightened-we are not trying to lead you into the Christian Science field under cover of Hermetic Philosophy. There is a Reconciliation of this apparently contradictory state of affairs. Be patient, we will reach it in time.

We see around us that which is called "Matter," which forms the physical foundation for all forms. Is **The All** merely Matter? Not at all! Matter cannot manifest Life or Mind, and as Life and Mind are manifested in the Universe, **The All** cannot be Matter, for nothing rises higher than its own source-nothing is ever manifested in an effect that is not in the cause-nothing is evolved as a consequent that is not involved as an antecedent. And then Modern Science informs us that there is really no such thing as Matter-that what we call Matter is merely "interrupted energy or force," that is, energy or force at a low rate of vibration. As a recent writer has said "Matter has melted into Mystery." Even Material Science has abandoned the theory of Matter, and now rests on the basis of "Energy."

Then is **The All** mere Energy or Force? Not Energy or Force as the materialists use the terms, for their energy and force are blind, mechanical things, devoid of Life or Mind. Life and Mind can never evolve from blind Energy or Force, for the reason given a moment ago: "Nothing can rise higher than its source-nothing is evolved unless it is involved-nothing manifests in the effect, unless it is in the cause." And so **The All** cannot be mere Energy or Force, for, if it were, then there would be no such things as Life and Mind in existence, and we know better than that, for we are Alive and using Mind to consider this very question, and so are those who claim that Energy or Force is Everything.

What is there then higher than Matter or Energy that we know to be existent in the Universe? _Life and Mind_! Life and Mind in all their varying degrees of unfoldment! "Then," you ask, "do you mean to tell us that **The All** is **Life** and **Mind**?" Yes! and No! is our answer. If you mean Life and Mind as we poor petty mortals know them, we say No! **The All** is not that! "But what kind of Life and Mind do you mean?" you ask.

The answer is "**Living Mind**," as far above that which mortals know by those words, as Life and Mind are higher than mechanical forces, or matter-*__Infinite living mind__* as compared to finite "Life and Mind." We mean that which the illumined souls mean when they reverently pronounce the word: "**Spirit!**"

" **The All**" is Infinite Living Mind-the Illumined call it SPIRIT!

v. The Mental Universe

*"The Universe is Mental-held in the Mind of **The All**."*

-The Kybalion.

The All is **Spirit**! But what is Spirit? This question cannot be answered, for the reason that its definition is practically that of **The All**, which cannot be explained or defined. Spirit is simply a name that men give to the highest conception of Infinite Living Mind-it means "the Real Essence"-it means Living Mind, as much superior to Life and Mind as we know them, as the latter are superior to mechanical Energy and Matter. Spirit transcends our understanding, and we use the term merely that we may think or speak of **The All**. For the purposes of thought and understanding, we are justified in thinking of Spirit as Infinite Living Mind, at the same time acknowledging that we cannot fully understand it. We must either do this or stop thinking of the matter at all.

Let us now proceed to a consideration of the nature of the Universe, as a whole and in its parts. What is the Universe? We have seen that there can be nothing outside of **The All**. Then is the Universe **The All**? No, this cannot be, because the Universe seems to be made up of *many*, and is constantly changing, and in other ways it does not measure up to the ideas that we are compelled to accept regarding **The All**, as stated in our last lesson. Then if the Universe is not **The All**, then it must be Nothing-such is the inevitable conclusion of the mind at first thought. But this will not satisfy the question, for we are sensible of the existence of the Universe. Then if the Universe is neither **The All**, nor Nothing, what can it be? Let us examine this question.

If the Universe exists at all, or seems to exist, it must proceed in some way from **The All** -it must be a creation of **The All**. But as something can never come from nothing, from what could **The All** have created it. Some philosophers have answered this question by saying that **The All** created the Universe from *itself* -that is, from the being and substance of **The All**. But this will not do, for **The All** cannot be subtracted from, nor divided, as we have seen, and then again if this be so, would not each particle in the Universe be aware of its being **The All - The All** could not lose its knowledge of itself, nor actually **become** an atom, or blind force, or lowly living thing. Some men, indeed, realizing that **The All** is indeed *All*, and also recognizing that they, the men, existed, have jumped to the conclusion that they and **The All** were identical, and they have filled the air with shouts of "I am God," to the amusement of the multitude and the sorrow of sages. The claim of the corpuscle that: "I am Man!" would be modest in comparison.

But, what indeed is the Universe, if it be not **The All**, not yet created by **The All** having separated itself into fragments? What else can it be- of what else can it be made? This is the great question. Let us examine it carefully. We find here that the "Principle of Correspondence" comes to our aid. The old Hermetic axiom, "*As above so below,*" may be pressed into service at this point. Let us endeavor to get a glimpse of the workings on higher planes by examining those on our own. The Principle of Correspondence must apply to this as well as to other problems.

Let us see! On his own plane of being, how does Man create? Well, first, he may create by making something out of outside materials. But this will not do, for there are no materials outside of **The All** with which it may create. Well, then, secondly, Man procreates or reproduces his kind by the process of begetting, which is self-multiplication accomplished by transferring a portion of his substance to his offspring. But this will not do, because **The All** cannot transfer or subtract a portion of itself, nor can it reproduce or multiply itself-in the first place there would be a taking away, and in the second case a multiplication or addition to **The All**, both thoughts being an absurdity. Is there no third way in which **man** creates? Yes, there is-he *creates mentally*! And in so doing he uses no outside materials, nor does he reproduce himself, and yet his Spirit pervades the Mental Creation.

Following the Principle of Correspondence, we are justified in considering that **The All** creates the Universe **Mentally**, in a manner akin to the process whereby Man creates Mental Images. And, here is where the report of Reason tallies precisely with the report of the Illumined, as shown by their teachings and writings. Such are the teachings of the Wise Men. Such was the Teaching of Hermes.

The All can create in no other way except mentally, without either using material (and there is none to use), or else reproducing itself (which is also impossible). There is no escape from this conclusion of the Reason, which, as we have said, agrees with the highest teachings of the Illumined. Just as you, student, may create a Universe of your own in your mentality, so does **The All** create Universes in its own Mentality. But your Universe is the mental creation of a Finite Mind, whereas that of **The All** is the creation of an Infinite. The two are similar in kind, but infinitely different in degree. We shall examine more closely into the process of creation and manifestation as we proceed. But this is the point to fix in your minds at this stage: *The Universe, and all it contains, is a mental creation of The All*. Verily indeed, **All is Mind**!

*"**The All** creates in its Infinite Mind countless Universes, which exist for aeons of Time-and yet, to **The All**, the creation, development, decline and death of a million Universes is as the time of the twinkling of an eye."*

                                        -The Kybalion.

*"The Infinite Mind of **The All** is the womb of Universes."*

                                        -The Kybalion.

The Principle of Gender is manifested on all planes of life, material mental and spiritual. But, as we have said before, "Gender" does not mean "Sex" sex is merely a material manifestation of gender. "Gender" means "relating to generation or creation." And whenever anything is generated or created, on any plane, the Principle of Gender must be manifested. And this is true even in the creation of Universes.

Now do not jump to the conclusion that we are teaching that there is a male and female God, or Creator. That idea is merely a distortion of the ancient teachings on the subject. The true teaching is that **The All**, in itself, is above Gender, as it is above every other Law, including those of Time and Space. It is the Law, from which the Laws proceed, and it is not subject to them. But when **The All** manifests on the plane of generation or creation, then it acts according to Law and Principle, for it is moving on a lower plane of Being. And consequently it manifests the Principle of Gender, in its Masculine and Feminine aspects, on the Mental Plane, of course.

This idea may seem startling to some of you who hear it for the first time, but you have all really passively accepted it in your everyday conceptions. You speak of the Fatherhood of God, and the Motherhood of Nature-of God, the Divine Father, and Nature the Universal Mother-and have thus instinctively acknowledged the Principle of Gender in the Universe. Is this not so?

But, the Hermetic teaching does not imply a real duality- **The All** is **One**-the Two Aspects are merely aspects of manifestation. The teaching is that The Masculine Principle manifested by **The All** stands, in a way, apart from the actual mental creation of the Universe. It projects its Will toward the Feminine Principle (which may be called "Nature") whereupon the latter begins the actual work of the evolution of the Universe, from simple "centers of activity" on to man, and then on and on still higher, all according to well-established and firmly enforced Laws of Nature. If you prefer the old figures of thought, you may think of the Masculine Principle as *God*, the Father, and of the Feminine Principle as *Nature,* the Universal Mother, from whose womb all things have been born. This is more than a mere poetic figure of speech-it is an idea of the actual process of the creation of the Universe. But always remember, that **The All** is but **One**, and that in its Infinite Mind the Universe is generated, created and exists.

It may help you to get the proper idea, if you will apply the Law of Correspondence to yourself, and your own mind. You know that the part of You which you call "I," in a sense, stands apart and witnesses the creation of mental Images in your own mind. The part of your mind in which the mental generation is accomplished may be called the "Me" in distinction from the "I" which stands apart and witnesses and examines the thoughts, ideas and images of the "Me." "As above, so below," remember, and the phenomena of one plane may be employed to solve the riddles of higher or lower planes.

Is it any wonder that You, the child, feel that instinctive reverence for **The All**, which feeling we call "religion"-that respect, and reverence for *The Father Mind*? Is it any wonder that, when you consider the works and wonders of Nature, you are overcome with a mighty feeling which has its roots away down in your inmost being? It is *The Mother Mind* that you are pressing close up to, like a babe to the breast.

Do not make the mistake of supposing that the little world you see around you-the Earth, which is a mere grain of dust in the Universe-is the Universe itself. There are millions upon millions of such worlds, and greater. And there are millions of millions of such Universes in existence within the Infinite Mind of THE ALL. And even in our own little solar system there are regions and planes of life far higher than ours, and beings compared to which we earth-bound mortals are as the slimy life-forms that dwell on the ocean's bed when compared to Man. There are beings with powers and attributes higher than Man has ever dreamed of the gods' possessing. And yet these beings were once as you, and still lower-and you will be even as they, and still higher, in time, for such is the Destiny of Man as reported by the Illumined.

And Death is not real, even in the Relative sense-it is but Birth to a new life-and You shall go on, and on, and on, to higher and still higher planes of life, for aeons upon aeons of time. The Universe is your home, and you shall explore its farthest recesses before the end of Time. You are dwelling in the Infinite Mind of **The All**, and your possibilities and opportunities are infinite, both in time and space. And at the end of the Grand Cycle of Aeons, when **The All** shall draw back into itself all of its creations-you will go gladly for you will then be able to know the Whole Truth of being At One with **The All**. Such is the report of the Illumined-those who have advanced well along The Path.

And, in the meantime, rest calm and serene-you are safe and protected by the Infinite Power of ***The Father-Mother Mind.***

"Within the Father-Mother Mind, mortal children are at home."

-The Kybalion.

"There is not one who is Fatherless, nor Motherless in the Universe."

-The Kybalion.

vi. The Divine Paradox

"The half-wise, recognizing the comparative unreality of the Universe, imagine that they may defy its Laws—such are vain and presumptuous fools, and they are broken against the rocks and torn asunder by the elements by reason of their folly. The truly wise, knowing the nature of the Universe, use Law against laws; the higher against the lower; and by the Art of Alchemy transmute that which is undesirable into that which is worthy, and thus triumph. Mastery consists not in abnormal dreams, visions and fantastic imaginings or living, but in using the higher forces against the lower —escaping the pains of the lower planes by vibrating on the higher. Transmutation, not presumptuous denial, is the weapon of the Master."

-The Kybalion.

This is the Paradox of the Universe, resulting from the Principle of Polarity which manifests when **The All** begins to Create -hearken to it for it points the difference between half-wisdom and wisdom. While to **The Infinite All**, the Universe, its Laws, its Powers, its life, its Phenomena, are as things witnessed in the state of Meditation or Dream; yet to all that is Finite, the Universe must be treated as Real, and life, and action, and thought, must be based thereupon, accordingly, although with an ever understanding of the Higher Truth. Each according to its own Plane and Laws. Were **The All** to imagine that the Universe were indeed Reality, then woe to the Universe, for there would be then no escape from lower to higher, divineward-then would the Universe become a fixity and progress would become impossible. And if Man, owing to half-wisdom, acts and lives and thinks of the Universe as merely a dream (akin to his own finite dreams) then indeed does it so become for him, and like a sleep-walker he stumbles ever around and around in a circle, making no progress, and being forced into an awakening at last by his falling bruised and bleeding over the Natural Laws which he ignored. Keep your mind ever on the Star, but let your eyes watch over your footsteps, lest you fall into the mire by reason of your upward gaze. Remember the Divine Paradox, that while the Universe **IS NOT**, still **IT IS**. Remember ever the Two Poles of Truth the Absolute and the Relative. Beware of Half-Truths.

What Hermetists know as "the Law of Paradox" is an aspect of the Principle of Polarity. The Hermetic writings are filled with references to the appearance of the Paradox in the consideration of the problems of Life and Being. The Teachers are constantly warning their students against the error of omitting the "other side" of any question. And their warnings are particularly directed to the problems of the Absolute and the Relative, which perplex all students of philosophy, and which cause so many to think and act contrary to what is generally known as "common sense." And we caution all students to be sure to grasp the Divine Paradox of the Absolute and Relative, lest they become entangled in the mire of the Half-Truth. With this in view this particular lesson has been written. Read it carefully!

The first thought that comes to the thinking man after he realizes the truth that the Universe is a Mental Creation of **The All**, is that the Universe and all that it contains is a mere illusion; an unreality; against which idea his instincts revolt. But this, like all other great truths, must be considered both from the Absolute and the Relative points of view. From the Absolute viewpoint, of course, the Universe is in the nature of an illusion, a dream, a phantasmagoria, as compared to **The All** in itself. We recognize this even in our ordinary view, for we speak of the world as "a fleeting show" that comes and goes, is born and dies-for the element of impermanence and change, finiteness and unsubstantiality, must ever be connected with the idea of a created Universe when it is contrasted with the idea of **The All,** no matter what may be our beliefs concerning the nature of both.

Philosopher, metaphysician, scientist and theologian all agree upon this idea, and the thought is found in all forms of philosophical thought and religious conceptions, as well as in the theories of the respective schools of metaphysics and theology.

So, the Hermetic Teachings do not preach the unsubstantiality of the Universe in any stronger terms than those more familiar to you, although their presentation of the subject may seem somewhat more startling. Anything that has a beginning and an ending must be, in a sense, unreal and untrue, and the Universe comes under the rule, in all schools of thought. From the Absolute point of view, there is nothing Real except **The All**, no matter what terms we may use in thinking of, or discussing the subject. Whether the Universe be created of Matter, or whether it be a Mental Creation in the Mind of **The All** -it is unsubstantial, non-enduring, a thing of time, space and change. We want you to realize this fact thoroughly, before you pass judgment on the Hermetic conception of the Mental nature of the Universe. Think over any and all of the other conceptions, and see whether this be not true of them.

But the Absolute point of view shows merely one side of the picture-the other side is the Relative one. Absolute Truth has been defined as "Things as the mind of God knows them," while Relative Truth is "Things as the highest reason of Man understands them." And so while to **The All** the Universe must be unreal and illusionary, a mere dream or result of meditation,-nevertheless, to the finite minds forming a part of that Universe, and viewing it through mortal faculties, the Universe is very real indeed, and must be so considered. In recognizing the Absolute view, we must not make the mistake of ignoring or denying the facts and phenomena of the Universe as they present themselves to our mortal faculties-we are not **The All**, remember.

To take familiar illustrations, we all recognize the fact that matter "exists" to our senses-we will fare badly if we do not. And yet, even our finite minds understand the scientific dictum that there is no such thing as Matter from a scientific point of view-that which we call Matter is held to be merely an aggregation of atoms, which atoms themselves are merely a grouping of units of force, called electrons or "ions," vibrating and in constant circular motion. We kick a stone and we feel the impact-it seems to be real, notwithstanding that we know it to be merely what we have stated above. But remember that our foot, which feels the impact by means of our brains, is likewise Matter, so constituted of electrons, and for that matter so are our brains. And, at the best, if it were not by reason of our Mind, we would not know the foot or stone at all.

Then again, the ideal of the artist or sculptor, which he is endeavoring to reproduce in stone or on canvas, seems very real to him. So do the characters in the mind of the author; or dramatist, which he seeks to express so that others may recognize them. And if this be true in the case of our finite minds, what must be the degree of Reality in the Mental Images created in the Mind of the Infinite? Oh, friends, to mortals this Universe of Mentality is very real indeed-it is the only one we can ever know, though we rise from plane to plane, higher and higher in it. To know it otherwise, but actual experience, we must be **The All** itself. It is true that the higher we rise in the scale-the nearer to "the mind of the Father" we reach-the more apparent becomes the illusory nature of finite things, but not until **The All** finally withdraws us into itself does the vision actually vanish.

So, we need not dwell upon the feature of illusion. Rather let us, recognizing the real nature of the Universe, seek to understand its mental laws, and endeavor to use them to the best effect in our upward progress through life, as we travel from plane to plane of being. The Laws of the Universe are none the less "Iron Laws" because of the mental nature. All, except **The All**, are bound by them. What is **In The Infinite Mind of The All** is **Real** in a degree second only to that Reality itself which is vested in the nature of **The All**.

So, do not feel insecure or afraid-we are all **held firmly in The Infinite Mind of The All**, and there is naught to hurt us or for us to fear. There is no Power outside of **The All** to affect us. So we may rest calm and secure. There is a world of comfort and security in this realization when once attained. Then "calm and peaceful do we sleep, rocked in the Cradle of the Deep"-resting safely on the bosom of the Ocean of Infinite Mind, which is **The All**. In **The All**, indeed, do "we live and move and have our being."

Matter is none the less Matter to us, while we dwell on the plane of Matter, although we know it to be merely an aggregation of "electrons," or particles of Force, vibrating rapidly and gyrating around each other in the formations of atoms; the atoms in turn vibrating and gyrating, forming molecules, which latter in turn form larger masses of Matter. Nor does Matter become less Matter, when we follow the inquiry still further, and learn from the Hermetic Teachings, that the "Force" of which the electrons are but units is merely a manifestation of the Mind of **The All**, and like all else in the Universe is purely Mental in its nature. While on the Plane of matter, we must recognize its phenomena- we may control Matter (as all Masters of higher or lesser degree do), but we do so by applying the higher forces. We commit a folly when we attempt to deny the existence of Matter in the relative aspect. We may deny its mastery over us-and rightly so-but we should not attempt to ignore it in its relative aspect, at least so long as we dwell upon its plane.

Nor do the Laws of Nature become less constant or effective, when we know them, likewise, to be merely mental creations. They are in full effect on the various planes. We overcome the lower laws, by applying still higher ones-and in this way only. But we cannot escape Law or rise above it entirely. Nothing but **The All** can escape Law-and that because **The All** is **Law** itself, from which all Laws emerge. The most advanced Masters may acquire the powers usually attributed to the gods of men; and there are countless ranks of being, in the great hierarchy of life, whose being and power transcends even that of the highest Masters among men to a degree unthinkable by mortals, but even the highest Master, and the highest Being, must bow to the Law, and be as Nothing in the eye of **The All**. So that if even these highest Beings, whose powers exceed even those attributed by men to their gods-if even these are bound by and are subservient to Law, then imagine the presumption of mortal man, of our race and grade, when he dares to consider the Laws of Nature as "unreal!" visionary and illusory, because he happens to be able to grasp the truth that the Laws are Mental in nature, and simply Mental Creations of **The All**. Those Laws which **The All** intends to be governing Laws are not to be defied or argued away. So long as the Universe endures, will they endure-for the Universe exists by virtue of these Laws which form its framework and which hold it together.

The Hermetic Principle of Mentalism, while explaining the true nature of the Universe upon the principle that all is Mental, does not change the scientific conceptions of the Universe, Life, or Evolution. In fact, science merely corroborates the Hermetic Teachings. The latter merely teaches that the nature of the Universe is "Mental," while modern science has taught that it is "Material"; or (of late) that it is "Energy" at the last analysis. The Hermetic Teachings have no fault to find with Herbert Spencer's basic principle which postulates the existence of an "Infinite and Eternal Energy, from which all things proceed." In fact, the Hermetics recognize in Spencer's philosophy the highest outside statement of the workings of the Natural Laws that have ever been promulgated, and they believe Spencer to have been a reincarnation of an ancient philosopher who dwelt in ancient Egypt thousands of years ago, and who later incarnated as Heraclitus, the Grecian philosopher who lived B. C.

500. And they regard his statement of the "Infinite and Eternal Energy" as directly in the line of the Hermetic Teachings, always with the addition of their own doctrine that his "Energy" is the Energy of the Mind of **The All**. With the Master Key of the Hermetic Philosophy, the student of Spencer will be able to unlock many doors of the inner philosophical conceptions of the great English philosopher, whose work shows the results of the preparation of his previous incarnations. His teachings regarding Evolution and Rhythm are in almost perfect agreement with the Hermetic Teachings regarding the Principle of Rhythm.

So, the student of Hermetics need not lay aside any of his cherished scientific views regarding the Universe. All he is asked to do is to grasp the underlying principle of " **The All** is Mind; the Universe is Mental-held in the mind of **The All**." He will find that the other six of the Seven Principles will "fit into" his scientific knowledge, and will serve to bring out obscure points and to throw light in dark corners. This is not to be wondered at, when we realize the influence of the Hermetic thought of the early philosophers of Greece, upon whose foundations of thought the theories of modern science largely rest. The acceptance of the First Hermetic Principle (Mentalism) is the only great point of difference between Modern Science and Hermetic students, and Science is gradually moving toward the Hermetic position in its groping in the dark for a way out of the Labyrinth into which it has wandered in its search for Reality.

The purpose of this lesson is to impress upon the minds of our students the fact that, to all intents and purposes, the Universe and its laws, and its phenomena, are just as **Real**, so far as Man is concerned, as they would be under the hypotheses of Materialism or Energism. Under any hypothesis the Universe in its outer aspect is changing, ever-flowing, and transitory-and therefore devoid of substantiality and reality. But (note the other pole of the truth) under the same hypotheses, we are compelled to **Act and Live** as if the fleeting things were real and substantial. With this difference, always, between the various hypotheses-that under the old views Mental Power was ignored as a Natural Force, while under Mentalism it becomes the Greatest Natural Force. And this one difference revolutionizes Life, to those who understand the Principle and its resulting laws and practice.

So, finally, students all, grasp the advantage of Mentalism, and learn to know, use and apply the laws resulting therefrom. But do not yield to the temptation which, as The Kybalion states, overcomes the half-wise and which causes them to be hypnotized by the apparent unreality of things, the consequence being that they wander about like dream-people dwelling in a world of dreams, ignoring the practical work and life of man, the end being that "they are broken against the rocks and torn asunder by the elements, by reason of their folly." Rather follow the example of the wise, which the same authority states, "use Law against Laws; the higher against the lower; and by the Art of Alchemy transmute that which is undesirable into that which is worthy, and thus triumph." Following the authority, let us avoid the half-wisdom (which is folly) which ignores the truth that: "Mastery consists not in abnormal dreams, visions, and fantastic imaginings or living, but in using the higher forces against the lower-escaping the pains of the lower planes by vibrating on the higher." Remember always, student, that "Transmutation, not presumptuous denial, is the weapon of the Master." The above quotations are from The Kybalion, and are worthy of being committed to memory by the student.

We do not live in a world of dreams, but in an Universe which while relative, is real so far as our lives and actions are concerned. Our business in the Universe is not to deny its existence, but to **live**, using the Laws to rise from lower to higher-living on, doing the best that we can under the circumstances arising each day, and living, so far as is possible, to our biggest ideas and ideals. The true Meaning of Life is not known to men on this plane, if, indeed, to any but the highest authorities, and our own intuitions, teach us that we will make no mistake in living up to the best that is in us, so far as is possible, and realizing the Universal tendency in the same direction in spite of apparent evidence to the contrary. We are all on The Path-and the road leads upward ever, with frequent resting places.

Read the message of The Kybalion-and follow the example of "the wise"-avoiding the mistake of "the half-wise" who perish by reason of their folly.

vii. The All in All

*"While All is in **The All**, it is equally true that **The All** is in All. To him who truly understands this truth hath come great knowledge."* -The Kybalion.

How often have the majority of people heard repeated the statement that their Deity (called by many names) was "All in All" and how little have they suspected the inner occult truth concealed by these carelessly uttered words? The commonly used expression is a survival of the ancient Hermetic Maxim quoted above. As the Kybalion says: *"To him who truly understands this truth, hath come great knowledge."* And, this being so, let us seek this truth, the understanding of which means so much. In this statement of truth-this Hermetic Maxim-is concealed one of the greatest philosophical, scientific and religious truths.

We have given you the Hermetic Teaching regarding the Mental Nature of the Universe-the truth that "the Universe is Mental-held in the Mind of **The All**." As the Kybalion says, in the passage quoted above: "All is in **The All**." But note also the co-related statement, that: "It is equally true that **The All** is in All." This apparently contradictory statement is reconcilable under the Law of Paradox. It is, moreover, an exact Hermetic statement of the relations existing between **The All** and its Mental Universe. We have seen how "All is in **The All** "-now let us examine the other aspect of the subject.

The Hermetic Teachings are to the effect that **The All** is Imminent in ("remaining within; inherent; abiding within") its Universe, and in every part, particle, unit, or combination, within the Universe. This statement is usually illustrated by the Teachers by a reference to the Principle of Correspondence. The Teacher instructs the student to form a Mental Image of something, a person, an idea, something having a mental form, the favorite example being that of the author or dramatist forming an idea of his characters; or a painter or sculptor forming an image of an ideal that he wishes to express by his art. In each case, the student will find that while the image has its existence, and being, solely within his own mind, yet he, the student, author, dramatist, painter, or sculptor, is, in a sense, immanent in; remaining within; or abiding within, the mental image also. In other words, the entire virtue, life, spirit, of reality in the mental image is derived from the "immanent mind" of the thinker. Consider this for a moment, until the idea is grasped.

To take a modern example, let us say that Othello, Iago, Hamlet, Lear, Richard III, existed merely in the mind of Shakespeare, at the time of their conception or creation. And yet, Shakespeare also existed within each of these characters, giving them their vitality, spirit, and action. Whose is the "spirit" of the characters that we know as Micawber, Oliver Twist, Uriah Heep-is it Dickens, or have each of these characters a personal spirit, independent of their creator? Have the Venus of Medici, the Sistine Madonna, the Apollo Belvidere, spirits and reality of their own, or do they represent the spiritual and mental power of their creators? The Law of Paradox explains that both propositions are true, viewed from the proper viewpoints. Micawber is both Micawber, and yet Dickens. And, again, while Micawber may be said to be Dickens, yet Dickens is not identical with Micawber. Man, like Micawber, may exclaim: "The Spirit of my Creator is inherent within me- and yet I am not *He*!" How different this from the shocking half-truth so vociferously announced by certain of the half-wise, who fill the air with their raucous cries of: "I am God!" Imagine poor Micawber, or the sneaky Uriah Heep, crying: "I Am Dickens"; or some of the lowly clods in one of Shakespeare's plays, eloquently announcing that: "I Am Shakespeare!" **The All** is in the earthworm, and yet the earth-worm is far from being **The All**. And still the wonder remains, that though the earth-worm exists merely as a lowly thing, created and having its being solely within the Mind of **The All** -yet **The All** is immanent in the earthworm, and in the particles that go to make up the earthworm. Can there be any greater mystery than this of "All in **The All**; and **The All** in All?"

The student will, of course, realize that the illustrations given above are necessarily imperfect and inadequate, for they represent the creation of mental images in finite minds, while the Universe is a creation of Infinite Mind-and the difference between the two poles separates them. And yet it is merely a matter of degree-the same Principle is in operation-the Principle of Correspondence manifests in each-"As above, so Below; as Below, so above."

And, in the degree that Man realizes the existence of the Indwelling Spirit immanent within his being, so will he rise in the spiritual scale of life. This is what spiritual development means-the recognition, realization, and manifestation of the Spirit within us. Try to remember this last definition-that of spiritual development. It contains the Truth of True Religion.

There are many planes of Being-many sub-planes of Life-many degrees of existence in the Universe. And all depend upon the advancement of beings in the scale, of which scale the lowest point is the grossest matter, the highest being separated only by the thinnest division from the **Spirit** of **The All**. And, upward and onward along this Scale of Life, everything is moving. All are on the Path, whose end is **The All**. All progress is a Returning Home. All is Upward and Onward, in spite of all seemingly contradictory appearances. Such is the message of the Illumined.

The Hermetic Teachings concerning the process of the Mental Creation of the Universe, are that at the beginning of the Creative Cycle, **The All**, in its aspect of Being, projects its Will toward its aspect of "Becoming" and the process of creation begins. It is taught that the process consists of the lowering of Vibration until a very low degree of vibratory energy is reached, at which point the grossest possible form of Matter is manifested. This process is called the stage of Involution, in which **The All** becomes "involved," or "wrapped up," in its creation. This process is believed by the Hermetists to have a Correspondence to the mental process of an artist, writer, or inventor, who becomes so wrapped up in his mental creation as to almost forget his own existence and who, for the time being, almost "lives in his creation," If instead of "wrapped" we use the word "rapt," perhaps we will give a better idea of what is meant.

This Involuntary stage of Creation is sometimes called the "Outpouring" of the Divine Energy, just as the Evolutionary state is called the "Indrawing." The extreme pole of the Creative process is considered to be the furthest removed from **The All**, while the beginning of the Evolutionary stage is regarded as the beginning of the return swing of the pendulum of Rhythm-a "coming home" idea being held in all of the Hermetic Teachings.

The Teachings are that during the "Outpouring," the vibrations become lower and lower until finally the urge ceases, and the return swing begins. But there is this difference, that while in the "Outpouring" the creative forces manifest compactly and as a whole, yet from the beginning of the Evolutionary or "Indrawing" stage, there is manifested the Law of Individualization-that is, the tendency to separate into Units of Force, so that finally that which left **The All** as unindividualized energy returns to its source as countless highly developed Units of Life, having risen higher and higher in the scale by means of Physical, Mental and Spiritual Evolution.

The ancient Hermetists use the word "Meditation" in describing the process of the mental creation of the Universe in the Mind of **The All**, the word "Contemplation" also being frequently employed. But the idea intended seems to be that of the employment of the Divine Attention. "Attention" is a word derived from the Latin root, meaning "to reach out; to stretch out," and so the act of Attention is really a mental "reaching out; extension" of mental energy, so that the underlying idea is readily understood when we examine into the real meaning of "Attention."

The Hermetic Teachings regarding the process of Evolution are that, **The All**, having meditated upon the beginning of the Creation-having thus established the material foundations of the Universe-having thought it into existence-then gradually awakens or rouses from its Meditation and in so doing starts into manifestation the process of Evolution, on the material mental and spiritual planes, successively and in order. Thus the upward movement begins-and all begins to move Spiritward. Matter becomes less gross; the Units spring into being; the combinations begin to form; Life appears and manifests in higher and higher forms; and Mind becomes more and more in evidence-the vibrations constantly becoming higher. In short, the entire process of Evolution, in all of its phases, begins, and proceeds according to the established "Laws of the Indrawing" process. All of this occupies aeons upon aeons of Man's time, each aeon containing countless millions of years, but yet the Illumined inform us that the entire creation, including Involution and Evolution, of an Universe, is but "as the twinkle of the eye" to **The All**. At the end of countless cycles of aeons of time, **The All** withdraws its Attention-its Contemplation and Meditation-of the Universe, for the Great Work is finished-and All is withdrawn into **The All** from which it emerged. But Mystery of Mysteries-the Spirit of each soul is not annihilated, but is infinitely expanded-the Created and the Creator are merged. Such is the report of the Illumined!

The above illustration of the "meditation," and subsequent "awakening from meditation," of **The All**, is of course but an attempt of the teachers to describe the Infinite process by a finite example. And, yet: "As Below, so Above." The difference is merely in degree. And just as **The All** arouses itself from the meditation upon the Universe, so does Man (in time) cease from manifesting upon the Material Plane, and withdraws himself more and more into the Indwelling Spirit, which is indeed "The Divine Ego."

There is one more matter of which we desire to speak in this lesson, and that comes very near to an invasion of the Metaphysical field of speculation, although our purpose is merely to show the futility of such speculation. We allude to the question which inevitably comes to the mind of all thinkers who have ventured to seek the Truth. The question is: "*Why* does **The All** create Universes?" The question may be asked in different forms, but the above is the gist of the inquiry.

Men have striven hard to answer this question, but still there is no answer worthy of the name. Some have imagined that **The All** had something to gain by it, but this is absurd, for what could **The All** gain that it did not already possess? Others have sought the answer in the idea that **The All** "wished something to love" and others that it created for pleasure, or amusement; or because it "was lonely" or to manifest its power;-all puerile explanations and ideas, belonging to the childish period of thought.

Others have sought to explain the mystery by assuming that **The All** found itself "compelled" to create, by reason of its own "internal nature"-its "creative instinct." This idea is in advance of the others, but its weak point lies in the idea of **The All** being "compelled" by anything, internal or external. If its "internal nature," or "creative instinct," compelled it to do anything, then the "internal nature" or "creative instinct" would be the Absolute, instead of **The All**, and so accordingly that part of the proposition falls. And, yet, **The All** does create and manifest, and seems to find some kind of satisfaction in so doing. And it is difficult to escape the conclusion that in some infinite degree it must have what would correspond to an "inner nature," or "creative instinct," in man, with correspondingly infinite Desire and Will. It could not act unless it Willed to Act; and it would not Will to Act, unless it Desired to Act and it would not Desire to

Act unless it obtained some Satisfaction thereby. And all of these things would belong to an "Inner Nature," and might be postulated as existing according to the Law of Correspondence. But, still, we prefer to think of **The All** as acting entirely *free* from any influence, internal as well as external. That is the problem which lies at the root of difficulty-and the difficulty that lies at the root of the problem.

Strictly speaking, there cannot be said to be any "Reason" whatsoever for **The All** to act, for a "reason" implies a "cause," and **The All** is above Cause and Effect, except when it Wills to become a Cause, at which time the Principle is set into motion. So, you see, the matter is Unthinkable, just as **The All** is Unknowable. Just as we say **The All** merely "**IS**"-so we are compelled to say that "**The All acts because It acts**." At the last, **The All** is All Reason in Itself; All Law in Itself; All Action in Itself-and it may be said, truthfully, that **The All** is Its Own Reason; its own Law; its own Act-or still further, that **The All**; Its Reason; Its Act; is Law; are ONE, all being names for the same thing. In the opinion of those who are giving you these present lessons, the answer is locked up in the **Inner Self** of **The All**, along with its Secret of Being. The Law of Correspondence, in our opinion, reaches only to that aspect of **The All**, which may be spoken of as "The Aspect of **Becoming**." Back of that Aspect is "The Aspect of **Being**" in which all Laws are lost in *Law* all Principles merge into *Principle*-and **The All**; *Principle*; and *Being*; are **identical**, **One and The Same**. Therefore, Metaphysical speculation on this point is futile. We go into the matter here, merely to show that we recognize the question, and also the absurdity of the ordinary answers of metaphysics and theology.

In conclusion, it may be of interest to our students to learn that while some of the ancient, and modern, Hermetic Teachers have rather inclined in the direction of applying the Principle of Correspondence to the question, with the result of the "Inner Nature" conclusion,-still the legends have it that **Hermes,** the Great, when asked this question by his advanced students, answered them by ***pressing his lips tightly together*** and saying not a word, indicating that there ***was no answer***. But, then, he may have intended to apply the axiom of his philosophy, that: "The lips of Wisdom are closed, except to the ears of Understanding," believing that even his advanced students did not possess the Understanding which entitled them to the Teaching. At any rate, if Hermes possessed the Secret, he failed to impart it, and so far as the world is concerned ***The Lips of Hermes are Closed*** regarding it. And where the Great Hermes hesitated to speak, what mortal may dare to teach?

But, remember, that whatever be the answer to this problem, if indeed there be an answer the truth remains that: "While All is in **The All**, it is equally true that **The All** is in All." The Teaching on this point is emphatic. And, we may add the concluding words of the quotation: "To him who truly understands this truth, hath come great knowledge."

viii. Planes of Correspondence

"As above, so below; as below, so above."-The Kybalion.

The great Second Hermetic Principle embodies the truth that there is a harmony, agreement, and correspondence between the several planes of Manifestation, Life and Being. This truth is a truth because all that is included in the Universe emanates from the same source, and the same laws, principles, and characteristics apply to each unit, or combination of units, of activity, as each manifests its own phenomena upon its own plane.

For the purpose of convenience of thought and study, the Hermetic Philosophy considers that the Universe may be divided into three great classes of phenomena, known as the Three Great Planes, namely:

1. The Great Physical Plane
2. The Great Mental Plane
3. The Great Spiritual Plane

These divisions are more or less artificial and arbitrary, for the truth is that all of the three divisions are but ascending degrees of the great scale of Life, the lowest point of which is undifferentiated Matter, and the highest point that of Spirit. And, moreover, the different Planes shade into each other, so that no hard and fast division may be made between the higher phenomena of the Physical and the lower of the Mental; or between the higher of the Mental and the lower of the Physical.

In short, the Three Great Planes may be regarded as three great groups of degrees of Life Manifestation. While the purposes of this little book do not allow us to enter into an extended discussion of, or explanation of, the subject of these different planes, still we think it well to give a general description of the same at this point.

At the beginning we may as well consider the question so often asked by the neophyte, who desires to be informed regarding the meaning of the word "Plane", which term has been very freely used, and very poorly explained, in many recent works upon the subject of occultism. The question is generally about as follows: "Is a Plane a place having dimensions, or is it merely a condition or state?" We answer: "No, not a place, nor ordinary dimension of space; and yet more than a state or condition. It may be considered as a state or condition, and yet the state or condition is a degree of dimension, in a scale subject to measurement." Somewhat paradoxical, is it not? But let us examine the matter. A "dimension," you know, is "a measure in a straight line, relating to measure," etc. The ordinary dimensions of space are length, breadth, and height, or perhaps length, breadth, height, thickness or circumference. But there is another dimension of "created things" or "measure in a straight line," known to occultists, and to scientists as well, although the latter have not as yet applied the term "dimension" to it-and this new dimension, which, by the way, is the much speculated -about "Fourth Dimension," is the standard used in determining the degrees or "planes."

This Fourth Dimension may be called "The Dimension of Vibration" It is a fact well known to modern science, as well as to the Hermetists who have embodied the truth in their "Third Hermetic Principle," that "everything is in motion; everything vibrates; nothing is at rest." From the highest manifestation, to the lowest, everything and all things Vibrate. Not only do they vibrate at different rates of motion, but as in different directions and in a different manner. The degrees of the rate of vibrations constitute the degrees of measurement on the Scale of Vibrations-in other words the degrees of the Fourth Dimension. And these degrees form what occultists call "Planes" The higher the degree of rate of vibration, the higher the plane, and the higher the manifestation of Life occupying that plane. So that while a plane is not "a place," nor yet "a state or condition," yet it possesses qualities common to both. We shall have more to say regarding the subject of the scale of Vibrations in our next lessons, in which we shall consider the Hermetic Principle of Vibration.

You will kindly remember, however, that the Three Great Planes are not actual divisions of the phenomena of the Universe, but merely arbitrary terms used by the Hermetists in order to aid in the thought and study of the various degrees and Forms of universal activity and life. The atom of matter, the unit of force, the mind of man, and the being of the arch -angel are all but degrees in one scale, and all fundamentally the same, the difference between solely a matter of degree, and rate of vibration-all are creations of **The All**, and have their existence solely within the Infinite Mind of **The All**.

The Hermetists subdivide each of the Three Great Planes into Seven Minor Planes, and each of these latter are also sub-divided into seven sub-planes, all divisions being more or less arbitrary, shading into each other, and adopted merely for convenience of scientific study and thought.

The Great Physical Plane, and its Seven Minor Planes, is that division of the phenomena of the Universe which includes all that relates to physics, or material things, forces, and manifestations. It includes all forms of that which we call Matter, and all forms of that which we call Energy or Force. But you must remember that the Hermetic Philosophy does not recognize Matter as a thing in itself, or as having a separate existence even in the Mind of **The All**. The Teachings are that Matter is but a form of Energy, that is, Energy at a low rate of vibrations of a certain kind. And accordingly the Hermetists classify Matter under the head of Energy, and give to it three of the Seven Minor Planes of the Great Physical Plane.

These Seven Minor Physical Planes are as follows:

1. The Plane of Matter (A)
2. The Plane of Matter (B)
3. The Plane of Matter (C)
4. The Plane of Ethereal Substance
5. The Plane of Energy (A)
6. The Plane of Energy (B)
7. The Plane of Energy (C)

The Plane of Matter (A) comprises the forms of Matter in its form of solids, liquids, and gases, as generally recognized by the text-books on physics. The Plane of Matter (B) comprises certain higher and more subtle forms of Matter of the existence of which modern science is but now recognizing, the phenomena of Radiant Matter, in its phases of radium, etc., belonging to the lower sub-division of this Minor Plane. The Plane of Matter (C) comprises forms of the most subtle and tenuous Matter, the existence of which is not suspected by ordinary scientists. The Plane of Ethereal Substance comprises that which science speaks of as "The Ether", a substance of extreme tenuity and elasticity, pervading all Universal Space, and acting as a medium for the transmission of waves of energy, such as light, heat, electricity, etc. This Ethereal Substance forms a connecting link between Matter (so-called) and Energy, and partakes of the nature of each. The Hermetic Teachings, however, instruct that this plane has seven sub-divisions (as have all of the Minor Planes), and that in fact there are seven ethers, instead of but one.

Next above the Plane of Ethereal Substance comes the Plane of Energy (A), which comprises the ordinary forms of Energy known to science, its seven sub-planes being, respectively, Heat; Light; Magnetism; Electricity, and Attraction (including Gravitation, Cohesion, Chemical Affinity, etc.) and several other forms of energy indicated by scientific experiments but not as yet named or classified. The Plane of Energy (B) comprises seven subplanes of higher forms of energy not as yet discovered by science, but which have been called "Nature's Finer Forces" and which are called into operation in manifestations of certain forms of mental phenomena, and by which such phenomena becomes possible. The Plane of Energy (C) comprises seven sub-planes of energy so highly organized that it bears many of the characteristics of "life," but which is not recognized by the minds of men on the ordinary plane of development, being available for the use on beings of the Spiritual Plane alone-such energy is unthinkable to ordinary man, and may be considered almost as "the divine power." The beings employing the same are as "gods" compared even to the highest human types known to us.

The Great Mental Plane comprises those forms of "living things" known to us in ordinary life, as well as certain other forms not so well known except to the occultist. The classification of the Seven Minor Mental Planes is more or less satisfactory and arbitrary (unless accompanied by elaborate explanations which are foreign to the purpose of this particular work), but we may as well mention them. They are as follows:

1. The Plane of Mineral Mind
2. The Plane of Elemental Mind (A)
3. The Plane of Plant Mind
4. The Plane of Elemental Mind (B)
5. The Plane of Animal Mind
6. The Plane of Elemental Mind (C)
7. The Plane of Human Mind

The Plane of Mineral Mind comprises the "states or conditions" of the units or entities, or groups and combinations of the same, which animate the forms known to us as "minerals, chemicals, etc." These entities must not be confounded with the molecules, atoms and corpuscles themselves, the latter being merely the material bodies or forms of these entities, just as a man's body is but his material form and not "himself." These entities may be called "souls" in one sense, and are living beings of a low degree of development, life, and mind-just a little more than the units of "living energy" which comprise the higher sub-divisions of the highest Physical Plane. The average mind does not generally attribute the possession of mind, soul, or life, to the mineral kingdom, but all occultists recognize the existence of the same, and modern science is rapidly moving forward to the point-of-view of the Hermetic, in this respect. The molecules, atoms and corpuscles have their "loves and hates"; "likes and dislikes"; "attractions and repulsions". "affinities and non-affinities," etc., and some of the more daring of modern scientific minds have expressed the opinion that the desire and will, emotions and feelings, of the atoms differ only in degree from those of men. We have no time or space to argue this matter here. All occultists know it to be a fact, and others are referred to some of the more recent scientific works for outside corroboration. There are the usual seven sub-divisions to this plane.

The Plane of Elemental Mind (A) comprises the state or condition, and degree of mental and vital development of a class of entities unknown to the average man, but recognized to occultists. They are invisible to the ordinary senses of man, but, nevertheless, exist and play their part of the Drama of the Universe. Their degree of intelligence is between that of the mineral and chemical entities on the one hand, and of the entities of the plant kingdom on the other. There are seven subdivisions to this plane, also.

The Plane of Plant Mind, in its seven sub-divisions, comprises the states or conditions of the entities comprising the kingdoms of the Plant World, the vital and mental phenomena of which is fairly well understood by the average intelligent person, many new and interesting scientific works regarding "Mind and Life in Plants" having been published during the last decade. Plants have life, mind and "souls," as well as have the animals, man, and super-man.

The Plane of Elemental Mind (B), in its seven sub-divisions, comprises the states and conditions of a higher form of "elemental" or unseen entities, playing their part in the general work of the Universe, the mind and life of which form a part of the scale between the Plane of Plant Mind and the Plane of Animal Mind, the entities partaking of the nature of both.

The Plane of Animal Mind, in its seven sub-divisions, comprises the states and conditions of the entities, beings, or souls, animating the animal forms of life, familiar to us all. It is not necessary to go into details regarding this kingdom or plane of life, for the animal world is as familiar to us as is our own.

The Plane of Elemental Mind (C), in its seven sub-divisions, comprises those entities or beings, invisible as are all such elemental forms, which partake of the nature of both animal and human life in a degree and in certain combinations. The highest forms are semi-human in intelligence.

The Plane of Human Mind, in its seven sub-divisions, comprises those manifestations of life and mentality which are common to Man, in his various grades, degrees, and divisions. In this connection, we wish to point out the fact that the average man of today occupies but the fourth sub-division of the Plane of Human Mind, and only the most intelligent have crossed the borders of the Fifth Sub-Division. It has taken the race millions of years to reach this stage, and it will take many more years for the race to move on to the sixth and seventh sub-divisions, and beyond. But, remember, that there have been races before us which have passed through these degrees, and then on to higher planes. Our own race is the fifth (with stragglers from the fourth) which has set foot upon The Path. And, then there are a few advanced souls of our own race who have outstripped the masses, and who have passed on to the sixth and seventh sub-division, and some few being still further on. The man of the Sixth Sub-Division will be "The Super-Man"; he of the Seventh will be "The Over-Man."

In our consideration of the Seven Minor Mental Planes, we have merely referred to the Three Elementary Planes in a general way. We do not wish to go into this subject in detail in this work, for it does not belong to this part of the general philosophy and teachings. But we may say this much, in order to give you a little clearer idea, of the relations of these planes to the more familiar ones-the Elementary Planes bear the same relation to the Planes of Mineral, Plant, Animal and Human Mentality and Life, that the black keys on the piano do to the white keys. The white keys are sufficient to produce music, but there are certain scales, melodies, and harmonies, in which the black keys play their part, and in which their presence is necessary. They are also necessary as "connecting links" of soul-condition; entity states, etc., between the several other planes, certain forms of development being attained therein-this last fact giving to the reader who can "read between the lines" a new light upon the processes of Evolution, and a new key to the secret door of the "leaps of life" between kingdom and kingdom. The great kingdoms of Elementals are fully recognized by all occultists, and the esoteric writings are full of mention of them. The readers of Bulwer's "Zanoni" and similar tales will recognize the entities inhabiting these planes of life.

Passing on from the Great Mental Plane to the Great Spiritual Plane, what shall we say? How can we explain these higher states of Being, Life and Mind, to minds as yet unable to grasp and understand the higher subdivisions of the Plane of Human Mind? The task is impossible. We can speak only in the most general terms. How may Light be described to a man born blind-how sugar, to a man who has never tasted anything sweet-how harmony, to one born deaf?

All that we can say is that the Seven Minor Planes of the Great Spiritual Plane (each Minor Plane having its seven sub-divisions) comprise Beings possessing Life, Mind and Form as far above that of Man of to-day as the latter is above the earth-worm, mineral or even certain forms of Energy or Matter. The Life of these Beings so far transcends ours, that we cannot even think of the details of the same; their minds so far transcend ours, that to them we scarcely seem to "think," and our mental processes seem almost akin to material processes; the Matter of which their forms are composed is of the highest Planes of Matter, nay, some are even said to be "clothed in Pure Energy." What may be said of such Beings?

On the Seven Minor Planes of the Great Spiritual Plane exist Beings of whom we may speak as Angels; Archangels; Demigods. On the lower Minor Planes dwell those great souls whom we call Masters and Adepts. Above them come the Great Hierarchies of the Angelic Hosts, unthinkable to man; and above those come those who may without irreverence be called "The Gods," so high in the scale of Being are they, their being, intelligence and power being akin to those attributed by the races of men to their conceptions of Deity. These Beings are beyond even the highest flights of the human imagination, the word "Divine" being the only one applicable to them. Many of these Beings, as well as the Angelic Host, take the greatest interest in the affairs of the Universe and play an important part in its affairs. These Unseen Divinities and Angelic Helpers extend their influence freely and powerfully, in the process of Evolution, and Cosmic Progress. Their occasional intervention and assistance in human affairs have led to the many legends, beliefs, religions and traditions of the race, past and present. They have superimposed their knowledge and power upon the world, again and again, all under the Law of **The All**, of course.

But, yet, even the highest of these advanced Beings exist merely as creations of, and in, the Mind of **The All**, and are subject to the Cosmic Processes and Universal Laws. They are still Mortal. We may call them "gods" if we like, but still they are but the Elder Brethren of the Race,-the advanced souls who have outstripped their brethren, and who have foregone the ecstasy of Absorption by **The All**, in order to help the race on its upward journey along The Path. But, they belong to the Universe, and are subject to its conditions-they are mortal-and their plane is below that of Absolute Spirit.

Only the most advanced Hermetists are able to grasp the Inner Teachings regarding the state of existence, and the powers manifested on the Spiritual Planes. The phenomena is so much higher than that of the Mental Planes that a confusion of ideas would surely result from an attempt to describe the same. Only those whose minds have been carefully trained along the lines of the Hermetic Philosophy for years-yes, those who have brought with them from other incarnations the knowledge acquired previously-can comprehend just what is meant by the Teaching regarding these Spiritual Planes. And much of these Inner Teachings is held by the Hermetists as being too sacred, important and even dangerous for general public dissemination. The intelligent student may recognize what we mean by this when we state that the meaning of "Spirit" as used by the Hermetists is akin to "Living Power"; "Animated Force;" "Inner Essence;" "Essence of Life," etc., which meaning must not be confounded with that usually and commonly employed in connection with the term, i.e., "religious; ecclesiastical; spiritual; ethereal; holy," etc., etc. To occultists the word "Spirit" is used in the sense of "The Animating Principle," carrying with it the idea of Power, Living Energy, Mystic Force, etc. And occultists know that that which is known to them as "Spiritual Power" may be employed for evil as well as good ends (in accordance with the Principle of Polarity), a fact which has been recognized by the majority of religions in their conceptions of Satan, Beelzebub, the Devil, Lucifer, Fallen Angels, etc. And so the knowledge regarding these Planes has been kept in the Holy of Holies in all Esoteric Fraternities and Occult Orders,-in the Secret Chamber of the Temple. But this may be said here, that those who have attained high spiritual powers and have misused them, have a terrible fate in store for them, and the swing of the pendulum of Rhythm will inevitably swing them back to the furthest extreme of Material existence, from which point they must retrace their steps Spiritward, along the weary rounds of The Path, but always with the added torture of having always with them a lingering memory of the heights from which they fell owing to their evil actions. The legends of the Fallen Angels have a basis in actual facts, as all advanced occultists know. The striving for selfish power on the Spiritual Planes inevitably results in the selfish soul losing its spiritual balance and falling back as far as it had previously risen. But to even such a soul, the opportunity of a return is given-and such souls make the return journey, paying the terrible penalty according to the invariable Law.

In conclusion we would again remind you that according to the Principle of Correspondence, which embodies the truth: "As Above so Below; as Below, so Above," all of the Seven Hermetic Principles are in full operation on all of the many planes, Physical Mental and Spiritual. The Principle of Mental Substance of course applies to all the planes, for all are held in the Mind of THE ALL. The Principle of Correspondence manifests in all, for there is a correspondence, harmony and agreement between the several planes. The Principle of Vibration manifests on all planes, in fact the very differences that go to make the "planes" arise from Vibration, as we have explained. The Principle of Polarity manifests on each plane, the extremes of the Poles being apparently opposite and contradictory. The Principle of Rhythm manifests on each Plane, the movement of the phenomena having its ebb and flow, rise and flow, incoming and outgoing. The Principle of Cause and Effect manifests on each Plane, every Effect having its Cause and every Cause having its effect. The Principle of Gender manifests on each Plane, the Creative Energy being always manifest, and operating along the lines of its Masculine and Feminine Aspects.

"As Above so Below; as Below, so Above." This centuries old Hermetic axiom embodies one of the great Principles of Universal Phenomena. As we proceed with our consideration of the remaining Principles, we will see even more clearly the truth of the universal nature of this great Principle of Correspondence.

ix. Vibration

"Nothing rests; everything moves; everything vibrates."
-The Kybalion.

The great Third Hermetic Principle-the Principle of Vibration-embodies the truth that Motion is manifest in everything in the Universe-that nothing is at rest-that everything moves, vibrates, and circles. This Hermetic Principle was recognized by some of the early Greek philosophers who embodied it in their systems. But, then, for centuries it was lost sight of by the thinkers outside of the Hermetic ranks. But in the Nineteenth Century physical science rediscovered the truth and the Twentieth Century scientific discoveries have added additional proof of the correctness and truth of this centuries-old Hermetic doctrine.

The Hermetic Teachings are that not only is everything in constant movement and vibration, but that the "differences" between the various manifestations of the universal power are due entirely to the varying rate and mode of vibrations. Not only this, but that even **The All**, in itself, manifests a constant vibration of such an infinite degree of intensity and rapid motion that it may be practically considered as at rest, the teachers directing the attention of the students to the fact that even on the physical plane a rapidly moving object (such as a revolving wheel) seems to be at rest. The Teachings are to the effect that Spirit is at one end of the Pole of Vibration, the other Pole being certain extremely gross forms of Matter. Between these two poles are millions upon millions of different rates and modes of vibration.

Modern Science has proven that all that we call Matter and Energy are but "modes of vibratory motion," and some of the more advanced scientists are rapidly moving toward the positions of the occultists who hold that the phenomena of Mind are likewise modes of vibration or motion. Let us see what science has to say regarding the question of vibrations in matter and energy.

In the first place, science teaches that all matter manifests, in some degree, the vibrations arising from temperature or heat. Be an object cold or hot-both being but degrees of the same things-it manifests certain heat vibrations, and in that sense is in motion and vibration. Then all particles of Matter are in circular movement, from corpuscle to suns. The planets revolve around suns, and many of them turn on their axes. The suns move around greater central points, and these are believed to move around still greater, and so on, ad infinitum. The molecules of which the particular kinds of Matter are composed are in a state of constant vibration and movement around each other and against each other. The molecules are composed of Atoms, which, likewise, are in a state of constant movement and vibration. The atoms are composed of Corpuscles, sometimes called "electrons," "ions," etc., which also are in a state of rapid motion, revolving around each other, and which manifest a very rapid state and mode of vibration. And, so we see that all forms of Matter manifest Vibration, in accordance with the Hermetic Principle of Vibration.

And so it is with the various forms of Energy. Science teaches that Light, Heat, Magnetism and Electricity are but forms of vibratory motion connected in some way with, and probably emanating from the Ether. Science does not as yet attempt to explain the nature of the phenomena known as Cohesion, which is the principle of Molecular Attraction; nor Chemical Affinity, which is the principle of Atomic Attraction; nor Gravitation (the greatest mystery of the three), which is the principle of attraction by which every particle or mass of Matter is bound to every other particle or mass. These three forms of Energy are not as yet understood by science, yet the writers incline to the opinion that these too are manifestations of some form of vibratory energy, a fact which the Hermetists have held and taught for ages past.

The Universal Ether, which is postulated by science without its nature being understood clearly, is held by the Hermetists to be but a higher manifestation of that which is erroneously called matter-that is to say, Matter at a higher degree of vibration-and is called by them "The Ethereal Substance." The Hermetists teach that this Ethereal Substance is of extreme tenuity and elasticity, and pervades universal space, serving as a medium of transmission of waves of vibratory energy, such as heat, light, electricity, magnetism, etc. The Teachings are that The Ethereal Substance is a connecting link between the forms of vibratory energy known as "Matter" on the one hand, and "Energy or Force" on the other; and also that it manifests a degree of vibration, in rate and mode, entirely its own.

Scientists have offered the illustration of a rapidly moving wheel, top, or cylinder, to show the effects of increasing rates of vibration. The illustration supposes a wheel, top, or revolving cylinder, running at a low rate of speed-we will call this revolving thing "the object" in following out the illustration. Let us suppose the object moving slowly. It may be seen readily, but no sound of its movement reaches the ear. The speed is gradually increased. In a few moments its movement becomes so rapid that a deep growl or low note may be heard. Then as the rate is increased the note rises one in the musical scale. Then, the motion being still further increased, the next highest note is distinguished. Then, one after another, all the notes of the musical scale appear, rising higher and higher as the motion is increased. Finally when the motions have reached a certain rate the final note perceptible to human ears is reached and the shrill, piercing shriek dies away, and silence follows. No sound is heard from the revolving object, the rate of motion being so high that the human ear cannot register the vibrations. Then comes the perception of rising degrees of Heat.

Then after quite a time the eye catches a glimpse of the object becoming a dull dark reddish color. As the rate increases, the red becomes brighter. Then as the speed is increased, the red melts into an orange. Then the orange melts into a yellow. Then follow, successively, the shades of green, blue, indigo, and finally violet, as the rate of sped increases. Then the violet shades away, and all color disappears, the human eye not being able to register them. But there are invisible rays emanating from the revolving object, the rays that are used in photographing, and other subtle rays of light. Then begin to manifest the peculiar rays known as the "X-Rays," etc., as the constitution of the object changes. Electricity and Magnetism are emitted when the appropriate rate of vibration is attained.

When the object reaches a certain rate of vibration its molecules disintegrate, and resolve themselves into the original elements or atoms. Then the atoms, following the Principle of Vibration, are separated into the countless corpuscles of which they are composed. And finally, even the corpuscles disappear and the object may be said to be composed of The Ethereal Substance. Science does not dare to follow the illustration further, but the Hermetists teach that if the vibrations be continually increased the object would mount up the successive states of manifestation and would in turn manifest the various mental stages, and then on Spiritward, until it would finally re-enter **The All**, which is Absolute Spirit. The "object," however, would have ceased to be an "object" long before the stage of Ethereal Substance was reached, but otherwise the illustration is correct inasmuch as it shows the effect of constantly increased rates and modes of vibration. It must be remembered, in the above illustration, that at the stages at which the "object" throws off vibrations of light, heat, etc., it is not actually "resolved" into those forms of energy (which are much higher in the scale), but simply that it reaches a degree of vibration in which those forms of energy are liberated, in a degree, from the confining influences of its molecules, atoms and corpuscles, as the case may be. These forms of energy, although much higher in the scale than matter, are imprisoned and confined in the material combinations, by reason of the energies manifesting through, and using material forms, but thus becoming entangled and confined in their creations of material forms, which, to an extent, is true of all creations, the creating force becoming involved in its creation.

But the Hermetic Teachings go much further than do those of modern science. They teach that all manifestation of thought, emotion, reason, will or desire, or any mental state or condition, are accompanied by vibrations, a portion of which are thrown off and which tend to affect the minds of other persons by "induction." This is the principle which produces the phenomena of "telepathy"; mental influence, and other forms of the action and power of mind over mind, with which the general public is rapidly becoming acquainted, owing to the wide dissemination of occult knowledge by the various schools, cults and teachers along these lines at this time.

Every thought, emotion or mental state has its corresponding rate and mode of vibration. And by an effort of the will of the person, or of other persons, these mental states may be reproduced, just as a musical tone may be reproduced by causing an instrument to vibrate at a certain rate-just as color may be reproduced in the same may. By a knowledge of the Principle of Vibration, as applied to Mental Phenomena, one may polarize his mind at any degree he wishes, thus gaining a perfect control over his mental states, moods, etc. In the same way he may affect the minds of others, producing the desired mental states in them. In short, he may be able to produce on the Mental Plane that which science produces on the Physical Plane-namely, "Vibrations at Will." This power of course may be acquired only by the proper instruction, exercises, practice, etc., the science being that of Mental Transmutation, one of the branches of the Hermetic Art.

A little reflection on what we have said will show the student that the Principle of Vibration underlies the wonderful phenomena of the power manifested by the Masters and Adepts, who are able to apparently set aside the Laws of Nature, but who, in reality, are simply using one law against another; one principle against others; and who accomplish their results by changing the vibrations of material objects, or forms of energy, and thus perform what are commonly called "miracles."

As one of the old Hermetic writers has truly said: "He who understands the Principle of Vibration, has grasped the scepter of Power."

x. Polarity

"Everything is dual; everything has poles; everything has its pair of opposites; like and unlike are the same; opposites are identical in nature, but different in degree; extremes meet; all truths are but half-truths; all paradoxes may be reconciled."-The Kybalion.

The great Fourth Hermetic Principle-the Principle of Polarity embodies the truth that all manifested things have "two sides"; "two aspects"; "two poles"; a "pair of opposites," with manifold degrees between the two extremes. The old paradoxes, which have ever perplexed the mind of men, are explained by an understanding of this Principle. Man has always recognized something akin to this Principle, and has endeavored to express it by such sayings, maxims and aphorisms as the following: "Everything is and isn't, at the same time"; "all truths are but half-truths"; "every truth is half-false"; "there are two sides to everything"-"there is a reverse side to every shield," etc., etc.

The Hermetic Teachings are to the effect that the difference between things seemingly diametrically opposed to each other is merely a matter of degree. It teaches that "the pairs of opposites may be reconciled," and that "thesis and anti-thesis are identical in nature, but different in degree"; and that the "universal reconciliation of opposites" is effected by a recognition of this Principle of Polarity. The teachers claim that illustrations of this Principle may be had on every hand, and from an examination into the real nature of anything. They begin by showing that Spirit and Matter are but the two poles of the same thing, the intermediate planes being merely degrees of vibration. They show that **The All** and The Many are the same, the difference being merely a matter of degree of Mental Manifestation. Thus the **Law** and Laws are the two opposite poles of one thing. Likewise, **Principle** and Principles. Infinite Mind and finite minds.

Then passing on to the Physical Plane, they illustrate the Principle by showing that Heat and Cold are identical in nature, the differences being merely a matter of degrees. The thermometer shows many degrees of temperature, the lowest pole being called "cold," and the highest "heat." Between these two poles are many degrees of "heat" or "cold," call them either and you are equally correct. The higher of two degrees is always "warmer," while the lower is always "colder." There is no absolute standard-all is a matter of degree. There is no place on the thermometer where heat ceases and cold begins. It is all a matter of higher or lower vibrations. The very terms "high" and "low," which we are compelled to use, are but poles of the same thing-the terms are relative. So with "East and West"-travel around the world in an eastward direction, and you reach a point which is called west at your starting point, and you return from that westward point. Travel far enough North, and you will find yourself traveling South, or vice versa.

Light and Darkness are poles of the same thing, with many degrees between them. The musical scale is the same-starting with "C" you move upward until you reach another "C" and so on, the differences between the two ends of the board being the same, with many degrees between the two extremes. The scale of color is the same-higher and lower vibrations being the only difference between high violet and low red. Large and Small are relative. So are Noise and Quiet; Hard and Soft follow the rule. Likewise Sharp and Dull. Positive and Negative are two poles of the same thing, with countless degrees between them.

Good and Bad are not absolute-we call one end of the scale Good and the other Bad, or one end Good and the other Evil, according to the use of the terms. A thing is "less good" than the thing higher in the scale; but that "less good" thing, in turn, is "more good" than the thing next below it-and so on, the "more or less" being regulated by the position on the scale.

And so it is on the Mental Plane. "Love and. Hate" are generally regarded as being things diametrically opposed to each other; entirely different; unreconcilable. But we apply the Principle of Polarity; we find that there is no such thing as Absolute Love or Absolute Hate, as distinguished from each other. The two are merely terms applied to the two poles of the same thing. Beginning at any point of the scale we find "more love," or "less hate," as we ascend the scale; and "more hate" or "less love" as we descend this being true no matter from what point, high or low, we may start. There are degrees of Love and Hate, and there is a middle point where "Like and Dislike" become so faint that it is difficult to distinguish between them. Courage and Fear come under the same rule. The Pairs of Opposites exist everywhere. Where you find one thing you find its opposite-the two poles.

And it is this fact that enables the Hermetist to transmute one mental state into another, along the lines of Polarization. Things belonging to different classes cannot be transmuted into each other, but things of the same class may be changed, that is, may have their polarity changed. Thus Love never becomes East or West, or Red or Violet-but it may and often does turn into Hate and likewise Hate may be transformed into Love, by changing its polarity. Courage may be transmuted into Fear, and the reverse. Hard things may be rendered Soft. Dull things become Sharp. Hot things become Cold. And so on, the transmutation always being between things of the same kind of different degrees. Take the case of a Fearful man. By raising his mental vibrations along the line of Fear- Courage, he can be filled with the highest degree of Courage and Fearlessness. And, likewise, the Slothful man may change himself into an Active, Energetic individual simply by polarizing along the lines of the desired quality.

The student who is familiar with the processes by which the various schools of Mental Science, etc., produce changes in the mental states of those following their teachings, may not readily understand the principle underlying many of these changes. When, however, the Principle of Polarity is once grasped, and it is seen that the mental changes are occasioned by a change of polarity-a sliding along the same scale-the hatter is readily understood. The change is not in the nature of a transmutation of one thing into another thing entirely different-but is merely a change of degree in the same things, a vastly important difference. For instance, borrowing an analogy from the Physical Plane, it is impossible to change Heat into Sharpness, Loudness, Highness, etc., but Heat may readily be transmuted into Cold, simply by lowering the vibrations. In the same way Hate and Love are mutually transmutable; so are Fear and Courage. But Fear cannot be transformed into Love, nor can Courage be transmuted into Hate. The mental states belong to innumerable classes, each class of which has its opposite poles, along which transmutation is possible.

The student will readily recognize that in the mental states, as well as in the phenomena of the Physical Plane, the two poles may be classified as Positive and Negative, respectively. Thus Love is Positive to Hate; Courage to Fear; Activity to Non-Activity, etc., etc. And it will also be noticed that even to those unfamiliar with the Principle of Vibration, the Positive pole seems to be of a higher degree than the Negative, and readily dominates it. The tendency of Nature is in the direction of the dominant activity of the Positive pole.

In addition to the changing of the poles of one's own mental states by the operation of the art of Polarization, the phenomena of Mental Influence, in its manifold phases, shows us that the principle may be extended so as to embrace the phenomena of the influence of one mind over that of another, of which so much has been written and taught of late years. When it is understood that Mental Induction is possible, that is that mental states may be produced by "induction" from others, then we can readily see how a certain rate of vibration, or polarization of a certain mental state, may be communicated to another person, and his polarity in that class of mental states thus changed. It is along this principle that the results of many of the "mental treatments" are obtained. For instance, a person is "blue," melancholy and full of fear. A mental scientist bringing his own mind up to the desired vibration by his trained will, and thus obtaining the desired polarization in his own case, then produces a similar mental state in the other by induction, the result being that the vibrations are raised and the person polarizes toward the Positive end of the scale instead toward the Negative, and his Fear and other negative emotions are transmuted to Courage and similar positive mental states. A little study will show you that these mental changes are nearly all along the line of Polarization, the change being one of degree rather than of kind.

A knowledge of the existence of this great Hermetic Principle will enable the student to better understand his own mental states, and those of other people. He will see that these states are all matters of degree, and seeing thus, he will be able to raise or lower the vibration at will-to change his mental poles, and thus be Master of his mental states, instead of being their servant and slave. And by his knowledge he will be able to aid his fellows intelligently and by the appropriate methods change the polarity when the same is desirable. We advise all students to familiarize themselves with this Principle of Polarity, for a correct understanding of the same will throw light on many difficult subjects.

xi. Rhythm

"Everything flows out and in; everything has its tides; all things rise and fall; the pendulum-swing manifests in everything; the measure of the swing to the right, is the measure of the swing to the left; rhythm compensates"

-The Kybalion.

The great Fifth Hermetic Principle-the Principle of Rhythm-embodies the truth that in everything there is manifested a measured motion; a to-and-from movement; a flow and inflow; a swing forward and backward; a pendulum-like movement; a tide-like ebb and flow; a high-tide and a low- tide; between the two-poles manifest on the physical, mental or spiritual planes. The Principle of rhythm is closely connected with the Principle of Polarity described in the preceding chapter. Rhythm manifests between the two poles established by the Principle of Polarity. This does not mean, however, that the pendulum of Rhythm swings to the extreme poles, for this rarely happens; in fact, it is difficult to establish the extreme polar opposites in the majority of cases. But the swing is ever "toward" first one pole and then the other.

There is always an action and reaction; an advance and a retreat; a rising and a sinking; manifested in all of the airs and phenomena of the Universe. Suns, worlds, men, animals, plants, minerals, forces, energy, mind and matter, yes, even Spirit, manifests this Principle. The Principle manifests in the creation and destruction of worlds; in the rise and fall of nations; in the life history of all things; and finally in the mental states of Man.

Beginning with the manifestations of Spirit-of **The All**-it will be noticed that there is ever the Outpouring and the Indrawing; the "Outbreathing and Inbreathing of Brahm," as the Brahmans word it. Universes are created; reach their extreme low point of materiality; and then begin in their upward swing. Suns spring into being, and then their height of power being reached, the process of retrogression begins, and after aeons they become dead masses of matter, awaiting another impulse which starts again their inner energies into activity and a new solar life cycle is begun. And thus it is with all the worlds; they are born, grow and die; only to be reborn. And thus it is with all the things of shape and form; they swing from action to reaction; from birth to death; from activity to inactivity-and then back again. Thus it is with all living things; they are born, grow, and die-and then are reborn. So it is with all great movements, philosophies, creeds, fashions, governments, nations, and all else-birth, growth, maturity, decadence, death-and then new-birth. The swing of the pendulum is ever in evidence.

Night follows day; and day night. The pendulum swings from Summer to Winter, and then back again. The corpuscles, atoms, molecules, and all masses of matter, swing around the circle of their nature. There is no such thing as absolute rest, or cessation from movement, and all movement partakes of rhythm. The principle is of universal application. It may be applied to any question, or phenomena of any of the many planes of life. It may be applied to all phases of human activity. There is always the Rhythmic swing from one pole to the other. The Universal Pendulum is ever in motion. The Tides of Life flow in and out, according to Law.

The Principle of rhythm is well understood by modern science, and is considered a universal law as applied to material things. But the Hermetists carry the principle much further, and know that its manifestations and influence extend to the mental activities of Man, and that it accounts for the bewildering succession of moods, feelings and other annoying and perplexing changes that we notice in ourselves. But the Hermetists by studying the operations of this Principle have learned to escape some of its activities by Transmutation.

The Hermetic Masters long since discovered that while the Principle of Rhythm was invariable, and ever in evidence in mental phenomena, still there were two planes of its manifestation so far as mental phenomena are concerned. They discovered that there were two general planes of Consciousness, the Lower and the Higher, the understanding of which fact enabled them to rise to the higher plane and thus escape the swing of the Rhythmic pendulum which manifested on the lower plane. In other words, the swing of the pendulum occurred on the Unconscious Plane, and the Consciousness was not affected. This they call the Law of Neutralization. Its operations consist in the raising of the Ego above the vibrations of the Unconscious Plane of mental activity, so that the negative-swing of the pendulum is not manifested in consciousness, and therefore they are not affected. It is akin to rising above a thing and letting it pass beneath you. The Hermetic Master, or advanced student, polarizes himself at the desired pole, and by a process akin to "refusing" to participate in the backward swing or, if you prefer, a "denial" of its influence over him, he stands firm in his polarized position, and allows the mental pendulum to swing back along the unconscious plane. All individuals who have attained any degree of self- mastery, accomplish this, more or less unknowingly, and by refusing to allow their moods and negative mental states to affect them, they apply the Law of Neutralization. The Master, however, carries this to a much higher degree of proficiency, and by the use of his Will he attains a degree of Poise and Mental Firmness almost impossible of belief on the part of those who allow themselves to be swung backward and forward by the mental pendulum of moods and feelings.

The importance of this will be appreciated by any thinking person who realizes what creatures of moods, feelings and emotion the majority of people are, and how little mastery of themselves they manifest. If you will stop and consider a moment, you will realize how much these swings of Rhythm have affected you in your life-how a period of Enthusiasm has been invariably followed by an opposite feeling and mood of Depression. Likewise, your moods and periods of Courage have been succeeded by equal moods of Fear. And so it has ever been with the majority of persons-tides of feeling have ever risen and fallen with them, but they have never suspected the cause or reason of the mental phenomena. An understanding of the workings of this Principle will give one the key to the Mastery of these rhythmic swings of feeling, and will enable him to know himself better and to avoid being carried away by these inflows and outflows. The Will is superior to the conscious manifestation of this Principle, although the Principle itself can never be destroyed. We may escape its effects, but the Principle operates, nevertheless. The pendulum ever swings, although we may escape being carried along with it.

There are other features of the operation of this Principle of Rhythm of which we wish to speak at this point. There comes into its operations that which is known as the Law of Compensation. One of the definitions or meanings of the word "Compensate" is, "to counterbalance" which is the sense in which the Hermetists use the term. It is this Law of Compensation to which the Kybalion refers when it says: "The measure of the swing to the right is the measure of the swing to the left; rhythm compensates."

The Law of Compensation is that the swing in one direction determines the swing in the opposite direction, or to the opposite pole-the one balances, or counterbalances, the other. On the Physical Plane we see many examples of this Law. The pendulum of the clock swings a certain distance to the right, and then an equal distance to the left. The seasons balance each other in the same way. The tides follow the same Law. And the same Law is manifested in all the phenomena of Rhythm. The pendulum, with a short swing in one direction, has but a short swing in the other; while the long swing to the right invariably means the long swing to the left. An object hurled upward to a certain height has an equal distance to traverse on its return. The force with which a projectile is sent upward a mile is reproduced when the projectile returns to the earth on its return journey. This Law is constant on the Physical Plane, as reference to the standard authorities will show you.

But the Hermetists carry it still further. They teach that a man's mental states are subject to the same Law. The man who enjoys keenly, is subject to keen suffering; while he who feels but little pain is capable of feeling but little joy. The pig suffers but little mentally, and enjoys but little-he is compensated. And on the other hand, there are other animals who enjoy keenly, but whose nervous organism and temperament cause them to suffer exquisite degrees of pain and so it is with Man. There are temperaments which permit of but low degrees of enjoyment, and equally low degrees of suffering; while there are others which permit the most intense enjoyment, but also the most intense suffering. The rule is that the capacity for pain and pleasure, in each individual, are balanced. The Law of Compensation is in full operation here.

But the Hermetists go still further in this matter. They teach that before one is able to enjoy a certain degree of pleasure, he must have swung as far, proportionately, toward the other pole of feeling. They hold, however, that the Negative is precedent to the Positive in this matter, that is to say that in experiencing a certain degree of pleasure it does not follow that he will have to "pay up for it" with a corresponding degree of pain; on the contrary, the pleasure is the Rhythmic swing, according to the Law of Compensation, for a degree of pain previously experienced either in the present life, or in a previous incarnation. This throws a new light on the Problem of Pain.

The Hermetists regard the chain of lives as continuous, and as forming a part of one life of the individual, so that in consequence the rhythmic swing is understood in this way, while it would be without meaning unless the truth of reincarnation is admitted.

But the Hermetists claim that the Master or advanced student is able, to a great degree, to escape the swing toward Pain, by the process of Neutralization before mentioned. By rising on to the higher plane of the Ego, much of the experience that comes to those dwelling on the lower plane is avoided and escaped.

The Law of Compensation plays an important part in the lives of men and women. It will be noticed that one generally "pays the price" of anything he possesses or lacks. If he has one thing, he lacks another-the balance is struck. No one can "keep his penny and have the bit of cake" at the same time Everything has its pleasant and unpleasant sides. The things that one gains are always paid for by the things that one loses. The rich possess much that the poor lack, while the poor often possess things that are beyond the reach of the rich. The millionaire may have the inclination toward feasting, and the wealth wherewith to secure all the dainties and luxuries of the table, while he lacks the appetite to enjoy the same; he envies the appetite and digestion of the laborer who lacks the wealth and inclinations of the millionaire, and who gets more pleasure from his plain food than the millionaire could obtain even if his appetite were not jaded, nor his digestion ruined, for the wants, habits and inclinations differ. And so it is through life. The Law of Compensation is ever in operation, striving to balance and counter-balance, and always succeeding in time, even though several lives may be required for the return swing of the Pendulum of Rhythm.

xii. Causation

"Every Cause has its Effect; every Effect has its Cause; everything happens according to Law; Chance is but a name for Law not recognized; there are many planes of causation, but nothing escapes the Law."-The Kybalion.

The great Sixth Hermetic Principle-the Principle of Cause and Effect-embodies the truth that Law pervades the Universe; that nothing happens by Chance; that Chance is merely a term indicating cause existing but not recognized or perceived; that phenomena is continuous, without break or exception.

The Principle of Cause and Effect underlies all scientific thought, ancient and modern, and was enunciated by the Hermetic Teachers in the earliest days. While many and varied disputes between the many schools of thought have since arisen, these disputes have been principally upon the details of the operations of the Principle, and still more often upon the meaning of certain words. The underlying Principle of Cause and Effect has been accepted as correct by practically all the thinkers of the world worthy of the name. To think otherwise would be to take the phenomena of the universe from the domain of Law and Order, and to relegate it; to the control of the imaginary something which men have called "Chance."

A little consideration will show anyone that there is in reality no such thing as pure chance. Webster defines the word "Chance" as follows: "A supposed agent or mode of activity other than a force, law or purpose; the operation or activity of such agent; the supposed effect of such an agent; a happening; fortuity; casualty, etc." But a little consideration will show you that there can be no such agent as "Chance," in the sense of something outside of Law-something outside of Cause and Effect. How could there be a something acting in the phenomenal universe, independent of the laws, order, and continuity of the latter? Such a something would be entirely independent of the orderly trend of the universe, and therefore superior to it. We can imagine nothing outside of **The All** being outside of the Law, and that only because **The All** is the **Law** in itself. There is no room in the universe for a something outside of and independent of **Law**. The existence of such a Something would render all Natural Laws ineffective, and would plunge the universe into chaotic disorder and lawlessness.

A careful examination will show that what we call "Chance" is merely an expression relating to obscure causes; causes that we cannot perceive; causes that we cannot understand. The word Chance is derived from a word Meaning "to fall" (as the falling of dice), the idea being that the fall of the dice (and many other happenings) are merely a "happening" unrelated to any cause. And this is the sense in which the term is generally employed. But when the matter is closely examined, it is seen that there is no chance whatsoever about the fall of the dice. Each time a die falls, and displays a certain number, it obeys a law as infallible as that which governs the revolution of the planets around the sun. Back of the fall of the die are causes, or chains of causes, running back further than the mind can follow. The position of the die in the box; the amount of muscular energy expended in the throw; the condition of the table, etc., etc., all are causes, the effect of which may be seen. But back of these seen causes there are chains of unseen preceding causes, all of which had a bearing upon the number of the die which fell uppermost.

If a die be cast a great number of times, it will be found that the numbers shown will be about equal, that is, there will be an equal number of one-spot, two-spot, etc., coming uppermost. Toss a penny in the air, and it may come down either "heads" or "tails"; but make a sufficient number of tosses, and the heads and tails will about even up. This is the operation of the law of average. But both the average and the single toss come under the Law of Cause and Effect, and if we were able to examine into the preceding causes, it would be clearly seen that it was simply impossible for the die to fall other than it did, under the same circumstances and at the same time. Given the same causes, the same results will follow. There is always a "cause" and a "because" to every event. Nothing ever "happens" without a cause, or rather a chain of causes.

Some confusion has arisen in the minds of persons considering this Principle, from the fact that they were unable to explain how one thing could cause another thing-that is, be the "creator" of the second thing. As a matter of fact, no "thing" ever causes or "creates" another "thing." Cause and Effect deals merely with "events." An "event" is "that which comes, arrives or happens, as a result or consequent of some preceding event." No event "creates" another event, but is merely a preceding link in the great orderly chain of events flowing from the creative energy of **The All**. There is a continuity between all events precedent, consequent and subsequent. There is a relation existing between everything that has gone before, and everything that follows. A stone is dislodged from a mountain side and crashes through a roof of a cottage in the valley below. At first sight we regard this as a chance effect, but when we examine the matter we find a great chain of causes behind it. In the first place there was the rain which softened the earth supporting the stone and which allowed it to fall; then back of that was the influence of the sun, other rains, etc., which gradually disintegrated the piece of rock from a larger piece; then there were the causes which led to the formation of the mountain, and its upheaval by convulsions of nature, and so on ad infinitum. Then we might follow up the causes behind the rain, etc. Then we might consider the existence of the roof In short, we would soon find ourselves involved in a mesh of cause and effect, from which we would soon strive to extricate ourselves.

Just as a man has two parents, and four grandparents, and eight great-grandparents, and sixteen great-great-grandparents, and so on until when, say, forty generations are calculated the numbers of ancestors run into many millions-so it is with the number of causes behind even the most trifling event or phenomena, such as the passage of a tiny speck of soot before your eye. It is not an easy matter to trace the bit of soot hack to the early period of the world's history when it formed a part of a massive tree-trunk, which was afterward converted into coal, and so on, until as the speck of soot it now passes before your vision on its way to other adventures. And a mighty chain of events, causes and effects, brought it to its present condition, and the later is but one of the chain of events which will go to produce other events hundreds of years from now. One of the series of events arising from the tiny bit of soot was the writing of these lines, which caused the typesetter to perform certain work; the proofreader to do likewise; and which will arouse certain thoughts in your mind, and that of others, which in turn will affect others, and so on, and on, and on, beyond the ability of man to think further-and all from the passage of a tiny bit of soot, all of which shows the relativity and association of things, and the further fact that *there is no great; there is no small, in the mind that causeth all."*

Stop to think a moment. If a certain man had not met a certain maid, away back in the dim period of the Stone Age-you who are now reading these lines would not now be here. And if, perhaps, the same couple had failed to meet, we who now write these lines would not now be here. And the very act of writing, on our part, and the act of reading, on yours, will affect not only the respective lives of yourself and ourselves, but will also have a direct, or indirect, affect upon many other people now living and who will live in the ages to come. Every thought we think, every act we perform, has its direct and indirect results which fit into the great chain of Cause and Effect.

We do not wish to enter into a consideration of Free Will, or Determinism, in this work, for various reasons. Among the many reasons, is the principal one that neither side of the controversy is entirely right-in fact, both sides are partially right, according to the Hermetic Teachings. The Principle of Polarity shows that both are but Half-Truths the opposing poles of Truth. The Teachings are that a man may be both Free and yet bound by Necessity, depending upon the meaning of the terms, and the height of Truth from which the matter is examined. The ancient writers express the matter thus: "The further the creation is from the Centre, the more it is bound; the nearer the Centre it reaches, the nearer Free is it."

The majority of people are more or less the slaves of heredity, environment, etc., and manifest very little Freedom. They are swayed by the opinions, customs and thoughts of the outside world, and also by their emotions, feelings, moods, etc. They manifest no Mastery, worthy of the name. They indignantly repudiate this assertion, saying, "Why, I certainly am free to act and do as I please-I do just what I want to do," but they fail to explain whence arise the "want to" and "as I please." What makes them "want to" do one thing in preference to another; what makes them "please" to do this, and not do that? Is there no "because" to their "pleasing" and "Wanting"? The Master can change these "pleases" and "wants" into others at the opposite end of the mental pole. He is able to "Will to will," instead of to will because some feeling, mood, emotion, or environmental suggestion arouses a tendency or desire within him so to do.

The majority of people are carried along like the falling stone, obedient to environment, outside influences and internal moods, desires, etc., not to speak of the desires and wills of others stronger than themselves, heredity, environment, and suggestion, carrying them along without resistance on their part, or the exercise of the Will. Moved like the pawns on the checkerboard of life, they play their parts and are laid aside after the game is over. But the Masters, knowing the rules of the game, rise above the plane of material life, and placing themselves in touch with the higher powers of their nature, dominate their own moods, characters, qualities, and polarity, as well as the environment surrounding them and thus become Movers in the game, instead of Pawns-Causes instead of Effects. The Masters do not escape the Causation of the higher planes, but fall in with the higher laws, and thus master circumstances on the lower plane. They thus form a conscious part of the Law, instead of being mere blind instruments. While they Serve on the Higher Planes, they Rule on the Material Plane.

But, on higher and on lower, the Law is always in operation. There is no such thing as Chance. The blind goddess has been abolished by Reason. We are able to see now, with eyes made clear by knowledge, that everything is governed by Universal Law-that the infinite number of laws are but manifestations of the One Great Law-the **Law** which is **The All**. It is true indeed that not a sparrow drops unnoticed by the Mind of **The All**-that even the hairs on our head are numbered-as the scriptures have said There is nothing outside of Law; nothing that happens contrary to it. And yet, do not make the mistake of supposing that Man is but a blind automaton-far from that. The Hermetic Teachings are that Man may use Law to overcome laws, and that the higher will always prevail against the lower, until at last he has reached the stage in which he seeks refuge in the **Law** itself, and laughs the phenomenal laws to scorn. Are you able to grasp the inner meaning of this?

xiii. Gender

"Gender is in everything; everything has its Masculine and Feminine Principles; Gender manifests on all planes." -The Kybalion.

The great Seventh Hermetic Principle-the Principle of Gender-embodies the truth that there is Gender manifested in everything-that the Masculine and Feminine principles are ever present and active in all phases of phenomena, on each and every plane of life. At this point we think it well to call your attention to the fact that Gender, in its Hermetic sense, and Sex in the ordinarily accepted use of the term, are not the same.

The word "Gender" is derived from the Latin root meaning "to beget; to procreate; to generate; to create; to produce." A moment's consideration will show you that the word has a much broader and more general meaning than the term "Sex," the latter referring to the physical distinctions between male and female living things. Sex is merely a manifestation of Gender on a certain plane of the Great Physical Plane-the plane of organic life. We wish to impress this distinction upon your minds, for the reason that certain writers, who have acquired a smattering of the Hermetic Philosophy, have sought to identify this Seventh Hermetic Principle with wild and fanciful, and often reprehensible, theories and teachings regarding Sex.

The office of Gender is solely that of creating, producing, generating, etc., and its manifestations are visible on every plane of phenomena. It is somewhat difficult to produce proofs of this along scientific lines, for the reason that science has not as yet recognized this Principle as of universal application. But still some proofs are forthcoming from scientific sources. In the first place, we find a distinct manifestation of the Principle of Gender among the corpuscles, ions, or electrons, which constitute the basis of Matter as science now knows the latter, and which by forming certain combinations form the Atom, which until lately was regarded as final and indivisible.

The latest word of science is that the atom is composed of a multitude of corpuscles, electrons, or ions (the various names being applied by different authorities) revolving around each other and vibrating at a high degree and intensity. But the accompanying statement is made that the formation of the atom is really due to the clustering of negative corpuscles around a positive one--the positive corpuscles seeming to exert a certain influence upon the negative corpuscles, causing the latter to assume certain combinations and thus "create" or "generate" an atom. This is in line with the most ancient Hermetic Teachings, which have always identified the Masculine principle of Gender with the "Positive," and the Feminine with the "Negative" Poles of Electricity (so called).

Now a word at this point regarding this identification. The public mind has formed an entirely erroneous impression regarding the qualities of the so-called "Negative" pole of electrified or magnetized Matter. The terms Positive and Negative are very wrongly applied to this phenomenon by science. The word Positive means something real and strong, as compared with a Negative unreality or weakness. Nothing is further from the real facts of electrical phenomenon. The so-called Negative pole of the battery is really the pole in and by which the generation or production of new forms and energies is manifested. There is nothing "negative" about it. The best scientific authorities now use the word "Cathode" in place of "Negative," the word Cathode coming from the Greek root meaning "descent; the path of generation, etc," From the Cathode pole emerge the swarm of electrons or corpuscles; from the same pole emerge those wonderful "rays" which have revolutionized scientific conceptions during the past decade. The Cathode pole is the Mother of all of the strange phenomena which have rendered useless the old textbooks, and which have caused many long accepted theories to be relegated to the scrap-pile of scientific speculation. The Cathode, or Negative Pole, is the Mother Principle of Electrical Phenomena, and of the finest forms of matter as yet known to science. So you see we are justified in refusing to use the term "Negative" in our consideration of the subject, and in insisting upon substituting the word "Feminine" for the old term. The facts of the case bear us out in this, without taking the Hermetic Teachings into consideration. And so we shall use the word "Feminine" in the place of "Negative" in speaking of that pole of activity.

The latest scientific teachings are that the creative corpuscles or electrons are Feminine (science says "they are composed of negative electricity"-we say they are composed of Feminine energy). A Feminine corpuscle becomes detached from, or rather leaves, a Masculine corpuscle, and starts on a new career. It actively seeks a union with a Masculine corpuscle, being urged thereto by the natural impulse to create new forms of Matter or Energy. One writer goes so far as to use the term "it at once seeks, of its own volition, a union," etc. This detachment and uniting form the basis of the greater part of the activities of the chemical world. When the Feminine corpuscle unites with a Masculine corpuscle, a certain process is begun. The Feminine particles vibrate rapidly under the influence of the Masculine energy, and circle rapidly around the latter. The result is the birth of a new atom. This new atom is really composed of a union of the Masculine and Feminine electrons, or corpuscles, but when the union is formed the atom is a separate thing, having certain properties, but no longer manifesting the property of free electricity. The process of detachment or separation of the Feminine electrons is called "ionization." These electrons, or corpuscles, are the most active workers in Nature's field. Arising from their unions, or combinations, manifest the varied phenomena of light, heat, electricity, magnetism, attraction, repulsion, chemical affinity and the reverse, and similar phenomena. And all this arises from the operation of the Principle of Gender on the plane of Energy.

The part of the Masculine principle seems to be that of directing a certain inherent energy toward the Feminine principle, and thus starting into activity the creative processes. But the Feminine principle is the one always doing the active creative work-and this is so on all planes. And yet, each principle is incapable of operative energy without the assistance of the other. In some of the forms of life, the two principles are combined in one organism. For that matter, everything in the organic world manifests both genders-there is always the Masculine present in the Feminine form, and the Feminine form. The Hermetic Teachings include much regarding the operation of the two principles of Gender in the production and manifestation of various forms of energy, etc., but we do not deem it expedient to go into detail regarding the same at this point, because we are unable to back up the same with scientific proof, for the reason that science has not as yet progressed thus far. But the example we have given you of the phenomena of the electrons or corpuscles will show you that science is on the right path, and will also give you a general idea of the underlying principles.

Some leading scientific investigators have announced their belief that in the formation of crystals there was to be found something that corresponded to "sex-activity" which is another straw showing the direction the scientific winds are blowing. And each year will bring other facts to corroborate the correctness of the Hermetic Principle of Gender. It will be found that Gender is in constant operation and manifestation in the field of inorganic matter, and in the field of Energy or Force. Electricity is now generally regarded as the "Something" into which all other forms of energy seem to melt or dissolve. The "Electrical Theory of the Universe" is the latest scientific doctrine, and is growing rapidly in popularity and general acceptance. And it thus follows that if we are able to discover in the phenomena of electricity-even at the very root and source of its manifestations a clear and unmistakable evidence of the presence of Gender and its activities, we are justified in asking you to believe that science at last has offered proofs of the existence in all universal phenomena of that great Hermetic Principle-the Principle of Gender.

It is not necessary to take up your time with the well known phenomena of the "attraction and repulsion" of the atoms; chemical affinity; the "loves and hates" of the atomic particles; the attraction or cohesion between the molecules of matter. These facts are too well known to need extended comment from us. But, have you ever considered that all of these things are manifestations of the Gender Principle? Can you not see that the phenomena is "on all fours" with that of the corpuscles or electrons? And more than this, can you not see the reasonableness of the Hermetic Teachings which assert that the very Law of Gravitation-that strange attraction by reason of which all particles and bodies of matter in the universe tend toward each other is but another manifestation of the Principle of Gender, which operates in the direction of attracting the Masculine to the Feminine energies, and vice versa? We cannot offer you scientific proof of this at this time-but examine the phenomena in the light of the Hermetic Teachings on the subject, and see if you have not a better working hypothesis than any offered by physical science. Submit all physical phenomena to the test, and you will discern the Principle of Gender ever in evidence.

Let us now pass on to a consideration of the operation of the Principle on the Mental Plane. Many interesting features are there awaiting examination.

xiv. Mental Gender

Students of psychology who have followed the modern trend of thought along the lines of mental phenomena are struck by the persistence of the dual-mind idea which has manifested itself so strongly during the past ten or fifteen years, and which has given rise to a number of plausible theories regarding the nature and constitution of these "two minds." The late Thomson J. Hudson attained great popularity in 1893 by advancing his well-known theory of the "objective and subjective minds" which he held existed in every individual. Other writers have attracted almost equal attention by the theories regarding the "conscious and subconscious minds"; the "voluntary and involuntary minds"; "the active and passive minds," etc., etc. The theories of the various writers differ from each other, but there remains the underlying principle of "the duality of mind."

The student of the Hermetic Philosophy is tempted to smile when he reads and hears of these many "new theories" regarding the duality of mind, each school adhering tenaciously to its own pet theories, and each claiming to have "discovered the truth." The student turns back the pages of occult history, and away back in the dim beginnings of occult teachings he finds references to the ancient Hermetic doctrine of the Principle of Gender on the Mental Plane-the manifestation of Mental Gender. And examining further he finds that the ancient philosophy took cognizance of the phenomenon of the "dual mind," and accounted for it by the theory of Mental Gender. This idea of Mental Gender may be explained in a few words to students who are familiar with the modern theories just alluded to. The Masculine Principle of Mind corresponds to the so-called Objective Mind; Conscious Mind; Voluntary Mind; Active Mind, etc. And the Feminine Principle of Mind corresponds to the so-called Subjective Mind; Sub-conscious Mind; Involuntary Mind; Passive Mind, etc. Of course the Hermetic Teachings do not agree with the many modern theories regarding the nature of the two phases of mind, nor does it admit many of the facts claimed for the two respective aspects-some of the said theories and claims being very far-fetched and incapable of standing the test of experiment and demonstration. We point to the phases of agreement merely for the purpose of helping the student to assimilate his previously acquired knowledge with the teachings of the Hermetic Philosophy. Students of Hudson will notice the statement at the beginning of his second chapter of "The Law of Psychic Phenomena," that: "The mystic jargon of the Hermetic philosophers discloses the same general idea" i.e., the duality of mind. If Dr. Hudson had taken the time and trouble to decipher a little of "the mystic jargon of the Hermetic Philosophy," he might have received much light upon the subject of "the dual mind"-but then, perhaps, his most interesting work might not have been written. Let us now consider the Hermetic Teachings regarding Mental Gender.

The Hermetic Teachers impart their instruction regarding this subject by bidding their students examine the report of their consciousness regarding their Self. The students are bidden to turn their attention inward upon the Self dwelling within each. Each student is led to see that his consciousness gives him first a report of the existence of his Self-the report is "I Am." This at first seems to be the final words from the consciousness, but a little further examination discloses the fact that this "I Am" may be separated or split into two distinct parts, or aspects, which while working in unison and in conjunction, yet, nevertheless, may be separated in consciousness.

While at first there seems to be only an "I" existing, a more careful and closer examination reveals the fact that there exists an "I" and a "Me." These mental twins differ in their characteristics and nature, and an examination of their nature and the phenomena arising from the same will throw much light upon many of the problems of mental influence.

Let us begin with a consideration of the Me, which is usually mistaken for the I by the student, until he presses the inquiry a little further back into the recesses of consciousness. A man thinks of his Self (in its aspect of Me) as being composed of certain feelings, tastes likes, dislikes, habits, peculiar ties, characteristics, etc., all of which go to make up his personality, or the "Self" known to himself and others. He knows that these emotions and feelings change; are born and die away; are subject to the Principle of Rhythm, and the Principle of Polarity, which take him from one extreme of feeling to another. He also thinks of the "Me" as being certain knowledge gathered together in his mind, and thus forming a part of himself. This is the "Me" of a man.

But we have proceeded too hastily. The "Me" of many men may be said to consist largely of their consciousness of the body and their physical appetites, etc. Their consciousness being largely bound up with their bodily nature, they practically "live there." Some men even go so far as to regard their personal apparel as a part of their "Me" and actually seem to consider it a part of themselves. A writer has humorously said that "men consist of three parts-soul, body and clothes." These "clothes conscious" people would lose their personality if divested of their clothing by savages upon the occasion of a shipwreck. But even many who are not so closely bound up with the idea of personal raiment stick closely to the consciousness of their bodies being their "Me" They cannot conceive of a Self independent of the body. Their mind seems to them to be practically "a something belonging to" their body-which in many cases it is indeed.

But as man rises in the scale of consciousness he is able to disentangle his "Me" from his idea of body, and is able to think of his body as "belonging to" the mental part of him. But even then he is very apt to identify the "Me" entirely with the mental states, feelings, etc., which he feels to exist within him. He is very apt to consider these internal states as identical with himself, instead of their being simply "things" produced by some part of his mentality, and existing within him-of him, and in him, but still not "himself." He sees that he may change these internal states of feelings by all effort of will, and that he may produce a feeling or state of an exactly opposite nature, in the same way, and yet the same "Me" exists. And so after a while he is able to set aside these various mental states, emotions, feelings, habits, qualities, characteristics, and other personal mental belongings-he is able to set them aside in the "not-me" collection of curiosities and encumbrances, as well as valuable possessions. This requires much mental concentration and power of mental analysis on the part of the student. But still the task is possible for the advanced student, and even those not so far advanced are able to see, in the imagination, how the process may be performed.

After this laying-aside process has been performed, the student will find himself in conscious possession of a "Self" which may be considered in its "I" and "Me" dual aspects. The "Me" will be felt to be a Something mental in which thoughts, ideas, emotions, feelings, and other mental states may be produced. It may be considered as the "mental womb," as the ancients styled it-capable of generating mental offspring. It reports to the consciousness as a "Me" with latent powers of creation and generation of mental progeny of all sorts and kinds. Its powers of creative energy are felt to be enormous. But still it seems to be conscious that it must receive some form of energy from either its "I" companion, or else from some other "I" ere it is able to bring into being its mental creations. This consciousness brings with it a realization of an enormous capacity for mental work and creative ability.

But the student soon finds that this is not all that he finds within his inner consciousness. He finds that there exists a mental Something which is able to Will that the "Me" act along certain creative lines, and which is also able to stand aside and witness the mental creation. This part of himself he is taught to call his "I." He is able to rest in its consciousness at will. He finds there not a consciousness of an ability to generate and actively create, in the sense of the gradual process attendant upon mental operations, but rather a sense and consciousness of an ability to project an energy from the "I" to the "Me"-a process of "willing" that the mental creation begin and proceed. He also finds that the "I" is able to stand aside and witness the operations of the "Me's" mental creation and generation. There is this dual aspect in the mind of every person. The "I" represents the Masculine Principle of Mental Gender-the "Me" represents the Female Principle. The "I" represents the Aspect of Being; the "Me" the Aspect of Becoming. You will notice that the Principle of Correspondence operates on this plane just as it does upon the great plane upon which the creation of Universes is performed. The two are similar in kind, although vastly different in degree. "As above, so below; as below, so above."

These aspects of mind-the Masculine and Feminine Principles-the "I" and the "Me"-considered in connection with the well-known mental and psychic phenomena, give the master-key to these dimly known regions of mental operation and manifestation. The principle of Mental Gender gives the truth underlying the whole field of the phenomena of mental influence, etc.

The tendency of the Feminine Principle is always in the direction of receiving impressions, while the tendency of the Masculine Principle is always in the direction of giving, out or expressing. The Feminine Principle has much more varied field of operation than has the Masculine Principle. The Feminine Principle conducts the work of generating new thoughts, concepts, ideas, including the work of the imagination. The Masculine Principle contents itself with the work of the "Will" in its varied phases. And yet, without the active aid of the Will of the Masculine Principle, the Feminine Principle is apt to rest content with generating mental images which are the result of impressions received from outside, instead of producing original mental creations.

Persons who can give continued attention and thought to a subject actively employ both of the Mental Principles-the Feminine in the work of the mental generation, and the Masculine Will in stimulating and energizing the creative portion of the mind. The majority of persons really employ the Masculine Principle but little, and are content to live according to the thoughts and ideas instilled into the "Me" from the "I" of other minds. But it is not our purpose to dwell upon this phase of the subject, which may be studied from any good text-book upon psychology, with the key that we have given you regarding Mental Gender.

The student of Psychic Phenomena is aware of the wonderful phenomena classified under the head of Telepathy; Thought Transference; Mental Influence; Suggestion; Hypnotism, etc. Many have sought for an explanation of these varied phases of phenomena under the theories of the various "dual mind" teachers. And in a measure they are right, for there is clearly a manifestation of two distinct phases of mental activity. But if such students will consider these "dual minds" in the light of the Hermetic Teachings regarding Vibrations and Mental Gender, they will see that the long sought for key is at hand.

In the phenomena of Telepathy it is seen how the Vibratory Energy of the Masculine Principle is projected toward the Feminine Principle of another person, and the latter takes the seed-thought and allows it to develop into maturity. In the same way Suggestion and Hypnotism operates. The Masculine Principle of the person giving the suggestions directs a stream of Vibratory Energy or Will-

Power toward the Feminine Principle of the other person, and the latter accepting it makes it its own and acts and thinks accordingly. An idea thus lodged in the mind of another person grows and develops, and in time is regarded as the rightful mental offspring of the individual, whereas it is in reality like the cuckoo egg placed in the sparrows nest, where it destroys the rightful offspring and makes itself at home. The normal method is for the Masculine and Feminine Principles in a person's mind to co-ordinate and act harmoniously in conjunction with each other, but, unfortunately, the Masculine Principle in the average person is too lazy to act-the display of Will-Power is too slight-and the consequence is that such persons are ruled almost entirely by the minds and wills of other persons, whom they allow to do their thinking and willing for them. How few original thoughts or original actions are performed by the average person? Are not the majority of persons mere shadows and echoes of others having stronger wills or minds than themselves? The trouble is that the average person dwells almost altogether in his "Me" consciousness and does not realize that he has such a thing as an "I." He is polarized in his Feminine Principle of Mind, and the Masculine Principle, in which is lodged the Will, is allowed to remain inactive and not employed.

The strong men and women of the world invariably manifest the Masculine Principle of Will, and their strength depends materially upon this fact. Instead of living upon the impressions made upon their minds by others, they dominate their own minds by their Will, obtaining the kind of mental images desired, and moreover dominate the minds of others likewise, in the same manner. Look at the strong people, how they manage to implant their seed-thoughts in the minds of the masses of the people, thus causing the latter to think thoughts in accordance with the desires and wills of the strong individuals. This is why the masses of people are such sheep like creatures, never originating an idea of their own, nor using their own powers of mental activity.

The manifestation of Mental Gender may be noticed all around us in everyday life. The magnetic persons are those who are able to use the Masculine Principle in the way of impressing their ideas upon others. The actor who makes people weep or cry as he wills, is employing this principle. And so is the successful orator, statesman, preacher, writer or other people who are before the public attention. The peculiar influence exerted by some people over others is due to the manifestation of Mental Gender, along the Vibrational lines above indicated. In this principle lies the secret of personal magnetism, personal influence, fascination, etc., as well as the phenomena generally grouped under the name of Hypnotism.

The student who has familiarized himself with the phenomena generally spoken of as "psychic" will have discovered the important part played in the said phenomena by that force which science has styled "Suggestion," by which term is meant the process or method whereby an idea is transferred to, or "impressed upon" the mind of another, causing the second mind to act in accordance therewith. A correct understanding of Suggestion is necessary in order to intelligently comprehend the varied psychical phenomena which Suggestion underlies. But, still more is a knowledge of Vibration and Mental Gender necessary for the student of Suggestion. For the whole principle of Suggestion depends upon the principle of Mental Gender and Vibration.

It is customary for the writers and teachers of Suggestion to explain that it is the "objective or voluntary" mind which make the mental impression, or suggestion, upon the "subjective or involuntary" mind. But they do not describe the process or give us any analogy in nature whereby we may more readily comprehend the idea. But if you will think of the matter in the light of the Hermetic Teachings you will be able to see that the energizing of the

Feminine Principle by the Vibratory Energy of the Masculine Principle Is in accordance to the universal laws of nature, and that the natural world affords countless analogies whereby the principle may be understood. In fact, the Hermetic Teachings show that the very creation of the Universe follows the same law, and that in all creative manifestations, upon the planes of the spiritual, the mental, and the physical, there is always in operation this principle of Gender-this manifestation of the Masculine and the Feminine Principles. "As above, so below; as below, so above." And more than this, when the principle of Mental Gender is once grasped and understood, the varied phenomena of psychology at once becomes capable of intelligent classification and study, instead of being very much in the dark. The principle "works out" in practice, because it is based upon the immutable universal laws of life.

We shall not enter into an extended discussion of, or description of, the varied phenomena of mental influence or psychic activity. There are many books, many of them quite good, which have been written and published on this subject of late years. The main facts stated in these various books are correct, although the several writers have attempted to explain the phenomena by various pet theories of their own. The student may acquaint himself with these matters, and by using the theory of Mental Gender he will be able to bring order out of the chaos of conflicting theory and teachings, and may, moreover, readily make himself a master of the subject if he be so inclined. The purpose of this work is not to give an extended account of psychic phenomena but rather to give to the student a master-key whereby He may unlock the many doors leading into the parts of the Temple of Knowledge which he may wish to explore. We feel that in this consideration of the teachings of The Kybalion, one may find an explanation which will serve to clear away many perplexing difficulties-a key that will unlock many doors. What is the use of going into detail regarding all of the many features of psychic phenomena and mental science, provided we place in the hands of the student the means whereby he may acquaint himself fully regarding any phase of the subject which may interest him. With the aid of The Kybalion one may go through any occult library anew, the old Light from Egypt illuminating many dark pages, and obscure subjects. That is the purpose of this book. We do not come expounding a new philosophy, but rather furnishing the outlines of a great world-old teaching which will make clear the teachings of others-which will serve as a Great Reconciler of differing: theories, and opposing doctrines.

xv. Hermetic Axioms

"The possession of Knowledge, unless accompanied by a manifestation and expression in Action, is like the hoarding of precious metals-a vain and foolish thing. Knowledge, like wealth, is intended for Use. The Law of Use is Universal, and he who violates it suffers by reason of his conflict with natural forces."-The Kybalion.

The Hermetic Teachings, while always having been kept securely locked up in the minds of the fortunate possessors thereof, for reasons which we have already stated, were never intended to be merely stored away and secreted. The Law of Use is dwelt upon in the Teachings, as you may see by reference to the above quotation from The Kybalion, which states it forcibly. Knowledge without Use and Expression is a vain thing, bringing no good to its possessor, or to the race. Beware of Mental Miserliness, and express into Action that which you have learned. Study the Axioms and Aphorisms, but practice them also.

We give below some of the more important Hermetic Axioms, from The Kybalion, with a few comments added to each. Make these your own, and practice and use them, for they are not really your own until you have used them.

"To change your mood or mental state-change your vibration."

-The Kybalion.

One may change his mental vibrations by an effort of Will, in the direction of deliberately fixing the Attention upon a more desirable state. Will directs the Attention, and Attention changes the Vibration. Cultivate the Art of Attention, by means of the Will, and you have solved the secret of the Mastery of Moods and Mental States.

"To destroy an undesirable rate of mental vibration, put into operation the principle of Polarity and concentrate upon the opposite pole to that

which you desire to suppress. Kill out the undesirable by changing its polarity."-The Kybalion.

This is one of the most important of the Hermetic Formulas. It is based upon true scientific principles. We have shown you that a mental state and its opposite were merely the two poles of one thing, and that by Mental Transmutation the polarity might be reversed. This Principle is known to modern psychologists, who apply it to the breaking up of undesirable habits by bidding their students concentrate upon the opposite quality. If you are possessed of Fear, do not waste time trying to "kill out" Fear, but instead cultivate the quality of Courage, and the Fear will disappear. Some writers have expressed this idea most forcibly by using the illustration of the dark room. You do not have to shovel out or sweep out the Darkness, but by merely opening the shutters and letting in the Light the Darkness has disappeared. To kill out a Negative quality, concentrate upon the Positive Pole of that same quality, and the vibrations will gradually change from Negative to Positive, until finally you will become polarized on the Positive pole instead of the Negative. The reverse is also true, as many have found out to their sorrow, when they have allowed themselves to vibrate too constantly on the Negative pole of things. By changing your polarity you may master your moods, change your mental states, remake your disposition, and build up character. Much of the Mental Mastery of the advanced Hermetics is due to this application of Polarity, which is one of the important aspects of Mental Transmutation. Remember the Hermetic Axiom (quoted previously), which says:

"Mind (as well as metals and elements) may be transmuted from state to state; degree to degree, condition to condition; pole to pole; vibration to vibration."-The Kybalion.

The mastery of Polarization is the mastery of the fundamental principles of Mental Transmutation or Mental Alchemy, for unless one acquires the art of changing his own polarity, he will be unable to affect his environment. An understanding of this principle will enable one to change his own Polarity, as well as that of others, if he will but devote the time, care, study and practice necessary to master the art. The principle is true, but the results obtained depend upon the persistent patience and practice of the student.

"Rhythm may be neutralized by an application of the Art of Polarization."-The Kybalion.

As we have explained in previous chapters, the Hermetists hold that the Principle of Rhythm manifests on the Mental Plane as well as on the Physical Plane, and that the bewildering succession of moods, feelings, emotions, and other mental states, are due to the backward and forward swing of the mental pendulum, which carries us from one extreme of feeling to the other. The Hermetists also teach that the Law of Neutralization enables one, to a great extent, to overcome the operation of Rhythm in consciousness. As we have explained, there is a Higher Plane of Consciousness, as well as the ordinary Lower Plane, and the Master by rising mentally to the Higher Plane causes the swing of the mental pendulum to manifest on the Lower Plane, and he, dwelling on his Higher Plane, escapes the consciousness of the swing backward. This is effected by polarizing on the Higher Self, and thus raising the mental vibrations of the Ego above those of the ordinary plane of consciousness. It is akin to rising above a thing and allowing it to pass beneath you. The advanced Hermetist polarizes himself at the Positive Pole of his Being-the "I Am" pole rather than the pole of personality and by "refusing" and "denying" the operation of Rhythm, raises himself above its plane of consciousness, and standing firm in his Statement of Being he allows the pendulum to swing back on the Lower Plane without changing his Polarity. This is accomplished by all individuals who have attained any degree of self-mastery, whether they understand the law or not. Such persons simply "refuse" to allow themselves to be swung back by the pendulum of mood and emotion, and by steadfastly affirming the superiority they remain polarized on the Positive pole. The Master, of course, attains a far greater degree of proficiency, because he understands the law which he is overcoming by a higher law, and by the use of his Will he attains a degree of Poise and Mental Steadfastness almost impossible of belief on the part of those who allow themselves to be swung backward and forward by the mental pendulum of moods and feelings.

Remember always, however, that you do not really destroy the Principle of Rhythm, for that is indestructible. You simply overcome one law by counter-balancing it with another and thus maintain an equilibrium. The laws of balance and counter-balance are in operation on the mental as well as on the physical planes, and an understanding of these laws enables one to seem to overthrow laws, whereas he is merely exerting a counterbalance.

"Nothing escapes the Principle of Cause and Effect, but there are many Planes of Causation, and one may use the laws of the higher to overcome the laws of the lower."-The Kybalion.

By an understanding of the practice of Polarization, the Hermetists rise to a higher plane of Causation and thus counter-balance the laws of the lower planes of Causation. By rising above the plane of ordinary Causes they become themselves, in a degree, Causes instead of being merely Caused. By being able to master their own moods and feelings, and by being able to neutralize Rhythm, as we have already explained, they are able to escape a great part of the operations of Cause and Effect on the ordinary plane. The masses of people are carried along, obedient to their environment; the wills and desires of others stronger than themselves; the effects of inherited tendencies; the suggestions of those about them; and other outward causes; which tend to move them about on the chess-board of life like mere pawns. By rising above these influencing causes, the advanced Hermetists seek a higher plane of mental action, and by dominating their moods, emotions, impulses and feelings, they create for themselves new characters, qualities and powers, by which they overcome their ordinary environment, and thus become practically players instead of mere Pawns. Such people help to play the game of life understandingly, instead of being moved about this way and that way by stronger influences and powers and wills. They use the Principle of Cause and Effect, instead of being used by it. Of course, even the highest are subject to the Principle as it manifests on the higher planes, but on the lower planes of activity, they are Masters instead of Slaves. As The Kybalion says:

"The wise ones serve on the higher, but rule on the lower. They obey the laws coming from above them, But on their own plane, and those below them they rule and give orders.

And, yet, in so doing, they form a part of the Principle, instead of opposing it. The wise man falls in with the Law, and by understanding its movements he operates it instead of being its blind slave. Just as does the skilled swimmer turn this way and that way, going and coming as he will, instead of being as the log which is carried here and there-so is the wise man as compared to the ordinary man-and yet both swimmer and log; wise man and fool, are subject to Law. He who understands this is well on the road to Mastery."-The Kybalion.

In conclusion let us again call your attention to the Hermetic Axiom:

"True Hermetic Transmutation is a Mental Art."-The Kybalion.

In the above axiom, the Hermetists teach that the great work of influencing one's environment is accomplished by Mental Power. The Universe being wholly mental, it follows that it may be ruled only by Mentality. And in this truth is to be found an explanation of all the phenomena and manifestations of the various mental powers which are attracting so much attention and study in these earlier years of the Twentieth Century. Back of and under the teachings of the various cults and schools, remains ever constant the Principle of the Mental Substance of the Universe. If the Universe be Mental in its substantial nature, then it follows that Mental Transmutation must change the conditions and phenomena of the Universe. If the Universe is Mental, then Mind must be the highest power affecting its phenomena. If this be understood then all the so-called "miracles" and "wonder-workings" are seen plainly for what they are.

"**The All is Mind;** The Universe is Mental."-The Kybalion.

The Emerald Tablet

By Hermes Trismegistus

Tabula Smaragdina

VERUM SINE MENDACIO CERTUM ET VERISSIMUM
QUOD EST INFERIUS EST SICUT QUOD EST SUPERIUS
ET QUOD EST SUPERIUS EST SICUT QUOD EST
INFERIUS AD PERPETRANDA MIRACULA REI UNIUS
ET SICUT RES OMNES FUERUNT AB UNO
MEDITATIONE UNIUS SIC OMNES RES NATAE AB
HAC UNA RE ADAPTATIONE PATER EIUS EST SOL
MATER EIUS EST LUNA PORTAVIT ILLUD VENTUS IN
VENTRE SUO NUTRIX EIUS TERRA EST PATER
OMNIS TELESMI TOTIUS MUNDI EST HIC VIRTUS EIUS
INTEGRA EST SI VERSA FUERIT IN TERRAM
SEPARABIS TERRAM AB IGNE SUBTILE AB SPISSO
SUAVITER MAGNO CUM INGENIO ASCENDIT A
TERRA IN COELUM ITERUMQUE DESCENDIT IN
TERRAM ET RECIPIT VIM SUPERIORUM ET
INFERIORUM SIC HABEBIS GLORIAM TOTIUS MUNDI
IDEO FUGIET A TE OMNIS OBSCURITAS HAEC EST
TOTIUS FORTITUDINIS FORTITUDO FORTIS QUIA
VINCET OMNEM REM SUBTILEM OMNEMQUE
SOLIDAM PENETRABIT SIC MUNDUS CREATUS EST
HINC ERUNT ADAPTATIONES MIRABILES QUARUM
MODUS EST HIC ITAQUE VOCATUS SUM HERMES
TRISMEGISTUS HABENS TRES PARTES
PHILOSOPHIAE TOTIUS MUNDI COMPLETUM EST
QUOD DIXI DE OPERATIONE SOLIS

Selected Variations and Translations

Issac Newton[*]

'Tis true without lying, certain and most true.

That which is below is like that which is above and that which is above is like that which is below to do ye miracles of one only thing.

Thus as all things have been and arose from one by the mediation of one: so all things have their birth from this one thing by adaptation.

The Sun is its father, the moon its mother, the wind hath carried it in its belly, the earth its nurse.

The father of all perfection in the whole world is here. Its force or power is entire if it be converted into earth.

Seperate thou the earth from the fire, the subtle from the gross sweetly with great industry.

It ascends from the earth to the heaven and again it descends to the earth and receives the force of things superior and inferior.

By this means you shall have the glory of the whole world and thereby all obscurity shall fly from you.

Its force is above all force. For it vanquishes every subtle thing and penetrates every solid thing.

So was the world created. From this are and do come admirable adaptations whereof the means is here in this.

Hence I am called Hermes Trismegistus, having the three parts of the philosophy of the whole world. That which I have said of the operation of the Sun is accomplished and ended.

---

[*] Translated into Modern English where required for clarity.

H.P. Blavatsky

- What is below is like that which is above, and what is above is similar to that which is below to accomplish the wonders of the one thing.

- As all things were produced by the mediation of one being, so all things were produced from this one by adaptation.

- Its father is the sun, its mother the moon.

- It is the cause of all perfection throughout the whole Earth.

- Its power is perfect if it is changed into Earth.

- Separate the Earth from the fire, the subtle from the gross, acting prudently and with judgment.

- Ascend with the greatest sagacity from earth to heaven, and unite together the power of things inferior and superior

- Thus you will possess the light of the whole world, and all obscurity will fly away from you.

- This thing has more fortitude than fortitude itself, because it will overcome every subtle thing and penetrate every solid thing.

- By it the world was formed.

Georgio Beato

1. This is true and remote from all cover of falsehood.
2. Whatever is below is similar to that which is above. Through this the marvels of the work of one thing are procured and perfected.
3. Also, as all things are made from one, by the consideration of one, so all things were made from this one, by conjunction.
4. The father of it is the sun, the mother the moon.
5. The wind bore it in the womb. Its nurse is the earth, the mother of all perfection.
6. Its power is perfected.
7. If it is turned into earth, separate the earth from the fire, the subtle and thin from the crude and coarse, prudently, with modesty and wisdom.
8. This ascends from the earth into the sky and again descends from the sky to the earth, and receives the power and efficacy of things above and of things below.
9. By this means you will acquire the glory of the whole world, and so you will drive away all shadows and blindness.
10. For this by its fortitude snatches the palm from all other fortitude and power. For it is able to penetrate and subdue everything subtle and everything crude and hard.
11. By this means the world was founded
12. And hence the marvelous conjunctions of it and admirable effects, since this is the way by which these marvels may be brought about.

13. And because of this they have called me Hermes Trismegistus since I have the three parts of the wisdom and Philosophy of the whole universe.
14. My speech is finished which I have spoken concerning the solar work.

The Divine Poemander
in Seventeen books.

Translated from the Latin *Corpus Hermeticum*
by John Everard

I: Introduction

Hermes Trismegistus speaks thusly to his son…
1. O my Son, write this first Book, both for humanity's sake, and for piety towards God. 2. For there can be no religion more true or just, than to know the things that are, and to acknowledge thanks for all things, to him that made them, which thing I shall not cease continually to do.

Tat, the son, replies: 3. What then should a man do, O Father, to lead his life well, seeing there is nothing here true ?

Hermes Trismegistus says: 4. Be pious and religious, O my son, for he that doth so, is the best and highest Philosopher, and without philosophy, it is impossible ever to attain to the height and exactness of piety or religion, 5. but he that shall learn and study the things that are, and how they are ordered and governed, and by whom and for what cause, or to what end, will acknowledge thanks to the Workman as to a good father, an excellent nurse and a faithful steward, and he that gives thanks shall be pious or religious, and he that is religious shall know both where the truth is, and what it is, and learning that, he will be yet more and more religious. 6. For never, O son, shall or can that Soul which while it is in the Body lightens and lifts up itself to know and comprehend that which is good and true, slide back to the contrary; for it is infinitely enamoured thereof, and forgetteth all Evils, and when it hath learned and known its Father and progenitor it can no more apostatize or depart from that Good. 7. And let this, O Son, be the end of religion and piety; whereunto when thou art once arrived, thou shalt both live well, and die blessedly, whilst thy Soul is not ignorant whether it must return and fly back again.

8. For this only, O Son, is the way to the Truth, which our progenitors traveled in; and by which, making their journey, they at length attained to the Good. It is a venerable way, and plain, but hard and difficult for the Soul to go in that is in the Body. 9. For first must it war against its own self, and after much strife and dissention it must be overcome of one part; for the contention is of one against two, whilst it flies away and they strive to hold and detain it. 10. But the victory of both is not like; for the one hasteth to that which is Good, but the other is a neighbour to the things that are Evil and that which is Good, desireth to be set at Liberty but the things that are Evil, love Bondage and Slavery. 11. And if the two parts be overcome, they become quiet, and are content to accept of it as their Ruler; but if the one be overcome of the two, it is by them led and carried to be punished by its being and continuance here.

12. This is, O Son, the guide in the way that leads thither for thou must first forsake the body before thy end, and get the victory in this contention and strifeful life, and when thou hast overcome, return. 13. But now, O my Son, I will by Heads run through the things that are: understand thou what I say, and remember what thou hearest. 14. All things that are, are moved; only that which is not, is unmovable. 15. Every Body is changeable. 16. Not every Body is dissolvable. 17. Some Bodies are dissolvable. 18. Every living thing is not mortal. 19. Not every living thing is immortal. 20. That which may be dissolved is also corruptible.21. That which abides always is unchangeable. 22. That which is unchangeable is eternal. 23. That which is always made is always corrupted. 24. That which is made but once, is never corrupted, neither becomes any other thing. 25. First, God; Secondly, the World; Thirdly, Man. 26. The World for Man, Man for God. 27. Of the Soul, that part which is Sensible is mortal, but that which is Reasonable is immortal. 28. Every essence is

immortal. 29. Every essence is unchangeable. 30. Every thing that is, is double. 31. None of the things that are stand still. 32. Not all things are moved by a Soul, but every thing that is, is moved by a Soul. 33. Every thing that suffers is Sensible, every thing that is Sensible suffereth. 34. Every thing that is sad rejoiceth also, and is a mortal living Creature. 35. Not every thing that joyeth is also sad, but is an eternal living thing. 36. Not every Body is sick; every Body that is sick is dissolvable. 37. The Mind in God. 38. Reasoning (or disputing or discoursing) in Man, 39. Reason in the Mind. 40. The Mind is void of suffering. 41. No thing in a Body true. 42. All that is incorporeal, is void of Lying. 43. Every thing that is made is corruptible. 44. Nothing good upon Earth, nothing evil in Heaven. 45. God is good, Man is evil. 46. Good is voluntary, or of its own accord. 47. Evil is involuntary or against its will.48. The Gods choose good things, as good things. 49. Time is a Divine thing. 50. Law is Humane. 51. Malice is the nourishment of the World. 52. Time is the Corruption of Man. 53. Whatsoever is in Heaven is unalterable. 54. All upon Earth is alterable. 55. Nothing in Heaven has servants, nothing upon Earth is free. 56. Nothing unknown in Heaven, nothing known upon Earth. 57. The things upon Earth communicate not with those in Heaven. 58. All things in Heaven are unblameable, all things upon Earth are subject to Reprehension. 59. That which is immortal, is not mortal: that which is mortal is not immortal. 60. That which is sown, is not always begotten; but that which is begotten always, is sown. 61. Of a dissolvable Body, there are two Times, one from sowing to generation, one from generation to death. 62. Of an everlasting Body, the time is only from the Generation. 63. Dissolvable Bodies are increased and diminished. 64. Dissolvable matter is altered into contraries; to wit, Corruption and Generation, but Eternal matter into its self, and its like. 65. The Generation of Man is Corruption, the Corruption of Man is the beginning of Generation. 66. That which off-springs or begetteth another, is itself an offspring or begotten by another. 67. Of things that are, some are in Bodies, some in their Ideas. 68. Whatsoever things belong to operation or working, are in a Body. 69. That which is immortal, partakes not of that which is mortal. 70. That which is mortal, cometh not into a Body immortal, but that which is immortal, cometh into that which is mortal. 71. Operations or Workings are not carried upwards, but descend downwards. 72. Things upon Earth do nothing advantage those in Heaven, but all things in Heaven do profit and advantage the things upon Earth. 73. Heaven is capable and a fit receptacle of everlasting Bodies, the Earth of corruptible Bodies. 74. The Earth is brutish, the Heaven is reasonable or rational. 75. Those things that are in Heaven are subjected or placed under it, but the things on Earth, are placed upon it. 76. Heaven is the first Element. 77. Providence is Divine Order. 78. Necessity is the Minister or Servant of Providence. 79. Fortune is the carriage or effect of that which is without Order; the Idol of operation, a lying fantasy or opinion.

80. What is God? The immutable or unalterable Good.

81. What is Man? An unchangeable Evil.

82. If thou perfectly remember these Heads, thou canst not forget those things which in more words I have largely expounded unto thee; for these are the Contents or Abridgment of them. 83. Avoid all Conversation with the multitude or common People, for I would not have thee subject to Envy, much less to be ridiculous unto the many. 84. For the like always takes to itself that which is like, but the unlike never agrees with the unlike: such Discourses as these have very few Auditors, and peradventure very few will have, but they have something peculiar unto themselves. 85. They do rather sharpen and whet evil men to their maliciousness, therefore it behoveth to avoid

the multitude and take heed of them as not understanding the virtue and power of the things that are said.

Tat questions his father: 86. How dost Thou mean, O Father?

Hermes replies: 87. Thus, O Son, the whole Nature and Composition of those living things called Men, is very prone to Maliciousness, and is very familiar, and as it were nourished with it, and therefore is delighted with it. Now this wight if it shall come to learn or know, that the world was once made, and all things are done according to Providence and Necessity, Destiny, or Fate, bearing Rule over all: Will he not be much worse than himself, despising the whole because it was made. And if he may lay the cause of evil upon Fate or Destiny, he will never abstain from any evil work. 88. Wherefore we must look warily to such kind of people, that being in ignorance, they may be less evil for fear of that which is hidden and kept secret.

II: Hermes Trismegestus tells of his vision of Poemander.

1. My Thoughts being once seriously busied about the things that are, and my Understanding lifted up, all my bodily Senses being exceedingly holden back, as it is with them that are very heavy of sleep, by reason either of fulness of meat, or of bodily labor. Me thought I saw one of an exceeding great stature, and an infinite greatness call me by my name, and say unto me, "What wouldest thou Hear and See? or what wouldest thou Understand, to Learn, and Know!"

2. Then said I, " Who art Thou?"
"I am," quoth he, "Poemander, the mind of the Great Lord, the most Mighty and absolute Emperor: I know what thou wouldest have, and I am always present with thee."

3. Then said I, "I would Learn the Things that art, and Understand the Nature of them and know God."
"How?" said he.
I answered, "That I would gladly hear."
Then he, "Have me again in thy mind, and whatsoever thou wouldst learn, I will teach thee."

4. When he had thus said, he was changed in his Idea or Form and straightway in the twinkling of an eye, all things were opened unto me: and I saw an infinite Sight, all things were become light, both sweet and exceedingly pleasant; and I was wonderfully delighted in the beholding it.

5. But after a little while, there was a darkness made in part, coming down obliquely, fearful and hideous, which seemed unto me to be changed into a Certain Moist Nature, unspeakably troubled, which

yielded a smoke as from fire; and from whence proceeded a voice unutterable, and very mournful, but inarticulate, insomuch that it seemed to have come from the Light.

6. Then from that Light, a certain Holy Word joined itself unto Nature, and out flew the pure and unmixed Fire from the moist Nature upward on high; it is exceeding Light, and Sharp, and Operative withal. And the Air which was also light, followed the Spirit and mounted up to Fire (from the Earth and the Water) insomuch that it seemed to hang and depend upon it.

7. And the Earth and the Water stayed by themselves so mingled together, that the Earth could not be seen for the Water, but they were moved, because of the Spiritual Word that was carried upon them.

8. Then said Poemander unto me, "Dost thou understand this Vision, and what it meaneth?"
"I shall know," said I.
Then said he, "I am that Light, the Mind, thy God, who am before that Moist Nature that appeareth out of Darkness, and that Bright and Lightful Word from the Mind is the Son of God."

9. "How is that?" quoth I.
"Thus," replied he, "Understand it, That which in thee Seeth and Heareth, the Word of the Lord, and the Mind, the Father, God, Differeth not One from the Other, and the Unison of these is Life."
Trismegistus: "I thank thee."
Poemander: "But first conceive well the Light in thy mind and know it."

10. When he had thus said, for a long time me looked steadfastly one upon the other, insomuch that I trembled at his Idea or Form.

11. But when he nodded to me, I beheld in my mind the Light that is in innumerable, and the truly indefinite Ornament or World; and that the Fire is comprehended or contained in or by a most great Power, and constrained to keep its station.

12. These things I understood, seeing the word of Poemander; and when I was mightily amazed, he said again unto me, "Hast thou seen in thy mind that Archetypal Form, which was before the Interminated and Infinite Beginning?" Thus Poemander to me. "But whence," quoth I, "or whereof are the Elements of Nature made?"
Poemander : "Of the Will and Counsel of God; which taking the Word, and beholding the beautiful World (in the Archetype thereof) imitated it, and so made this World, by the principles and vital Seeds or Soul-like productions of itself."

13. For the Mind being God, Male and Female, Life and Light, brought forth by his Word; another Mind, the Workman: Which being God of the Fire, and the Spirit, fashioned and formed seven other Governors, which in their Circles contain the Sensible World, whose Government or Disposition is called Fate or Destiny.

14. Straightway leaped out, or exalted itself front the downward born Elements of God, the Word of God into the clean and pure Workmanship of Nature, and was united to the Workman, Mind, for it was Consubstantial; and so the downward born Elements of Nature were left without Reason, that they might be the only Matter.

15. But the Workman, Mind, together with the Word, containing the Circles and Whirling them about, turned round as a Wheel his own Workmanships, and suffered them to be turned from an indefinite Beginning to an undeterminable End; for they always begin where they end.

16. And the Circulation or running round of these, as the Mind willeth, out of the lower or downward-born Elements brought forth unreasonable or brutish creatures, for they had no reason, the Air flying things, and the Water such as swim.

17. And the Earth and the Water was separated, either from the other, as the Mind would: and the Earth brought forth from herself such Living Creatures as she had, four-footed and creeping Beasts, wild and tame.

18. But the Father of all things, the Mind being Life and Light, brought forth Man, like unto himself, whom he loved as his proper Birth, for he was all beauteous, having the Image of his Father.

19. For indeed God was exceedingly enamoured of his own Form or Shape, and delivered unto it all his own Workmanships. But he seeing and understanding the Creation of the Workman in the whole, would needs also himself Fall to Work, and so was separated from the Father, being in the sphere of Generation or operation.

20. Having all Power, he considered the Operations or Workmanships of the Seven; but they loved him, and every one made him partaker of his own Order.

21. And he learning diligently and understanding their Essence, and partaking their nature, resolved to pierce and break through the Circumference of the Circles, and to understand the Power of him that sits upon the Fire.

22. And having already all power of mortal things, of the Living, and of the unreasonable Creatures of the World, stooped down and peeped through the Harmony, and breaking through the strength of the Circles, so shewed and made manifest the downward-born Nature, the fair and beautiful Shape or Form of God.

23. Which when he saw, having in itself the unsatiable Beauty and all the Operation of the Seven Governors, and the Form or Shape of God, he Smiled for love, as if he had seen the Shape or Likeness in the Water, or the shadow upon the Earth of the fairest Human form.

24. And seeing in the Water a shape, a shape like unto himself in himself he loved it, and would cohabit with it; and immediately upon the resolution, ensued the Operation, and brought forth the unreasonable Image or Shape.

25. Nature presently laying hold of what it so much loved, did wholly wrap herself about it, and they were mingled, for they loved one another.

26. And for this cause, Man above all things that live upon Earth, is double; Mortal because of his Body, and Immortal because of the substantial Man: For being immortal, and having power of all things, he yet suffers mortal things, and such as are subject to Fate or Destiny.

27. And therefore being; above all Harmony, he is made and become a servant to Harmony. And being Hermaphrodite, or Male and Female, and watchful, he is governed by and subjected to a Father, that is both Male and Female and watchful.

28. After these things, I said: "Thou art my Mind and I am in love with Reason."

29. Then said Poemander, "This is the Mystery that to this day is hidden, and kept secret; for Nature being mingled with Man brought forth a Wonder most wonderful; for he having the Nature of the Harmony of the Seven, from him whom I told thee, the Fire and the Spirit, Nature continued not, but forth with brought forth seven Men all Males and Females and sublime, or on high, according to the Natures of the Seven Governors."

30. "And after these things, O Poemander," quoth I, "I am now come into a great desire, and longing to hear, do not digress, or run out."

31. But he said, "Keep silence, for I have not yet finished the first speech."

Trismegistus: 32. "Behold, I am silent."

Poemander: 33. "The Generation therefore of these Seven was after this manner, the Air being Feminine and the Water desirous of Copulation, took from the Fire its ripeness, and from the aether Spirit; and so Nature produced bodies after the Species and Shape of men."

34. And Man was made of Life and Light into Soul and Mind, of Life the Soul, of Light the Mind.

35. And so all the Members of the Sensible World, continued unto the period of the end, bearing rule, and generating.

36. Hear now the rest of that speech, thou so much desirest to hear.

37. "When that Period was fulfilled, the bond of all things was loosed and untied by the Will of God; for all living Creatures being Hermaphroditical, or Male and Female, were loosed and untied together with Man; and so the Males were apart by themselves and the Females likewise.

38. And straightway God said to the Holy Word,. Increase in Increasing, and Multiply in Multitude all you my Creatures and Workmanships. And let Him that is endued with Mind, know Himself to be Immortal; and that the cause of Death is the Love of the Body, and let Him Learn all Things that are.

39. When he had thus said, Providence by Fate and Harmony, made the mixtures, and established the Generations, and all things were multiplied according to their kind, and he that knew himself, came at length to the Superstantial of every way substantial good.

40. But he that through the Error of Love, loved the Body, abideth wandering in darkness, sensible, suffering the things of death."

Trismegistus: 41. "But why do they that are ignorant sin so much, that they should therefore be deprived of immortality."

Poemander: 42. "Thou seemest not to have understood what thou hast heard."

Trismegistus: 43. "Peradventure I seem so to thee, but I both understand and remember them."

Poemander: 44. "I am glad for thy sake, if thou understoodest them."

Trismegistus: 45. "Tell me, why are they worthy of death, that are in death?"

Poemander: 46. "Because there goeth a sad and dismal darkness before its Body; of which darkness is the moist Nature, of which moist Nature, the Body consisteth in the sensible World, from whence death is derived. Hast thou understood this aright!"

Trismegistus: 47. "But why or how doth he that understands himself, go or pass into God!"

Poemander: 48. "That which the Word of God said, say I: Because the Father of all things consists of Life and Light, whereof Man is made."

Trismegistus: 49. "Thou sayest very well."

Poemander: 50. "God and the Father is Light and Life, of which Man is made. If therefore thou learn and believe thyself to be of the Life and Light, thou shalt again pass into Life."

Trismegistus: 51. "But yet tell me more, O my Mind, how I shall go into Life."

Poemander: 52. "God saith, Let the Man endued with a Mind, mark, consider, and know himself well."

Trismegistus: 53. "Have not all Men a mind?"

Poemander: 54. "Take heed what thou sayest, for I the Mind come unto men that are holy and good, pure and merciful, and that live piously and religiously; and my presence is a help unto them. And forthwith they know all things, and lovingly they supplicate and propitiate the Father; and blessing him, they give him thanks, and sing hymns unto him, being ordered and directed by filial Affection, and natural Love: And before they give up their Bodies to the death of them, they hate their Senses, knowing their Works and Operations.

55. "Rather I that am the Mind itself, will not suffer the Operations or Works, which happen or belong to the body, to be finished and brought to perfection in them; but being the Porter and Door-keeper, I will shut up the entrances of Evil, and cut off the thoughtful desires of filthy works.

56. "But to the foolish, and evil, and wicked, and envious and covetous, and murderous, and profane, I am far off giving place to the avenging Demon, which applying unto him the sharpness of fire, tormenteth such a man sensibly, and armeth him the more to all wickedness, that he may obtain the greater punishment.

57. "And such a one never ceaseth, having unfulfillable desires and unsatiable concupiscences, and always fighting in darkness for the Demon afflicts and tormenteth him continually, and increaseth the fire upon him more and more."

Trismegistus: 58. "Thou hast, O Mind, most excellently taught me all things, as I desired; but tell me moreover, after the return is made, what then?"

Poemander: 59. "First of all, in the resolution of the material Body, the Body itself is given up to alteration, and the form which it had, becometh invisible; and the idle manners are permitted, and left to the Demon, and the Senses of the Body return into their Fountains, being parts, and again made up into Operations.

60. "And Anger and Concupiscence go into the brutish or unreasonable Nature; and the rest striveth upward by Harmony.

61. "And to the first Zone it giveth the power it had of increasing and diminishing.

62. "To the second, the machination or plotting of evils, and one effectual deceit or craft.

63. "To the third, the idle deceit of Concupiscence.

64. "To the fourth, the desire of Rule, and unsatiable Ambition.

65. "To the fifth, profane Boldness, and headlong rashness of Confidence.

66. "To the sixth, Evil and ineffectual occasions of Riches.

67. "And to the seventh zone, subtle Falsehood always lying in wait.

68. "And then being made naked of all the Operations of Harmony it cometh to the eighth Nature, having its proper power, and singeth praises to the Father with the things that are, and all they that are present rejoice, and congratulate the coming of it; and being made like to them with whom it converseth, it heareth also the Powers that are above the eighth Nature, singing praise to God in a certain voice that is peculiar to them.

69. "And then in order they return unto the Father, and themselves deliver themselves to the powers, and becoming powers they are in God.

70. "This is the Good, and to them that know to be deified.

71. "Furthermore, why sayest thou, What resteth, but that understanding all men, thou become a guide, and way-leader to them that are worthy; that the kind of Humanity or Mankind, may be saved by God!"

72. When Poemander had thus said unto me, he was mingled among the Powers.

73. But I giving thanks, and blessing the Father of all things, rose up, being enabled by him, and taught the Nature, of the Nature of the whole and having seen the greatest sight or spectacle.

74. And I began to Preach unto men, the beauty and fairness of Piety and Knowledge.

75. O ye People, Men, born and made of the Earth, which have given Yourselves over to Drunkenness, and Sleep, and to the Ignorance of

God, be Sober, and Cease your Surfeit, whereto you are allured, and invited by Brutish and Unreasonable Sleep.

76. And they that heard me, come willingly, and with one accord, and then I said further.

77. Why, O Men of the Off-spring of the Earth, why have you delivered Yourselves over unto Death, having Power to Partake of Immortality; Repent and Change your Minds, you that have together Walked in Error, and have been Darkened in Ignorance.

78. Depart from that dark Light, be Partakers of Immortality, and Leave or Forsake Corruption.

79. And some of Them That Heard Me, mocking and scorning, went away and delivered themselves up to the way of death.

80. But others, casting themselves down before my feet, besought me that they might be taught; but I causing them to rise up, became a guide of mankind, teaching them the reasons how, and by what means they may be saved. And I sowed in them the words of Wisdom, and nourished them with Ambrosian Water of Immortality.

81. And when it was Evening, and the Brightness of the same began wholly to go down, I commanded them to give thanks to God; and when they had finished their thanksgiving, everyone returned to his own lodging.

82. But I wrote in myself the bounty and beneficence of Poemander; and being filled with what I most desired, I was exceeding glad.

83. For the sleep of the Body was the sober watchfulness of the mind; and the shutting of my eyes the true Sight, and my silence great with child and full of good; and the pronouncing of my words, the blossoms and fruits of good things.

84. And thus came to pass or happened unto me, which I received from my mind, that is, Poemander, the Lord of the Word; whereby I became inspired by God with the Truth.

85. For which cause, with my Soul, and whole strength, I give praise and blessing unto God the Father.

86. Holy is God the Father of All Things.

87. Holy is God Whose Will is Performed and Accomplished by His Own Powers.

88. Holy is God, that Determineth to be Known, and is Known of His Own, or Those that are His.

89. Holy art Thou, that by Thy Word hast established all Things.

90. Holy art Thou of Whom all Nature is the Image.

91. Holy art Thou Whom Nature hath not Formed.

92. Holy art Thou that art Stronger than all Power.

93. Holy art Thou, that art Greater than all Excellency.

94. Holy art Thou, Who art Better than all Praise.

95. Accept these Reasonable Sacrifices from a Pure Soul, and a Heart stretched out unto Thee.

96. O Thou Unspeakable, Unutterable, to be Praised with Silence!

97. I beseech Thee, that I may never Err from the Knowledge of Thee, Look Mercifully upon Me, and Enable Me, and Enlighten with this Grace, those that .are in Ignorance, the Brothers of my Kind, but Thy Sons.

98. Therefore I Believe Thee, and Bear Witness, and go into the Life and Light.

98. Blessed art Thou, O Father, Thy Man would be Sanctified with Thee, as Thou hast given Him all Power.

III. The Sermon

1. The glory of all things, God and that which is Divine, and the Divine Nature, the beginning of things that are.

2. God, and the Mind, and Nature, and Matter, and Operation, or Working and Necessity, and the End and Renovation.

3. For there were in the Chaos, an infinite darkness in the Abyss or bottomless Depth, and Water, and a subtle Spirit intelligible in Power; and there went out the Holy Light, and the Elements were coagulated from the Sand out of the moist Substance.

4. And all the Gods distinguished the Nature full of Seeds.

5. And when all things were interminated and unmade up, the light things were divided on high. And the heavy things were founded upon the moist sand, all things being Terminated or Divided by Fire; and being sustained or hung up by the Spirit they were so carried, and the Heaven was seen in Seven Circles.

6. And the Gods were seen in their Ideas of the Stars, with all their Signs, and the Stars were numbered, with the Gods in them. And the Sphere was all lined with Air, carried about in a circular, motion by the Spirit of God.

7. And every God by his internal power, did that which was commanded him; and there were made four footed things, and creeping things, and such as live in the Water, and such as fly, and every fruitful Seed, and Grass, and the Flowers of all Greens, and which had sowed in themselves the Seeds of Regeneration.

8. As also the Generations of men to the knowledge of the Divine Works, and a lively or working Testimony of Nature, and a multitude of men, and the Dominion of all things under Heaven and the knowledge of good things, and to be increased in increasing, and multiplied in multitude.

9. And every Soul in flesh, by the wonderful working of the Gods in the Circles, to the beholding of Heaven, the Gods, Divine Works, and the Operations of Nature; and for Signs of good things, and the knowledge of the Divine Power, and to find out every cunning workmanship of good things.

10. So it beginneth to live in them, and to be wise according to the Operation of the course of the circular Gods; and to be resolved into that which shall be great Monuments; and Remembrances of the cunning Works done upon Earth, leaving them to be read by the darkness of times.

11. And every generation of living flesh, of Fruit, Seed, and all Handicrafts, though they be lost, must of necessity be renewed by the renovation of the Gods, and of the Nature of a Circle, moving in number; for it is a Divine thing, that every world temperature should be renewed by nature, for in that which is Divine, is Nature also established.

IV. The Key

1. Yesterday's Speech, O Asclepius, I dedicated to thee, this day's it is fit to dedicate to Tat, because it is an Epitome of those general speeches that were spoken to him.

2. God therefore, and the Father, and the Good, O Tat, have the same Nature, or rather also the same Act and Operation.3. For there is one name or appellation of Nature and Increase which concerneth things changeable, and another about things unchangeable, and about things unmoveable, that is to say, Things Divine and Human; every one of which, himself will have so to be; but action or operation is of another thing, or elsewhere, as we have taught in other things, Divine and Human, which must here also be understood.4. For his Operation or Act, is his Will, and his Essence, to Will all Things to be.

5. For what is God, and the Father, and the Good, but the Being of all things that yet are not, and the existence itself, of those things that are. 6. This is God, this is the Father, this is the Good, whereunto no other thing is present or approacheth.

7. For the World, and the Sun, which is also a Father by Participation, is not for all that equally the cause of Good, and of Life, to living Creatures: And if this be so, he is altogether constrained by the Will of the Good, without which it is not possible, either to be, or to be begotten or made.8. But the Father is the cause of his Children, who hath a will both to sow and nourish that which is good by the Son. 9. For Good is always active or busy in making; and this cannot he in any other, but in him that taketh nothing, and yet willeth all things to be; for I will not say, O Tat, making them; for he that maketh is defective in much time, in which sometimes he maketh not, as also of quantity and quality; for sometimes he maketh

those things that have quantity and quality and sometimes the contrary.

10. But God is the Father, and the Good, in being all things; for he both will be this, and is it, and yet all this for himself(as is true) in him that can see it. 11. For all things else are for this, it is the property of Good to be known: This is the Good, O Tat.

Tat: 12. Thou hast filled us, O Father, with a sight both good and fair, and the eye of my mind is almost become more holy by the sight or spectacle.

Trismegistus: 13. I Wonder not at It, for the Sight of Good is not like the Beam of the Sun, which being of a fiery shining brightness, maketh the eye blind by his excessive Light, that gazeth upon it; rather the contrary, for it enlighteneth, and so much increaseth the light of the eye, as any man is able to receive the influence of this Intelligible clearness. 14. For it is more swift and sharp to pierce, and innocent or harmless withal, and full of immortality, and they that are capable and can draw any store of this spectacle, and sight do many times fall asleep from the Body, into this most fair and beauteous Vision ; which thing Celius and Saturn our Progenitors obtained unto.

Tat: 15. I would we also, O Father, could do so.

Trismegistus: 16. I would have could, O Son; but for the present we are less intent to the Vision, and cannot yet open the eyes of our minds to behold the incorruptible, and incomprehensible Beauty of that Good: But then shall we see it, when we have nothing at all to say of it. 17. For the knowledge of it, is a Divine Silence, and the rest of all the Senses; For neither can he that understands that understand anything else, nor he that sees that, see any thing else, nor hear any other thing, nor in sum, move the Body.

18. For shining steadfastly upon, and round about the whole Mind it enlighteneth all the Soul ; and loosing it from the Bodily Senses and Motions, it draweth it from the Body, and changeth it wholly into the Essence of God. 19. For it is Possible for the Soul, O Son, to be Deified while yet it Lodgeth in the Body of Man, if it Contemplate the Beauty of the Good.

Tat: 20. How dost thou mean deifying, Father!

Trismegistus: 21. There are differences, O Son, of every Soul.

Tat: 22. But how dost thou again divide the changes?

Trismegistus: 23. Hast thou not heard in the general Speeches, that from one Soul of the Universe, are all those Souls, which in all the world are tossed up and down, as it were, and severally divided? Of these Souls there are many changes, some into a more fortunate estate, and some quite contrary; for they which are of creeping things, are changed into those of watery things and those of things living in the water, to those of things living upon the Land; and Airy ones are changed into men, and human Souls, that lay hold of immortality, are changed into Demons. 24. And so they go on into the Sphere or Region of the fixed Gods, for there are two choirs or companies of Gods, one of them that wander, and another of them that are fixed. And this is the most perfect glory of the Soul.

25. But the Soul entering into the Body of a Man, if it continue evil, shall neither taste of immortality, nor is partaker of the good.26. But being drawn back the same way, it returneth into creeping things. And this is the condemnation of an evil Soul.

27. And the wickedness of a Soul is ignorance; for the Soul that knows nothing of the things that are, neither the Nature of them, nor that which is good, but is blinded, rusheth and dasheth against the bodily Passions, and unhappy as it is, not knowing itself, it serveth strange Bodies, and evil ones, carrying the Body as a burthen, and not ruling, but ruled. And this is the mischief of the Soul.28. On the contrary, the virtue of the Soul is Knowledge; for he that knows is both good and religious, and already Divine.

Tat: 29. But who is such a one, O Father!

Trismegistus: 30. He that neither speaks, nor hears many things; for he, O Son, that heareth two speeches or hearings, fighteth in the shadow. 31. For God, and the Father, and Good, is neither spoken nor heard.32. This being so in all things that are, are the Senses, because they cannot be without them.33. But Knowledge differs much from Sense; for Sense is of things that surmount it, but Knowledge is the end of Sense. 34. Knowledge is the gift of God ; for all Knowledge is unbodily but useth the Mind as an Instrument, as the Mind useth the Body.35. Therefore both intelligible and material things go both of them into bodies; for, of contraposition, That is Setting One against Another, and Contrariety, all Things must Consist. And it is impossible it should be otherwise.

Tat: 36. Who therefore is this material God?

Trismegistus: 37. The fair and beautiful world, and yet it is not good; for it is material and easily passible, nay, it is the first of all passible things; and the second of the things that are, and needy or wanting somewhat else. And it was once made and is always, and is ever in generation, and made, and continually makes, or generates things that have quantity and quality. 38. For it is moveable, and every material motion is generation; but the intellectual stability moves the material motion after this manner.

39. Because the World Is a Sphere, that is a Head, and above the head there is nothing material, as beneath the feet there is nothing intellectual.40. The whole universe is material; The Mind is the head, and it is moved spherically, that is like a head. 41. Whatsoever therefore is joined or united to the Membrane or Film of this head, wherein the Soul is, is immortal, and as in the Soul of a made Body, hath its Soul full of the Body; but those that are further from that Membrane, have the Body full of Soul.

42. The whole is a living wight, and therefore consisteth of material and intellectual. 43. And the World is the first, and Man the second living wight after the World; but the first of things that are mortal and therefore hath whatsoever benefit of the Soul all the others have: And yet for all this, he is not only not good, but flatly evil, as being mortal.44. For the World is not good as it is moveable; nor evil as it is immortal. 45. But man is evil, both as he is moveable, and as he is mortal.

46. But the Soul of Man is carried in this manner, The Mind is in Reason, Reason in the Soul, the Soul in the Spirit, the Spirit in the Body. 47. The Spirit being diffused and going through the veins, and arteries, and blood, both moveth the living Creature, and after a

certain manner beareth it. 48. Wherefore some also have thought the Soul to be blood, being deceived in Nature, not knowing that first the Spirit must return into the Soul, and then the blood is congealed, the veins and arteries emptied, and then the living thing dieth: And this is the death of the Body.

49. All things depend of one beginning, and- the beginning depends of that which is one and alone. 50. And the beginning is moved, that it may again be a beginning; but that which is one, standeth and abideth, and is not moved. 51. There are therefore these three, God the Father, and the Good, the World and Man: God hath the World, and the World hath Man; and the World is the Son of God, and Man as it were the Offspring of the World. 52. For God is not ignorant of Man, but knows him perfectly, and will be known by him. This only is healthful to man; the Knowledge of God: this is the return of Olympus; by this only the Soul is made good, and not sometimes good, and sometimes evil, but of necessity Good.

Tat: 53. What meanest thou, O Father?

Trismegistus: 54. Consider, O Son, the Soul of a Child, when as yet it hath received no dissolution of its Body, which is not yet grown, but is very small; how then if it look upon itself, it sees itself beautiful, as not having been yet spotted with the Passions of the Body, but as it were depending yet upon the Soul of the World. 55. But when the Body is grown and distracteth, the Soul it engenders Forgetfulness, and partakes no more of the Fair and the Good, and Forgetfulness is Evilness. 56. The like also happeneth to them that go out of the Body: for when the Soul runs back into itself the Spirit is contracted into the blood and the Soul into the Spirit; but the Mind being made pure, and free from these clothings; and being Divine by Nature, taking a fiery Body rangeth abroad in every place, leaving the Soul to judgment, and to the punishment it hath deserved.

Tat: 57. Why dost thou say so, O Father, that the Mind is separated from the Soul, and the Soul from the Spirit? When even now thou saidst the Soul was the Clothing or Apparel of the Mind, and the Body of the Soul.

Trismegistus: 58. O Son, he that hears must co-understand and conspire in thought with him that speaks; yea, he must have his hearing swifter and sharper than the voice of the speaker. 59. The disposition of these Clothings or Covers, is done in an Earthly Body; for it is impossible, that the mind should establish or rest itself, naked, and of itself; in an Earthly Body; neither is the Earthly Body able to bear such immortality; and therefore that it might suffer so great virtue the Mind compacted as it were, and took to itself the passible Body of the Soul, as a Covering or Clothing. And the Soul being also in some sort Divine, useth the Spirit as her Minister and Servant, and the Spirit governeth the living thing.

60. When therefore the Mind is separated, and departeth from the earthly Body, presently it puts on its Fiery Coat, which it could not do having to dwell in an Earthly Body. 61. For the Earth cannot suffer fire, for it is all burned of a small spark; therefore is the water poured round about the Earth, as a Wall or defence, to withstand the flame of fire.

62. But the Mind being the most sharp or swift of all the Divine Cogitations, and more swift than all the Elements, hath the fire for its Body. 63. For the Mind which is the Workman of all useth the fire as his instrument in his Workmanship; and he that is the Workman of

all, useth it to the making of all things, as it is used by man, to the making of Earthly things only; for the Mind that is upon Earth, void, or naked of fire, cannot do the business of men. nor that which is otherwise the affairs of God.

64. But the Soul of Man, and yet not everyone, but that which is pious and religious, is Angelical and Divine. And such a Soul, after it is departed from the Body, having striven the strife of Piety, becomes either Mind or God. 65. And the strife of Piety is to know God, and to injure no Man, and this way it becomes Mind. 66. But an impious Soul abideth in its own essence, punished of itself, and seeking an earthly and human Body to enter into. 67. For no other Body is capable of a Human Soul, neither is it lawful for a Man's Soul to fall into the Body of an unreasonable living thing: for it is the Law or Decree of God, to preserve a Human Soul from so great a contumely and reproach.

Tat: 68. How then is the Soul of Man punished, O Father; and what is its greatest torment.

Hermes: 69. Impiety, O my Son; for what Fire hath so great a flame as it? Or what biting Beast doth so tear the Body as it doth the Soul.70. Or dost thou not see how many evils the wicked Soul suffereth, roaring and crying out, I am Burned, I am Consumed, I know not what to Say, or Do, I am Devoured, Unhappy Wretch, of the Evils that compass and lay-hold upon me; Miserable that I am, I neither See nor Hear anything.

71. These are the voices of a punished and tormented Soul, and not as many; and thou, O Son, thinkest that the Soul going out of the Body grows brutish or enters into a Beast: which is a very great

Error, for the Soul punished after this manner. 72. For the Mind, when it is ordered or appointed to get a fiery Body for the services of God, coming down into the wicked Soul, torments it with the whips of Sins, wherewith the wicked Soul being scourged, turns itself to Murders, and Contumelies, and Blasphemies, and diverse violences, and other things by which men are injured.73. But into a pious Soul, the Mind entering, leads it into the Light of Knowledge. 74. And such a Soul is never satisfied with singing praise to God, and speaking well of all men; and both in words and deeds, always doing good in imitation of her Father.

75. Therefore, O Son, we must give thanks, and pray, that we may obtain a good mind. 76. The Soul therefore may be altered or changed into the better, but into the worse it is impossible. 77. But there is a communion of Souls, and those of Gods, communicate with those of men; and those of men, with those of Beasts. 78. And the better always take of the worse, Gods of Men, Men of brute Beasts, but God of all: For he is the best of all, and all things are less than he. 79. Therefore is the World subject unto God, Man unto the World and unreasonable things to Man. 80. But God is above all, and about all; and the beams of God are operations; and the beams of the World are Natures; and the beams of Man are Arts and Sciences. 81. And Operations do act by the World, and upon man by the natural beams of the World, but Natures work by the Elements, and man by Arts and Sciences. 82. And this is the Government of the whole, depending upon the Nature of the One, and piercing or coming down by the One Mind, than which nothing is more Divine, and more efficacious or operative; and nothing more uniting, or nothing is more One. The Communion of Gods to Men, and of Men to God. 83. This is the Bonus Genius, or good Demon, blessed Soul that is fullest of it! and unhappy Soul that is empty of it!

Tat: 84. And wherefore Father?

Trismegistus: 85. Know Son, that every Soul hath the Good Mind; for of that it is we now speak, and not of that Minister of which we said before, That he was sent from the Judgment. 86. For the Soul without the Mind, can neither do, nor say any thing; for many times the Mind flies away from the Soul, and in that hour the Soul neither seeth nor heareth, but is like an unreasonable thing; so great is the power of the Mind. 87. But neither brooketh it an idle or lazy Soul, but leaves such a one fastened to the Body, and by it pressed down.88. And such a Soul, O Son, hath no mind, wherefore neither must such a one be called a Man. 89. For man is a Divine living thing and is not to be compared to any brute Beast that lives upon Earth, but to them that are above in Heaven, that are called Gods. 90. Rather, if we shall be bold to speak the truth, he that is a man indeed, is above them, or at least they are equal in power, one to the other, For none of the things in Heaven will come down upon Earth, and leave the limits of Heaven, but a man ascends up into Heaven, and measures it. 91. And he knoweth what things are on high, and what below, and learneth all other things exactly.92. And that which is the greatest of all, he leaveth not the Earth, and yet is above: So great is the greatness of his Nature.

93. Wherefore we must be bold to say, That an Earthly Man is a Mortal God, and That the Heavenly God is an Immortal Man. 94. Wherefore, by these two are all things governed, the World and Man; but they and all things else, of that which is One.

V: The God that be manifest and not manifest.

Hermes: 1. This Discourse I will also make to thee, O Tat, that thou mayest not be ignorant of the more excellent Name of God. 2. But do thou contemplate in thy Mind, how that which to many seems hidden and unmanifest, may be most manifest unto thee.

3. For it were not all, if it were apparent, for whatsoever is apparent, is generated or made; for it was made manifest, but that which is not manifest is ever. 4. For it needeth not to be manifested, for it is always. 5. And he maketh all other things manifest, being unmanifest as being always, and making other things manifest, he is not made manifest.

9. Himself is not made, yet in fantasy he fantasieth all things, or in appearance he maketh them appear, for appearance is only of those things that are generated or made, for appearance is nothing but generation. 7. But he is that One, that is not made nor generated, is also unapparent and unmanifest. 8. But making all things appear, he appeareth in all and by all; but especially he is manifested to or in those things wherein himself listeth.

9. Thou therefore, O Tat, my Son, pray first to the Lord and Father, and to the Alone and to the One from whom is one to be merciful to thee, that thou mayest knowest and understand so great a God; and that he would shine one of his beams upon thee In thy understanding. 10. For only the Understanding sees that which is not manifest or apparent, as being itself not manifest or apparent; and if thou canst, O Tat, it will appear to the eyes of thy Mind. 11. For the Lord, void of envy, appeareth through the whole world. Thou mayest see the intelligence, and take it in thy hands, and contemplate the Image of God. 12. But if that which is in thee, be not

known or apparent unto thee, how shall he in thee be seen, and appear unto thee by the eyes?

13. But if thou wilt see him, consider and understand the Sun, consider the course of the Moon, consider the order of the Stars. 14. Who is he that keepeth order? for all order is circumscribed or terminated in number and place. 15. The Sun is the greatest of the Gods in heaven, to whom all the heavenly Gods give place, as to a King and potentate; and yet he being such a one, greater than the Earth or the Sea, is content to suffer infinite lesser stars to walk and move above himself; whom doth he fear the while, O Son? 16. Every one of these Stars that are in Heaven, do not make the like, or an equal course; who is it that hath prescribed unto every one, the manner and the greatness of their course! 17. This Bear that turns round about its own self; and carries round the whole World with her, who possessed and made such an Instrument. 18. Who hath set the Bounds to the Sea? who hath established the Earth? for there is some body, O Tat, that is the Maker and Lord of these things.

19. For it is impossible, O Son, that either place, or number, or measure, should be observed without a Maker. 20. For no order can be made by disorder or disproportion. 21. I would it were possible for thee, O my Son, to have wings, and to fly into the Air, and being taken up in the midst, between Heaven and Earth, to see the stability of the Earth, the fluidness of the Sea, the courses of the Rivers, the largeness of the Air, the sharpness or swiftness of the Fire, the motion of the Stars; and the speediness of the Heaven, by which it goeth round about all these.

22. O Son, what a happy sight it were, at one instant, to see all these, that which is unmovable moved, and that which is hidden appear

and be manifest. 23. And if thou wilt see and behold this Workman, even by mortal things that are upon Earth, and in the deep. Consider, O Son, how Man is made and framed in the Womb; and examine diligently the skill and cunning of the Workman, and learn who it was that wrought and fashioned the beautiful and Divine shape of Man; who circumscribed and marked out his eyes? Who bored his nostrils and ears? Who opened his mouth? Who stretched out and tied together his sinews? Who channeled the veins? Who hardened and made strong the bones? Who clothed the flesh with skin? Who divided the fingers and the joints? Who flattened and made broad the soles of the feet? Who dug the pores? Who stretched out the spleen? Who made the heart like a Pyramid? Who made the Liver broad! Who made the Lights spongy, and full of holes! Who made the belly large and capacious? Who set to outward view the more honorable parts and hid the filthy ones?

24. See how many Arts in one Matter, and how many Works in one Superscription, and all exceedingly beautiful, and all done in measure, and yet all differing.25. Who hath made all these things? What Mother, what Father? Save only God that is not manifest? That made all things by his own Will. 26. And no man says that a statue or an image is made without a Carver or a Painter, and was this Workmanship made without a Workman? O great Blindness, O great Impiety, O great Ignorance.

27. Never, O Son Tat, canst thou deprive the Workmanship of the Workman, rather it is the best Name of all the Names of God, to call him the Father of all, for so he is alone; and this is his Work to be the Father.

28. And if thou wilt force me to say anything more boldly, it is his Essence to be pregnant, or great with all things, and to make them. 29. And as without a Maker, it is impossible that anything should be made, so it is that he should not always be, and always be making all things in Heaven, in the Air, in the Earth, in the Deep, in the whole World, and in every part of the whole that is, or that is not. 30. For there is nothing in the whole World, that is not himself both the things that are and the things that are not. 31. For the things that are, he hath made manifest; and the things that are not, he hath hid in himself. 32. This is God that is better than any name; this is he that is secret; this is he that is most manifest; this is he that is to be seen by the Mind ; this is he that is visible to the eye; this is he that hath no body; and this is he that hath many bodies, rather there is nothing of any body, which is not He. 33. For he alone is all things.

34. And for this cause He hath all Names, because He is the One Father; and therefore He hath no Name, because He is the Father of all. 35. Who therefore can bless thee, or give thanks for thee, or to thee. 36. Which way shall I look, when I praise thee? upward? downward? outward? inward? 37. For about thee there is no manner, nor place, nor anything else of all things that are. 38. But all things are in thee; all things from thee, thou givest all things, and takest nothing; for thou hast all things and there is nothing that thou hast not. 39. When shall I praise thee, O Father; for it is neither possible to comprehend thy hour, nor thy time? 40. For what shall I praise thee? For what thou hast made, or for what thou hast not made? For those things thou hast manifested, or for those things thou hast hidden? 41. Wherefore shall I praise thee as being of myself, or having anything of mine own, or rather being another's?

42. For thou art what I am, thou art what I do, thou art what I say. 43. Thou Art All Things, and there is nothing Thou art not. 44. Thou Art Thou, All that is Made, and all that is not Made. 45. The Mind that Understandeth. 46. The Father that Maketh and Frameth. 47. The Good that Worketh. 48. The Good that doeth All Things.

VI: In God there is only good.

1. Good, O Asciepius, is in nothing but in God alone; or rather God himself is the Good always. 2. And if it be so, then must he be an Essence or Substance void of all motion and generation; but nothing is void or empty of him. 3. And this Essence hath about or in himself a Stable, and firm Operation, wanting nothing, most full, and giving abundantly. 4. One thing is the Beginning of all things, for it giveth all things; and when I name the Good, I mean that which is altogether and always Good. 5. This is present to none, but God alone; for he wanteth nothing, that he should desire to have it, nor can anything be taken from him; the loss whereof may grieve him; for sorrow is a part of evilness.

6. Nothing is stronger than he, that he should be opposed by it; nor nothing equal to him, that he should be in love with it; nothing unheard of to be angry, with nothing wiser to be envious at. 7. And none of these being in his Essence, what remains, but only the Good? 8. For as in this, being such an Essence, there is none of the evils; so in none of the other things shall the Good be found. 9. For in all other things, are all those other things. as well in the small as the great ; and as well in the particulars as in this living Creature the greater and mightiest of all. 10. For all things that are made or generated are full of Passion, Generation itself being a Passion; and where Passion is there is not the Good; where the Good is, there is no Passion; where it is day, it is not night, and where it is night, it is not day.

11. Wherefore it is impossible, that in Generation should be the Good, but only in that which is not generated or made. 12. Yet as the Participation of all things is in the Matter bound, so also of that which is Good. After this manner is the World good, as it maketh all things, and in the part of making or doing it is Good, but in all other

things not good. 13. For it is passible, and movable, and the Maker of passible things.

14. In Man also the Good is ordered (or Taketh Denomination) in comparison of that which is evil; for that which is not very evil, is here good; and that which is here called Good, is the least particle, or proportion of evil. 15. It is impossible therefore, that the Good should be here pure from Evil; for here the Good groweth Evil, and growing Evil, it doth not still abide Good; and not abiding Good it becomes Evil. 16. Therefore in God alone is the Good, or rather God is the Good. 17. Therefore, O Asclepius, there is nothing in men (or among Men) but the name of Good, the thing itself is not, for it is impossible; for a material Body receiveth (or Comprehendeth), is not as being on every side encompassed and coarcted with evilness, and labors, and griefs, and desires, and wrath, and deceits, and foolish opinions.

18. And in that which is the worst of all, Asclepius, every one of the forenamed things, is here believed to be the greatest good, especially that supreme mischief the pleasures of the Belly, and the ring-leader of all evils; Error is here the absence of the Good. 19. And I give thanks unto God, that concerning the knowledge of Good, put this assurance in my mind, that it is impossible it should be in the World. 20. For the World is the fulness of evilness ; but God is the fulness of Good, or Good of God.

21. For the eminencies of all appearing Beauty, are in the Essence more pure, more sincere, and peradventure they are also the Essence of it. 22. For we must be bold to say, Asclepius, that the Essence of God, if he have an Essence, is that which is fair or beautiful; but no good is comprehended in this World. 23. For all things that are

subject to the eye, are Idols, and as it were shadows; but those things that are not subject to the eye, are ever, especially the Essence of the Fair and the Good. 24. And as the eye cannot see God, so neither the Fair, and the Good.

25. For these are the parts of God that partake the Nature of the whole, proper, and familiar unto him alone, inseparable, most lovely, whereof either God is enamoured, or they are enamoured of God. 26. If thou canst understand God, thou shalt understand the Fair, and the Good which is most shining, and enlightening, and most enlightened by God. 27. For that Beauty is above comparison, and that Good is inimitable, as God himself. 28. As therefore thou understandest God, so understand the Fair and the Good, for these are incommunicable to any other living Creatures because they are inseparable from God.

29. If thou seek concerning God, thou seekest or askest also of the Fair, for there is one way that leads to the same thing, that is Piety with Knowledge. 30. Wherefore, they that are ignorant, and go not in the way of Piety, dare call Man Fair and Good, never seeing so much as in a dream, what Good is; but being enfolded and wrapped upon all evil, and believing that the evil is the Good, they by that means, both use it unsatiably, and are afraid to be deprived of it; and therefore they strive by all possible means, that they may not only have it, but also increase it. 31. Such, O Asclepius, are the Good and Fair things of men, which we can neither love nor hate, for this is the hardest thing of all, that we have need of them, and cannot live without them.

VII: The Profession of Silence

Tat: 1. In the general Speeches, O Father, discoursing of the Divinity, thou speakest enigmatically, and didst not clearly reveal thyself, saying, That no man can be saved before Regeneration. 2. And when I did humbly entreat thee, at the going up the Mountain after thou hadst discoursed unto me, having a great desire, to learn this Argument of Regeneration ; because among all the rest, I am ignorant only of this thou toldst me thou wouldst impart it unto me, when I would estrange myself from the World: whereupon I made myself ready, and have vindicated the understanding that is in me, from the deceit of the World. 3. Now then fulfill my defects, and as thou saidst instruct me of Regeneration, either by word of mouth or secretly; for I know not, O Trismegistus, of what Substance, or what Womb or what Seed a Man is thus born.

Hermes: 4. O Son, this Wisdom is to be understood in silence, and the Seed is the true Good.

Tat: 5. Who soweth it, O Father . for I am utterly ignorant and doubtful.

Hermes: 6. The Will of God, O Son.

Tat: 7. And what manner of Man is he that is thus born? for in this point, I am clean deprived of the Essence that understandeth in me.

Hermes: 8. The Son of God will be another, God made the universe, that in everything consisteth of all powers.

Tat: 9. Thou tellest me a Riddle, Father, and dost not speak as a Father to his Son.

Hermes: 10. Son, things of this kind are not taught, but are by God, when he pleaseth, brought to remembrance.

Tat: 11. Thou speakest of things strained, or far fetched, and impossible, Father; and therefore I will directly contradict them.

Hermes: 12. Wilt thou prove a stranger, Son, to thy Father's kind?

Tat: 13. Do not envy me, Father, or pardon me, I am thy Natural Son; discourse unto me the manner of Regeneration.

Hermes: 14. What shall I say, O my Son? I have nothing to say more than this, that I see in myself an unfeigned sight or spectacle, made by the mercy of God, and I am gone out of myself into an immortal body, and am riot now what I was before, but was begotten in Mind. 15. This thing is not taught, nor is it to be seen in this formed Element; for which the first compound form was neglected by me; and that I am now separated from it ; for I have both the touch and the measure of it, yet am I now estranged from them. 16. Thou seest, O Son, with thine eyes; but though thou look never so steadfastly upon me, with the Body, and bodily sight, thou canst not see, nor understand what I am now.

Tat: 17. Thou hast driven me, O Father, into no small fury and distraction of mind, for I do not now see my self.

Hermes: 18. I would, O Son, that thou also wert gone out of thyself, like them that dream in their sleep.

Tat: 19. Then tell me this, who is the Author and Maker of Regeneration ?

Hermes: 20. The child of God, one Man by the Will of God.

Tat: 21. Now, O Father, thou hast put me to silence for ever and all my former thoughts have quite left and forsaken me, for I see the greatness, and shape of all things here below, and nothing but falsehood in them all. 22. And since this mortal Form is daily changed, and turned by this time into increase, and diminution, as being falsehood; what therefore is true, O Trismegistus?

Trismegistus: 23. That, O Son, which is not troubled, nor bounded; not color ed, not figured, not changed; that which is naked, bright, comprehensible only of itself, unalterable, unbodily.

Tat: 24. Now I am mad, indeed, Father; for when I thought me to have been made a wise man by thee, with these thoughts thou hast quite dulled all my senses.

Hermes: 25. Yet is it so, as I say, O Son, He that Looketh Only upon that which is carried upward as Fire, that which is carried downward as Earth, that which is moist as Water, and that which bloweth or is subject to blast as Air; how can he sensibly understand that which is neither hard, nor moist, nor tangible, nor perspicuous, seeing it is only understood in power and operation; but I beseech and pray to the Mind which alone can understand the Generation, which is in God.

Tat: 26. Then am I, O Father, utterly unable to do it.

Hermes: 27. God forbid, Son, rather draw or pull him unto thee (or Study to Know Him) and he will come, be but Willing, and it shall be done; quiet (or make idle) the Senses of the Body, purging thyself from unreasonable brutish torments of matter.

Tat: 28. Have I any revengers or tormentors in myself, Father ?

Hermes: 29. Yes, and those, not a few, but many and fearful ones.

Tat: 30. I do not know them, Father.

Hermes: 31. One Torment, Son, is Ignorance, a second, Sorrow, a third, Intemperance, a fourth Concupiscence, a fifth, Injustice, a sixth, Covetousness, a seventh, Deceit, an eighth, Envy, a ninth, Fraud or Guile, a tenth, Wrath, an eleventh, Rashness, a twelfth, Maliciousness. 32. They are in number twelve, and under these many more; some which through the prison of the body, do force the inwardly placed Man to suffer sensibly. 33. And they do not suddenly, or easily depart from him, that hath obtained mercy of God; and herein consists, both the manner and the reason of Regeneration. 34. For the rest, O Son, hold thy peace, and praise God in silence, and by that means, the mercy of God will not cease, or be wanting unto us. 35. Therefore rejoice, my Son, from henceforward, being purged by the powers of God, to the Knowledge of the Truth. 36. For the revelation of God is come to us, and when that came all Ignorance was cast out. 37. The knowledge of Joy is come unto us, and when that comes, Sorrow shall fly away to them that are capable of it.

38. I call unto Joy, the power of Temperance, a power whose Virtue is most sweet; Let us take her unto ourselves, O Son, most willingly, for how at her coming hath she put away Intemperance. 39. Now I call the fourth, Continence, the power which is over Concupiscence.

This, O Son, is the stable and firm foundation of Justice. 40. For see, how without labor, she hath chased away injustice and we are justified, O Son, when Injustice is away. 41. The sixth Virtue which comes into us, I call Communion, which is against Covetousness. 42. And when that (Covetousness) is gone, I call Truth ; and when she cometh, Error and Deceit vanisheth. 43. See, O Son, how the Good is fulfilled by the access of Truth; for by this means, Envy is gone from us; for Truth is accompanied with the Good, together also with Life and Light. 44. And there came no more any torment of Darkness, but being overcome, they are all fled away suddenly, and tumultuarily.

45. Thou hast understood, O Son, the manner of Regeneration; for upon the coming of these Ten, the Intellectual Generation is perfected, and then it driveth away the twelve; and we have seen it in the Generation itself. 46. Whosoever therefore hath of Mercy obtained this Generation which is according to God, he leaving all bodily sense, knoweth himself to consist of divine things, and rejoiceth, being made by God stable and immutable.

Tat: 47. O Father, I conceive and understand, not by the sight of mine eyes, but by the Intellectual Operation, which is by the Powers. I am in Heaven, in the Earth, in the Water, in the Air, I am in living Creatures, in the Plants, in the Womb, everywhere. 48. Yet tell me further, this one thing, How are the torments of Darkness, being in number Twelve, driven away and expelled by the Ten powers. What is the manner of it, Trismegistus?

Hermes: 49. This Tabernacle, O Son, consists of the Zodiacal Circle; and this consisting of twelve numbers, the Idea of one; but all formed Nature admit of divers Conjugations to the deceiving of Man. 50. And though they be different in themselves, yet are they united in practice (as for example, Rashness is inseparable from Anger) and they are also indeterminate: Therefore with good Reason, do they make their departure, being driven away by the Ten powers; that is to say, By the dead.

51. For the number of Ten, O Son, is the Begetter of Souls. And there Life and Light are united, where the number of Unity is born of the Spirit. 52. Therefore according to Reason, Unity bath the number of Ten, and the number of Ten hath Unity.

Tat: 53. O Father, I now see the Universe, and myself in the Mind.

Hermes: 54.This is Regeneration, O Son, that we should not any longer fix our imagination upon this Body, subject to the three dimensions, according to this Speech which we have now commented. That we may not at all calumniate the Universe.

Tat: 55. Tell me, O Father, This Body that consists of Powers shall it ever admit of any Dissolution?

Hermes: 56. Good words, Son, and speak not things impossible; for so thou shalt sin, and the eye of thy mind grow wicked. 57. The sensible Body of Nature is far from the Essential Generation; for that is subject to Dissolution, but this not; and that is mortal, but this immortal. Dost thou not know that thou art born a God and the Son of the One, as I am.

Tat: 58. How fain would I, O Father, hear that praise given by a Hymn, which thou saidst, thou heardst from the Powers when I was in the Octonary.

Hermes: 59. As Poemander said by way of Oracle to the Octonary, Thou dost well, O Son, to desire the Solution of the Tabernacle, for thou art purified. 60. Poemander, the Mind of absolute Power and Authority, hath delivered no more unto me, than those that are written; knowing that of myself, I can understand all things, and hear, and see what I will. And he commanded me to do those things that are good; and therefore all the Powers that are in me sing.

Tat: 61. I would hear thee, O Father, and understand these things.

Hermes: 62. Be quiet, O Son, and now hearken to that harmonious blessing and thanksgiving: the hymn of Regeneration, which I did not determine to have spoken of so plainly, but to thyself in the end of all. 63. Wherefore this is not taught, but hid in silence. 64. So then, O Son, do thou standing in the open Air, worship looking to the North Wind, about the going down of the Sun, and to the South, when the Sun ariseth; And now keep silence, Son.

Hermes speaks the secret hymn: 65. Let all the Nature of the world entertain the hearing of this Hymn.66. Be opened, O Earth, and let all the Treasure of the Rain be opened. 67. You Trees tremble not, for I will sing and praise the Lord of the Creation, and the All and the One.68. Be opened you Heavens, ye Winds stand still, and let the Immortal Circle of God receive these words.
69. For I will sing, and praise him that created all things, that fixed the Earth, and hung up the Heavens, and commanded the sweet Water to come out of the Ocean; into all the World inhabited, and not inhabited, to the use and nourishment of all things, or men. 70. That commanded the fire to shine for very action, both to Gods and Men. 71. Let us altogether give him blessing, which rideth upon the Heavens, the Creator of all Nature. 72. This is he that is the Eye of

the Mind, and Will accept the praise of my Powers. 73. O all ye Powers that are in me, praise the One and the All. 74. Sing together with my Will, all you Powers that are in me. 75. O Holy Knowledge, being enlightened by thee, I magnify the intelligible Light, and rejoice in the Joy of the Mind. 76. All my Powers sing praise with me, and thou my Continence, sing praise my Righteousness by me; praise that which is righteous. 77. O Communion which is in me, praise the All. 78. By me the Truth sings praise to the Truth, the Good praiseth the Good. 79. O Life, O Light from us, unto you comes this praise and thanksgiving. 80. I give thanks unto thee, O Father, the operation or act of my Powers. 81. I give thanks unto thee, O God, the power of my operations. 82. By me thy Word sings praise unto thee, receive by me this reasonable (or verbal) sacrifice in words. 83. The powers that are in me cry these things, they praise the All, they fulfill thy Will; thy Will and Counsel is from thee unto thee. 84. O All, receive a reasonable Sacrifice from all things. 85. O Life, save all that is in us: O Light enlighten, O God the Spirit; for the Mind guideth or feedeth the Word ; O Spirit bearing Workman. 86. Thou art God, thy Man crieth these things unto thee through by the Fire, by the Air, by the Earth, by the Water, by the Spirit, by thy Creatures. 87. From eternity I have found (means to) bless and praise thee, and I have what I seek, for I rest in thy Will.

Tat: 88. O Father, I see thou hast sung this Song of praise and blessing with thy whole Will; and therefore have I put and placed it in my World.

Hermes: 89. Say in thy intelligible World, O Son.

Tat: 90. I do mean in my Intelligible World, for by thy Hymn and Song of Praise my mind is enlightened: and gladly would I send from my Understanding a Thanksgiving unto God.

Hermes: 91. Not rashly, O Son.

Tat: 92. In my mind, O Father.

Hermes: 93. Those things that I see and contemplate, I infuse into thee; and therefore say, thou son Tat, the Author of thy succeeding Generations, I send unto God these reasonable Sacrifices. 94. O God, Thou art the Father, Thou art the Lord, Thou art the Mind, accept these reasonable Sacrifices which Thou requirest of Me. 95. For all things are done as the Mind willeth. 96. Thou, O Son, send this acceptable Sacrifice to God, the Father of all things; but propound it also, O Son, by Word.

Tat: 97. I thank thee, Father, thou hast advised and instructed me thus to give praise and thanks.

Hermes: 98. I am glad, O Son, to see the Truth bring forth the Fruits of Good things, and such immortal branches. 99. And learn this of me: Above all other virtues entertain Silence, and impart unto no man, O Son, the tradition of Regeneration, lest we be reputed Calumniators; For we both have now sufficiently meditated, I in speaking, thou in hearing. And now thou dost intellectually know thyself and our Father.

VIII: The Greatest Evil in Man.

1. Whither are you carried, O Men, drunken with drinking up the strong Wine of Ignorance? Which seeing you cannot bear: Why do you not vomit it up again? 2. Stand, and be sober, and look up again with the eyes of your heart; and if you cannot all do so, yet do as many as you can. 3. For the malice of Ignorance surroundeth all the Earth, and corrupteth the Soul, shut up in the Body not suffering it to arrive at the Havens of Salvation. 4. Suffer not yourselves to be carried with the great stream, but stem the tide, you that can lay hold of the Haven of Safety, and make your full course towards it.

5. Seek one that may lead you by the hand, and conduct you to the door of Truth and Knowledge, where the clear Light is that is pure from Darkness, where there is not one drunken, but all are sober and in their heart look up to him, whose pleasure it is to be seen. 6. For he cannot be heard with ears, nor seen with eyes, nor expressed in words; but only in mind and heart.

7. But first thou must tear to pieces and break through the garment thou wearest; the web of Ignorance, the foundation of all Mischief; the bond of Corruption ; the dark Coverture; the living Death ; the sensible Carcass, the Sepulchre, carried about with us; the domestical Thief which in what he loves us, hates us, envies us. 8. Such is the hurtful Apparel, wherewith thou art clothed, which draws and pulls thee downward by its own self; lest looking up, and seeing the beauty of Truth, and the Good that is reposed therein, thou shouldst hate the wickedness of this garment, and understand the traps and ambushes, which it bath laid for thee.

9. Therefore doth it labor to make good those things that seem and are by the Senses, judged and determined; and the things that are

truly, it hides, and envelopeth in such matter, filling what it presents unto thee, with hateful pleasure, that thou canst neither hear what thou shouldst hear, nor see what thou shouldst see.

VIX: Sermon to Asclepius

Hermes: 1. All that is moved, O Asclepius, is it not moved in some thing, and by some thing?

Asclepius: 2. Yes, indeed.

Hermes: 3. Must not that, in which a thing is moved, of necessity be greater than the thing that is moved?

Asclepius: 4. Of necessity.

Hermes: 5. And that which moveth, is it not stronger than that which is moved?

Asclepius: 6. It is stronger.

Hermes: 7. That in which a thing is moved, must it not needs have a Nature, contrary to that of the thing that is moved?

Asclepius: 8. It must needs.

Hermes: 9. Is not this great World a Body, than which there is no greater?

Asclepius: 10. Yes, confessedly.

Hermes: 11. And is it not solid, as filled with many great Bodies, and indeed, with all the Bodies that are

Asclepius: 12. It is so.

Hermes: 13. And is not the World a Body, and a Body that is moved.

Asclepius: 14. It is.

Hermes: 15. Then what kind of a place must it be, wherein it is moved, and of what Nature? Must it not he much bigger, that it may receive the continuity of Motion? and lest that which is moved should for want of room, be stayed, and hindered in the Motion ?

Asclepius: 16. It must needs be an immense thing, Trismegistus, but of what Nature.

Hermes: 17. Of a contrary Nature, O Asclepius; but is not the Nature of things unbodily, contrary to a Body.

Asclepius: 18. Confessedly.

Hermes: 19. Therefore the place is unbodily; but that which is unbodily, is either some Divine thing or God himself. And by some thing Divine, I do not mean that which was made or begotten.20. If therefore it be Divine, it is an Essence or Substance but if it be God, it is above Essence; but he is otherwise intelligible. 21. For the first, God is intelligible, not to himself, but to us, for that which is intelligible, is subject to that which understandeth by Sense.

22. Therefore God is not intelligible to himself, for not being any other thing from that which is understood, he cannot be understood by himself. 23. But he is another thing from us, and therefore he is understood by us. 24. If therefore Place be intelligible, it is not Place but God, but if God be intelligible, he is intelligible not as Place, but as a capable Operation.

25. Now everything that is moved, is moved, not in or by that which is moved, but in that which standeth or resteth, and that which moveth standeth or resteth, for it is impossible it should be moved with it.

Asclepius: 26. How then, O Trismegistus, are those things that are here moved with the things that moved? For thou sayest that the Spheres that wander are moved by the Sphere that wanders not.

Hermes: 27. That, O Asclepius, is not a moving together, but a countermotion, for they are not moved after a like manner, but contrary one to the other; and contrariety hath a standing resistance of motion for resistance is a staying of motion. 28. Therefore the wandering Spheres being moved contrarily to that Sphere which wandereth not, shall have one from another contrariety standing of itself. 29. For this Bear which thou seest neither rise nor go down, but turning always about the same; dost thou think it moveth or standeth still?

Asclepius: 30. I think it moves, Trismegistus.

Hermes: 31. What motion, O Asclepius?

Asclepius: 32. A motion that is always carried about the same.

Hermes: 33. But the Circulation which is about the same, and the motion about the same, are both hidden by Station; for that which is about the same forbids that which is above the same, if it stand to that which is about the same. 34. And so the contrary motion stands fast always, being always established by the contrariety. 35. But I will give thee concerning this matter, an earthly example that may be seen with eyes.

36. Look upon any of these living Creatures upon Earth, as Man for example, and see him swimming; for as the Water is carried one way, the reluctation or resistance of his feet and hands is made a station to the man, that he should not be carried with the Water, nor sink underneath it.

Asclepius: 37. Thou hast laid down a very clear example, Trismegistus.

Hermes: 38. Therefore every motion is in station, and is moved of station. 39. The motion then of the World, and of every material living thing, happeneth not to be done by those things that are without the World, but by those things within it, a Soul, or Spirit, or some other unbodily thing, to those things which are without it. 40. For an inanimated Body, doth not now, much less a Body if it be wholly inanimate.

Asclepius: 41. What meaneth thou by this, O Trismegistus, Wood and Stones, and all other inanimate things, are they not moving Bodies?

Hermes: 42. By no means, O Asclepius, for that within the Body which moves the inanimate thing, is not the Body, that moves both as well the Body of that which beareth, as the Body of that which is born; for one dead or inanimate thing, cannot move another; that which moveth, must needs be alive if it move. 43. Thou seest therefore how the Soul is surcharged, when it carrieth two Bodies.

44. And now it is manifest, that the things that are moved are moved in something, and by something.

Asclepius: 45. The things that are, O Trismegistus, must needs be moved in that which is void or empty, Vacuum. 46. Be advised, O Asclepius, for of all the things that are, there is nothing empty, only that which is not, is empty and a stranger to existence or being. 47. But that which is, could not be if it were not full of existence, for that which is in being or existence can never be made empty.

Asclepius: 48. Are there not therefore some things that are empty, O Trismegistus, as an empty Barrel, an empty Hogshead, an empty Well, an empty Wine- Press, and many such like?

Hermes: 49. O the grossness of thy Error, O Asclepius, those things that are most full and replenished, dost thou account them void and empty.

Asclepius: 50. What may be thy meaning, Trismegistus?

Hermes: 51. Is not the Air a Body?

Asclepius: 52. It is a Body.

Hermes: 53. Why then this Body doth it not pass through all things that are and passing through them, fill them? and that Body doth it not consist of the mixture of the four? Therefore all things which thou callest empty are full of Air. 54. Therefore those things that thou callest empty, thou oughtest to call them hollow, not empty, for they exist and are full of Air and Spirit.

Asclepius: 55. This reason is beyond all contradiction, O Trismegistus, but what shall we call the Place in which the whole Universe is moved?

Hermes: 56. Call it incorporeal, O Asclepius.

Asclepius: 57. What is that incorporeal or unbodily?

Hermes: 58. The Mind and Reason, the whole, wholly comprehending itself, free from all Body, undeceivable, invisible, impassible from a Body itself, standing fast in itself, capable of all things, and that favour of the things that are. 59. Whereof the Good, the Truth, the Archetypal Light, the Archetype of the Soul, are as it were Beams.

Asclepius: 60. Why then, what is God?

Hermes: 61. That which is none of these things, yet is, and is the cause of Being to all; and every one of the things that are; for he left nothing destitute of Being. 62. And all things are made of things that are, and not of things that are not; for the things that are not, have not the nature to be able to be made; and again, the things that are, have not the nature never to be, or not to be at all.

Asclepius: 63. What dost thou then say at length, that God is?

Hermes: 64. God is not a Mind, but the Cause that the Mind is; not a Spirit, but the Cause that the Spirit is; not Light, but the Cause that Light is. 65. Therefore we must worship God by these two Appellations which are proper to him alone, and to no other 66. For neither of all the other, which are called Gods, nor of Men, nor

Demons, or Angels, can anyone be, though never so little, good, save only God alone. 67. And this He is, and nothing else; but all other things are separable from the nature of Good. 68. For the Body and the Soul have no place that is capable of or can contain the Good. 69. For the greatness of Good, is as great as the Existence of all things, that are both bodily and Unbodily, both sensible and intelligible. 70. This is the Good, even God.

71. See therefore that thou do not at any time, call ought else Good, for so thou shalt be impious, or any else God, but only the Good, for so thou shalt again be impious. 72. In Word it is often said by all men the Good, but all men do not understand what it is; but through Ignorance they call both the Gods, and some men Good, that can never either be or be made so. 73. Therefore all the other Gods are honoured with the title and appellation of God, but God is the Good, not according to Heaven, but Nature. 74. For there is one Nature of God, even the Good, and one kind of them both, from whence are all kinds. 75. For he that is Good, is the giver of all things, and takes nothing and therefore God gives all things and receives nothing. 76. The other title and appellation, is the Father, because of his making all things; for it is the part of a Father to make.

77. Therefore it hath been the greatest and most Religious care in this life, to them that are wise, and well-minded, to beget children. 78. As likewise it is the greatest misfortune and impiety for any to be separated from men, without children; and this man is punished after death by the Demons, and the punishment is this, To have the Soul of this childless man, adjudged and condemned to a Body, that neither bath the nature of a man, nor of a woman, which is an accursed thing under the Sun. 79. Therefore, O Asclepius, never congratulate any man that is childless; but on the contrary, pity his

misfortune, knowing what punishment abides, and is prepared for him.

80. Let so many, and such manner of things, O Asclepius, be said as a certain precognition of all things in Nature.

X: "The Long Sermon"

1. Forbear thy speech, O Hermes Trismegistus, and call to mind those things that are said: but I will not delay to speak what comes into my mind, since many men have spoken many things, and those very different, concerning the Universe and Good; but I have not learned the Truth. 2. Therefore, the Lord make it plain to me in this point ; for I will believe thee only, for the manifestation of these things.

3. Then said the Mind how the case stands… 4. God and all. 5. God, Eternity, the World, Time, Generation, 6. God made Eternity, Eternity the World; the World Time, and Time Generation. 7. Of God, as it were the Substance, is the Good, the Fair, Blessedness, Wisdom. 8. Of Eternity, Identity, or Selfness. 9. Of the World, Order. 10. Of Time, Change. 11. Of Generation, Life, and Death. 12. But the Operation of God, is Mind and Soul. 13. Of Eternity, Permanence, or Long-lasting, and Immortality. 14. Of the World, Restitution, and Decay or Destruction. 15. Of Time, Augmentation and Diminution. 16. And of Generation, Qualities. 17. Therefore Eternity is in God. 18. The World in Eternity. 19. Time in the World. 20. And Generation in Time. 21. And Eternity standeth about God. 22. The World is moved in Eternity. 23. Time is determined in the World. 24. Generation is done in Time. 25. Therefore the Spring and Fountain of all things is God.

26. The Substance Eternity. 27. The Matter is the World. 28. The Power of God is Eternity. 29. And the Work of Eternity is the World not yet made, and yet ever made by Eternity. 30. Therefore shall nothing be at any time destroyed, for Eternity is incorruptible. 31. Neither can anything perish, or be destroyed in the World, the World being contained and embraced by eternity. 32. But what is the

Wisdom of God? Even the Good, and the Fair and Blessedness, and every Virtue, and Eternity. 33. Eternity therefore put into the Matter Immortality and Everlastingness; for the Generation of that depends upon Eternity, even as Eternity doth of God. 34. For Generation and Time, in Heaven, and in Earth, are of a double Nature; in Heaven they are unchangeable and incorruptible, but on Earth they are changeable and corruptible. 35. And the Soul of Eternity is God; and the Soul of the World Eternity; and of the Earth, Heaven. 36. God is in the Mind, the Mind in the Soul1 the Soul in the Matter, all things by Eternity. 37. All this Universal Body, in which are all Bodies, is full of Soul, the Soul full of Mind, the Mind full of God. 38. For within he fills them, and without he contains them, quickening the Universe.

39. Without he quickens this perfect living thing the World, and within all living Creatures.40. And above in Heaven he abides in Identity or Selfness, but below upon Earth he changeth Generation. 41. Eternity comprehendeth the World, either by Necessity, or Providence, or Nature. 42. And if any man shall think any other thing, it is God that actuateth, or operateth this All. 43. But the operation or Act of God, is power insuperable, to which none may compare anything, either Human or Divine. 44. Therefore, O Hermes, think none of these things below, or the things above, in any wise like unto God, for if thou dost thou errest from the Truth. 45. For nothing can be like the unlike, and only and One; nor mayest thou think that he bath given of his Power to any other thing. 46. For who after him can make anything, either of Life, or Immortality; of Change or of Quality, and himself what other thing should he make.

47. For God is not idle, for then all things would be idle ; for all things are full of God. 48. But there is not anywhere in the world

such a thing as Idleness; for Idleness is a name that implieth a thing void or empty, both of a Doer and a thing done. 49. But all things must necessarily be made or done both always and according to the nature of every place. 50. For he that maketh or doth is in all things, yet not fastened or comprehended in anything, nor making or doing one thing, but all things. 51. For being an active or operating Power and sufficient of himself for the things that are made, and the things that are made are under him. 52. Look upon, through me, the World is subject to thy sight, and understand exactly the Beauty thereof.

53. A Body immarcescible, than the which, there is nothing more ancient, yet always vigorous and young.

54. See also the seven Worlds set over us, adorned with an everlasting Order, and filling Eternity, with a different course. 55. For all things are full of Light, but the Fire is nowhere. 56. For the friendship and commixture of contraries and unlike became Light shining from the Act or Operation of God, the Father of all Good, the Prince of all Order, and the Ruler of the seven Worlds. 57. Look also upon the Moon, the forerunner of them all, the Instrument of Nature, and which changeth the Matter here below.

58. Behold the Earth, the middle of the whole, the firm and stable Foundation of the Fair World, the Feeder and Nurse of Earthly things. 59. Consider moreover, how great the multitude is of immortal living things, and of mortal ones also; and see the Moon going about in the midst of both, to wit, of things immortal and mortal. 60. But all things are full of Soul, and all things are properly moved by it; some things about the Heaven, and some things about the Earth, and neither of those on the right hand to the left; nor those

on the left hand to the right; nor those things that are above, down.
ward; nor those things that are below, upwards.

61. And that all these things are made, O beloved Hermes, thou
needst not learn of me. 62. For they are Bodies, and have a Soul, and
are moved. 63. And that all these should come together into one, it is
impossible without some thing, to gather them together. 64.
Therefore there must be some such ones, and he altogether One.

65. For seeing that the motions are diverse, and many, and the
Bodies not alike, and yet one ordered swiftness among them all; It is
impossible there should be two or more Makers. 66. For one order is
not kept by many.

67. But in the weaker, there would be jealousy of the stronger and
thence also Contentions. 68. And if there were one Maker of mutable
and mortal living wights, he would desire also to make immortal
ones, as he that were the Maker of immortal ones, would do to make
mortal. 69. Moreover also, if there were two, the Matter being one,
who should be chief, or have the disposing of the facture? 70. Or if
both of them, which of them the greater part?

71. But think thus that every living Body hath its consistence of
Matter and Soul; and of that which is immortal, and that which is
mortal, and unreasonable. 72. For all living Bodies have a Soul; and
those things that are not living are only matter by itself.

73. And the Soul likewise of itself drawing near her Maker, is the
Cause of Life and Being and Being the cause of Life, is after a
manner, the cause of immortal things.

74. How then are mortal wights, other from immortal? 75. Or how cannot he make living wights that causeth immortal things and immortality? 76. That there is some Body that doth these things it is apparent, and that he is also one, it is most manifest. 77. For there is one Soul, one Life and one Matter.

78. Who is this? Who can it be? Other than the One God. 79. For whom else can it benefit, to make living things, save only God alone? 80. There is therefore one God.

81. For it is a ridiculous thing to confess the World to be one Sun, one Moon, one Divinity; and yet to have I know not how many gods. 82. He therefore being One, doth all things in many things. 83. And what great thing is it for God to make Life and Soul, and Immortality, and Change, when thy self dost so many things?

84. For thou both seest, speakest and hearest, smellest, tastest and touchest, walkest, understandest, and breathest. 85. And it is not one that seeth, and another that heareth, and another that speaketh, and another that toucheth, and another that smelleth, and another that walketh, and another that understandeth, and another that breatheth, but One that doth all these things. 86. Yet neither can these things possibly be without God.

87. For as thou, if thou shouldst cease from doing these things, were not a living wight; so if God should cease from those, he were not (which is not lawful to say) any longer God. 88. For if it be already demonstrated, that nothing can be idle or empty, how much more may be affirmed of God? 89. For if there be any thing which he doth not do, then is he (if it were lawful to say so) imperfect.90. Whereas feeling he is not idle, but perfect, certainly he doth all things.

91. Now give thy self unto me, O Hermes, for a little while thou shalt the more easily understand, that it is the necessary work of God that all things should be made or done that are done or were once done, or shall be done.92. And this, O best Beloved, is life. 93. And this is the Fair. 94. And this is the Good. 95. And this is God.

96. And if thou wilt understand this by work also, mark what happens to thy self, when thou wilt generate. 97. And yet this is not like unto him; for he is not sensible of pleasure, for neither bath he any other Fellow workman. 98. But being himself the only Workman he is always in the Work, himself being that which he doth or maketh. 99. For all things, if they were separated from him, must needs fall and die, as there being no life in them.

100. And again, if all things be living wights, both which are in Heaven, and upon Earth; and that there be one Life in all things which are made by God, and that is God, then certainly all things are made, or done by God. 101. Life is the union of the Mind and the Soul. 102. But death is not the destruction of those things that were gathered together, but a dissolving of the Union. 103. The Image therefore of God is Eternity, of Eternity the World, of the World the Sun, of the Sun, Man.104. But the people say, That changing is Death, because the Body is dissolved, and the Life goeth into that which appeareth not.

105. By this discourse, my dearest Hermes, I affirm as thou hearest, That the World is changed, because every day part thereof becomes invisible ; but that it is never dissolved. 106. And these are the Passions of the World, Revolutions and Occultations, and Revolution is a turning, but Occultation is Renovation.107. And the World being

188

all formed, bath not the forms lying without it, but itself changeth in itself.

108. Seeing then the World is all formed, what must he be that made it? for without form he cannot be. 109. And if he be all formed, he will be kept like the World, but if he have but one form, he shall be in this regard less than the World. 110. What do we then say that he is? We will not raise any doubts by our speech; for nothing that is doubtful concerning God, is yet known.

111. He hath therefore one Idea which is proper to him, which because it is unbodily is not subject to the sight, and yet shews all forms by the Bodies. 112. And do not wonder, if there be an incorruptible Idea. 113. For they are like the Margents of that Speech which is in writing; for they seem to be high and swelling, hut they are by nature smooth and even.

114. But understand well this that I say, more boldly, for it is more true; As a man cannot live without life, so neither can God live, not doing good. 115. For this is, as it were, the Life and Motion of God, to move all things, and quicken them.

116. But some of the things I have said, must have a particular explication; Understand then what I say. 117. All things are in God, not as lying in a place; for Place is both a Body, and unmoveable, and those things that are there placed, have no motion. 118. For they lie otherwise in that which is unbodily, than in the fantasy or to appearance. 119. Consider him that contains all things, and understand, that nothing is more capacious, than that which is incorporeal, nothing more swift, nothing more powerful, but it is most capacious, most swift and most strong.

120. And judge of this by thyself, command thy Soul to go into India, and sooner than thou canst bid it, it will be there. 121. Bid it likewise pass over the Ocean, and suddenly it will be there; Not as passing from place to place, but suddenly it will be there. 122. Command it to fly into Heaven, and it will need no Wings, neither shall anything hinder it; not the fire of the Sun, not the Aether, not the turning of the Spheres, not the bodies of any of the other Stars, but cutting through all, it will fly up to the last, and furthest Body. 123. And if thou wilt even break the whole, and see those things that are without the World (if there be any thing without) thou mayest.

124. Behold how great power, how great swiftness thou hast! Canst thou do all these things, and cannot God? 125. After this manner therefore contemplate God to have all the whole World to himself, as it were all thoughts, or intellections. 126. If therefore thou wilt not equal thy self to God, thou canst not understand God. 127. For the like is intelligible by the like. 128. Increase thy self into an immeasurable greatness, leaping beyond every Body; and transcending all Time, become Eternity and thou shalt understand God: If thou believe in thyself that nothing is impossible, but accountest thy self immortal, and that thou canst understand all things, every Art, every Science and the manner and custom of every living thing.

129. Become higher than all height, lower than all depths, comprehend in thy self, the qualities of all the Creatures, of the Fire, the Water, the Dry and Moist; and conceive likewise, that thou canst at once be everywhere in the Sea, in the Earth. 130. Thou shalt at once understand thy self, not yet begotten in the Womb, young, old, to be dead, the things after death, and all these together as also times, places, deeds, qualities, quantities, or else thou canst not yet

understand God. 131. But if thou shut up thy Soul in the Body and abuse it, and say, I understand nothing, I can do nothing, I am afraid of the Sea, I cannot climb up into Heaven, I know not who I am, I cannot tell what I shall be; what hast thou to do with God; for thou canst understand none of those Fair and Good things; be a lover of the Body, and Evil.

132. For it is the greatest evil, not to know God.133. But to be able to know and to will, and to hope, is the straight way, and Divine way, proper to the Good; and it will everywhere meet thee, and everywhere be seen of thee, plain and easy, when thou dost not expect or look for it; it will meet thee, waking, sleeping, sailing, travelling, by night, by day, when thou speakest, and when thou keepest silence. 134. For there is nothing which is not the Image of God. 135. And yet thou sayest, God is invisible, but be advised, for who is more manifest than He. 136. For therefore hath he made all things, that thou by all things mayest see him.

137. This is the Good of God, this is his Virtue, to appear, and to be seen in all things. 138. There is nothing invisible, no, not of those things that are incorporeal. 139. The Mind is seen in Understanding, and God is seen in doing or making.

140. Let these things thus far forth, be made manifest unto thee, O Trismegistus.141. Understand in like manner, all other things by thy self, and thou shalt not be deceived.

XI: Of the Common Mind.

1. The Mind, O Tat, is of the very Essence of God, if yet there be any Essence of God. 2. What kind of Essence that is, he alone knows himself exactly. 3. The Mind therefore is not cut off, or divided from the essentiality of God, but united as the light of the sun. 4. And this mind in men, is God, and therefore are some men Divine, and their Humanity is near Divinity.

5. For the good Demon called the Gods immortal men, and men mortal Gods. 6. But in the brute Beasts, or unreasonable living wights, the Mind is their Nature. 7. For where there is a Soul, there is the Mind, as where there is Life, there is also a Soul. 8. In living Creatures therefore, that are without Reason, the Soul is Life, void of the operations of the Mind. 9. For the Mind is the Benefactor of the Souls of men, and worketh to the proper Good. 10. And in unreasonable things it cooperateth with the Nature of everyone of them, but in men it worketh against their Natures. 11. For the Soul being in the Body, is straightway made Evil by Sorrow, and Grief and Pleasure or Delight. 12. For Grief and Pleasure flow like Juices from the compound Body, whereinto, when the Soul entereth, or descendeth, she is moistened and tincted with them.

13. As many Souls therefore, as the Mind governeth or overruleth, to them it shows its own Light, resisting their prepossessions or presumptions. 14. As a good Physician grieveth the Body, prepossessed of a disease, by burning or lancing it for health's sake. 15. After the same manner also, the Mind grieveth the Soul, by drawing it out of Pleasure, from whence every disease of the Soul proceedeth. 16. But the great Disease of the Soul is Atheism because that opinion followeth to all Evil and no Good. 17. Therefore the

Mind resisting it procureth Good to the Soul, as a Physician health to the Body.

18. But as many Souls of Men, as do not admit or entertain the Mind for their Governor, do suffer the same thing that the Soul of unreasonable living things. 19. For the Soul being a cooperator with them, permits or leaves them to their concupiscences, whereunto they are carried by the torrent of their Appetite, and so tend to brutishness. 20. And as Brute Beasts, they are angry without reason, and they desire without reason, and never cease, nor are satisfied with evil. 21. For unreasonable Angers and Desires, are the most exceeding Evils. 22. And therefore hath God set the Mind over these, as a Revenger and Reprover of them.

Tat: 23. Here, O Father, that discourse of Fate or Destiny which thou madest to me, is in danger to be overthrown; For if it be fatal for any man to commit Adultery or Sacrilege or do any evil, he is punished also, though he of necessity do the work of Fate or Destiny.

Hermes: 24. All things, O Son, are the work of Fate, and without it, can no bodily thing, either Good or Evil, be done. 25. For it is decreed by Fate, that he that cloth any evil, should also suffer for it. 26. And therefore he cloth it, that he may suffer that which he suffereth, because he did it. 27. But for the present let alone that speech, concerning Evil and Fate, for at other times we have spoken of it.

28. Now our discourse is about the Mind, and what it can do, and how it differs, and is in men such a one, but in brute Beasts changed. 29. And again, in Brute Beasts it is not beneficial, but in men by quenching both their Anger and Concupiscences. 30. And of men

thou must understand some to be rational or governed by reason, and some irrational.

31. But all men are subject to Fate, and to Generation, and Changes, for these are the beginning and end of Fate or Destiny. 32. And all men suffer those things that are decreed by Fate. 33. But rational men, over whom as we said, the Mind bears rule, do not suffer like unto other men, but being free from viciousness, and being not evil, they do suffer evil.

Tat: 34. How sayest thou this again, Father? An Adulterer, is he not evil? a Murderer, is he not evil? and so all others.

Hermes: 35. But the rational man, O Son, will not suffer for Adultery, but as the Adulterer, nor for Murder, but as the Murderer. 36. And it is impossible to escape the Quality of Change, as of Generation, but the Viciousness, he that hath the Mind, may escape. 37. And therefore, O Son, I have always heard the good Demon say, and if he had delivered it in writing, he had much profited all mankind: For he alone, O Son. as the first born, God, seeing all things, truly spake Divine words. I have heard him say sometimes, That all Things are one thing, Especially Intelligible Bodies, or that all Especially Intelligible Bodies are one. 38. We live in Power, in Act and in Eternity. 39. Therefore a good Mind, is that which the Soul of him is. 40. And if this be so, then no intelligible thing differs from intelligible things. 41. As therefore it is possible, that the Mind, the Prince of all things; so likewise, that the Soul that is of God, can do whatsoever it will.

42. But understand thou well, for this Discourse I have made to the question which thou askest of me before, I mean concerning Fate and

the Mind. 43. First, if, O Son, thou shalt diligently withdraw thy self from all Contentious speeches, thou shalt find that in Truth, the Mind, the Soul of God bears rule over all things, both over Fate and Law and all other things.

44. And nothing is impossible to him, no not of the things that are of Fate. 45. Therefore, though the Soul of man be above it, let it not neglect the things that happen to be under Fate. 46. And these thus far, were the excellent sayings of the good Demon.

Tat: 47. Most divinely spoken, O Father, and truly and profitably, yet clear this one thing unto me… 48. Thou sayest, that in brute Beasts the Mind worketh or acteth after the manner of Nature, co-operating also with their (impetus) inclinations. 49. Now the impetuous inclinations of brute Beasts, as I conceive, are Passions. If therefore the Mind do co-operate with these impetuous Inclinations, and that they are the Passions in brute Beasts, certainly the Mind is also a Passion, conforming itself to Passions.

Hermes: 50. Well done, Son, thou askest nobly, and yet it is just that I should answer thee.

51. All incorporeal things, O Son, that are in the Body, are possible, nay, they are properly Passions. 52. Everything that moveth is incorporeal; everything that is moved is a Body, and it is moved into the Bodies by the Mind. Now motion is Passion, and there they both suffer; as well that which moveth, as that which is moved, as well that which ruleth, as that which is ruled. 53. But being freed from the Body, it is freed likewise from Passion. 54. But especially, O Son, there is nothing impassible, but all things are passible. 55. But

Passion differs from that which is passible, for that (Passion) acteth but this suffers.

56. Bodies also of themselves do act, for either they are unmovable, or else are moved, and which soever it be, it is a Passion. 57. But incorporeal things do always act, or work, and therefore they are passible. 58. Let not therefore the appellations or names trouble thee, for Action and Passion are the same thing, but that it is not grievous to use the more honourable name.

Tat: 59. O Father. thou has delivered this Discourse most plainly.

Hermes: 60. Consider this also, O Son, That God hath freely bestowed upon man, above all other living things, these two, to wit, Mind and Speech, or Reason, equal to immortality. 61. These if any man use, or employ upon what he ought, he shall differ nothing from the Immortals. 62. Yea, rather going out of the Body, he shall be guided and led by them, both into the Choir and Society of the Gods, and blessed Ones.

Tat: 63. Do not other living Creatures use Speech, O Father?

Hermes: 64. NO, Son, but only Voice; now Speech and Voice do differ exceeding much; for Speech is common to all men, but Voice is proper unto every kind of living thing.

Tat: 65. Yea, but the Speech of men is different. O Father, every man according to his Nation.

Hermes: 66. It is true, O Son, they do differ: Yet as man is one so is Speech one also; and it is interpreted and found the same, both in

Egypt, Persia, and Greece. 67. But thou seemest unto me, Son, to be ignorant of the Virtue or Power, and Greatness of Speech. 68. For the blessed God, the good Demon said or commanded the Soul to be in the Body, the Mind, in the Soul, the Word, or Speech, or Reason in the Mind, and the Mind in God, and that God is the Father of them all. 69. Therefore the Word is the Image of the Mind, and the Mind of God, and the Body of the Idea, and the Idea of the Soul.

70. Therefore of the Matter, the subtlest or smallest part is Air, of the Air the Soul, of the Soul the Mind, of the Mind God. 71. And God is about all things, and through all things, but the Mind about the Soul, the Soul about the Air, and the Air about the Matter. 72. But Necessity, and Providence, and Nature, are the Organs or Instruments of the World, and of the Order of Matter. 73. For of those things that are intelligible, every one is but the Essence of them in Identity.

74. But of the Bodies of the whole, or universe, every one is many things.75: For the Bodies that are put together, and that have, and make their changes into other, having this Identity, do always save and preserve the uncorruption of the Identity. 76. But in every one of the compound Bodies, there is a number. 77. For without number it is impossible there should be consistence or constitution, or composition, or dissolution. 78. But Unities do both beget and increase Numbers, and again being dissolved, come into themselves. 79. And the Matter is One.

80. But this whole World, the great God, and the Image of the Greater, and united unto him, and conserving the Order and Will of the Father, is the fullness of Life. 81. And there is nothing therein, through all the Eternity of the Revolutions, neither of the whole, nor

of the parts which doth not live. 82. For there is nothing dead, that either hath been, or is, or shall be in the World. 83. For the Father would have it as long as it lasts, to be a living thing; and therefore it must needs be God also.

84, How therefore, O Son, can there be in God, in the Image of the Universe, in the fulness of Life, any dead things?

85. For dying is corruption, and corruption is destruction. 86. How then can any part of the incorruptible be corrupted, or of God be destroyed?

Tat: 87. Therefore, O Father, do not the living things in the World die, though they be parts thereof.

Hermes: 88. Be wary in thy Speech, O Son, and not deceived in the names of things. 89. For they do not die, O Son, but as compound Bodies they are dissolved. 90. But dissolution is not death; and they are dissolved, not that they may be destroyed, but that they may be made new.

Tat: 91. What then is the operation of Life? Is it not Motion?

Hermes: 92. And what is there in the World unmovable? Nothing at all, O Son.

Tat: 93. Why, doth not the Earth seem unmovable to thee, O Father?

Hermes: 94. No, but subject to many motions, though after a manner it alone be stable. 95. What a ridiculous thing it were, that the Nurse of all things should be unmovable, which beareth and bringeth forth all things. 96. For it is impossible, that anything that bringeth forth, should bring forth without Motion. 97. And a ridiculous question it is, Whether the fourth part of the whole, be idle: For the word immovable, or without Motion, signifies nothing else, but idleness.

98. Know generally, O Son, That whatsoever is in the World is moved either according to Augmentation or Diminution. 99. But that which is moved, liveth also, yet it is not necessary, that a living thing should be or continue the same. 100. For while the whole World is together, it is unchangeable, O Son, but all the parts thereof are changeable. 101. Yet nothing is corrupted or destroyed, and quite abolished but the names trouble men.

102. For Generation is not Life, but Sense; neither is Change Death, but Forgetfulness, or rather Occultation, and lying hid. Or better thus. For Generation is not a Creation of Life, but a Production of Things to Sense, and making them Manifest. Neither is Change Death, but an Occultation or Hiding of that which was. 103. These things being so, all things are Immortal, Matter, Life, Spirit, Soul, Mind, whereof every living thing consisteth. 104. Every living thing therefore is Immortal, because of the Mind, but especially Man, who both receiveth God, and converseth with him. 105. For with this living wight alone is God familiar; in the night by dreams, in the day by Symbols or Signs. 106. And by all things cloth he foretell him of things to come, by Birds, by Fowls, by the Spirit, or Wind, and by an Oak.

107. Wherefore also Man professeth to know things that: have been, things that are present, and things to come. 108. Consider this also, O Son, That every living Creature goeth upon one part of the World, Swimming things in Water, Land wights upon the Earth, Flying

Fowls in the Air.109. But Man useth all these, the Earth, the Water, the Air, and the Fire, nay, he seeth and toucheth Heaven by his Sense. 110. But God is both about all things, and through all things, for he is both Act and Power.

111. And it is no hard thing, O Son, to understand God. 112. And if thou wilt also see him, look upon the Necessity of things that appear, and the Providence of things that have been, and are done. 113. See the Matter being most full of Life, and so great a God moved with all Good, and Fair, both Gods, and Demons, and Men.

Tat: 114. But these, O Father, are wholly Acts or Operations.

Hermes: 115. If they be therefore wholly Acts or Operations, O Son, by whom are they acted or operated, but by God?

116. Or art thou ignorant, that as the parts of the World, are Heaven, and Earth, and Water, and Air; after the same manner the Members of God, are Life, and Immortality, and Eternity, and Spirit, and Necessity, and Providence, and Nature, and Soul, and Mind, and the Continuance or Perseverance of all these which is called Good. 117. And there is not any thing of all that hath been, and al1 that is, where God is not.

Tat: 118. What in the Matter, O Father?

Hermes: 119. The Matter, Son, what is it without God, that thou shouldst ascribe a proper place to it? 120. Or what cost thou think it to be? peradventure some heap that is not actuated or operated. 121. But if it be actuated, by whom is it actuated? for we have said, that Acts or Operations, are the parts of God.

122. By whom are all living things quickened? and the Immortal, by whom are they immortalized? the things that are changeable, by whom are they changed? 123. Whether thou speak of Matter, or Body, or Essence, know that all these are acts of God. 124. And that the Act of Matter is materiality, and of the Bodies corporality, and of Essence essentiality; and this is God the whole.

125. And in the whole, there is nothing that is not God. 126. Wherefore about God, there is neither Greatness, Place, Quality, Figure, or Time; for he is All, and the All, through all, and about all. 127. This Word, O Son, worship and adore. And the only service of God, is not to be evil.

XII: Crater

1. The Workman made this Universal World, not with his Hands, but his Word. 2. Therefore thus think of him, as present everywhere, and being always, and making all things, and one above, that by his Will hath framed the things that are.

3. For that is his Body, not tangible, nor visible, nor measurable, nor extensible, nor like any other body. 4. For it is neither Fire, nor Water, nor Air, nor Wind, but all these things are of him, for being Good, he hath dedicated that name unto himself alone.

5. But he would also adorn the Earth, but with the Ornament of a Divine Body. 6. And he sent Man an Immortal and a Mortal wight. 7. And Man had more than all living Creatures, and the World, because of his Speech, and Mind.

8. For Man became the spectator of the Works of God, and wondered, and acknowledged the Maker. 9. For he divided Speech among all men, but not Mind, and yet he envied not any, for Envy comes not thither, but is of abode here below in the Souls of men, that have not the Mind.

Tat: 10. But wherefore, Father, did not God distribute the Mind to all men?

Hermes: 11. Because it pleased him, O Son, to set that in the middle among all souls as a reward to strive for.

Tat: 12. And where hath he set it?

Hermes: 13. Filling a large Cup or Bowl therewith, he sent it down, giving also a Cryer or Proclaimer. 14. And he commanded him to proclaim these things to the souls of men. 15. Dip and wash thyself, thou that art able, in this Cup or Bowl; Thou that believes", that thou shalt return to him that sent this Cup; thou that acknowledgest whereunto thou wert made. 16. As many therefore as understood the Proclamation, and were baptized or dowsed into the Mind, these were made partakers of Knowledge, and became perfect men, receiving the Mind.

17. But as many as missed of the Proclamation, they received Speech, but not Mind, being ignorant whereunto they were made, or by whom. 18. But their senses are just like to brute Beasts, and having their temper in Anger and Wrath, they do not admire the things worthy of looking on. 19. But wholly addicted to the pleasures and desires of the Bodies, they believe that man was made for them.

20. But as many as partook of the gift of God, these, O Tat, in comparison of their works, are rather immortal than mortal men. 21. Comprehending all things in their Mind, which are upon the Earth, which are in Heaven, and if there be anything above Heaven. 22. And lifting up themselves so high, they see the Good, and seeing it, they account it a miserable calamity to make their abode here. 23. And despising all things bodily and unbodily, they make haste to the One and Only.

24. Thus, O Tat, is the Knowledge of the Mind, the beholding of Divine Things, and the Understanding of God, the Cup itself being Divine.

Tat: 25. And I, O Father, would be baptized and drenched therein.

Hermes: 26. Except thou first hate thy body, O Son, thou canst not love thy self; but loving thy self, thou shalt have the Mind, and having the Mind, thou shalt also partake the Knowledge or Science.

Tat: 27. How meanest thou that, O Father?

Hermes: 28. Because it is impossible, O Son, to be conversant about things Mortal and Divine. 29. For the things that are, being two Bodies, and things incorporeal, wherein is the Mortal and the Divine, the Election or Choice of either is left to him that will choose; For no man can choose both. 30. And of which soever the choice is made, the other being diminished or overcome, magnifieth the act and operation of the other. 31. The choice of the hefter therefore is not only best for him that chooseth it, by deifying a man; but it also sheweth Piety and Religion towards God. 32. But the choice of the worse destroys a man, but cloth nothing against God; save that as Pomps or Pageants, when they come abroad, cannot do any thing themselves, but hinder; after the same manner also do these make Pomps or Pageants in the World, being seduced by the pleasures of the Body.

33. These things being so, O Tat, that things have been, and are so plenteously ministered to us from God; let them proceed also from us, without any scarcity or sparing. 34. For God is innocent or guiltless, but we are the causes of Evil, preferring them before the Good. 35. Thou seest, O Son, how many Bodies we must go beyond, and how many choirs of Demons, and what continuity and courses of Stars, that we may make haste to the One, and only God.

36. For the Good is not to be transcended, it is unbounded and infinite; unto itself without beginning, but unto us, seeming to have

a beginning, even our knowledge of it. 37. For our knowledge is not the beginning of it, but shews us the beginning of its being known unto us. 38. Let us therefore lay hold of the beginning and we shall quickly go through all things.

39. It is indeed a difficult thing, to leave those things that are accustomable, and present, and turn us to those things that are ancient, and according to the original. 40. For these things that appear, delight us, but make the things that appear not, hard to believe, or the Things that Appear not, are Hard to believe. 41. The things most apparent are Evil, but the Good is secret, or hid in, or to the things that appear for it hath neither Form nor Figure.

42. For this cause it is like to itself, but unlike every thing else; for it is impossible, that any thing incorporeal, should be made known, or appear to a Body. 43. For this is the difference between the like and the unlike, and the unlike wanteth always somewhat of the like. 44. For the Unity, Beginning, and Root of all things, as being the Root and Beginning. 45. Nothing is without a beginning, but the Beginning is of nothing, but of itself; for it is the Beginning of all other things.

46. Therefore it is, seeing it is not from another beginning. 47. Unity therefore being the Beginning, containeth every number, but itself is contained of none, and begetteth every number, itself being begotten of no other number. 48. Every thing that is begotten (or made) is imperfect, and may be divided, increased, diminished. 49. But to the perfect, there happeneth none of these.50. And that which is increased, is increased by Unity, but is consumed and vanished through weakness, being not able to receive the Unity.

51. This Image of God, have I described to thee, O Tat, as well as I could; which if thou do diligently consider, and view by the eyes of thy mind, and heart, believe me, Son, thou shalt find the way to the things above, or rather the Image itself will lead thee. 52. But the spectacle or sight, hath this peculiar and proper; Them that can see, and behold it, it holds fast and draws unto it, as they say, the Loadstone cloth Iron.

XIII: Sense and Understanding

1. Yesterday, Asclepius, I delivered a perfect Discourse; but now I think it necessary, in suite of that, to dispute also of Sense.

2. For Sense and Understanding seem to differ, because the one is material, the other essential. 3. But unto me, they appear to be both one, or united, and not divided in men, I mean.

4. For in other living Creatures, Sense is united unto Nature but in men to Understanding. 5. But the Mind differs from Understanding, as much as God from Divinity.

6. For Divinity is from or under God, and Understanding from the Mind, being the sister of the Word or Speech, and they the Instruments one of another.

7. For-neither is the Word pronounced without Understanding, neither is Understanding manifested without the Word.

8. Therefore Sense and Understanding do both flow together into a man, as if they were infolded one within another. 9. For neither is it possible without Sense to Understand, nor can we have Sense without Understanding. 10. And yet it is possible (for the Time being) that the Understanding may understand without Sense, as they that fantasy Visions in their Dreams. 11. But it seems unto me, that both the operations are in the Visions of Dreams, and that the Sense is stirred up out of sleep, unto awaking.

12. For man is divided into a Body and a Soul; when both parts of the Sense accord one with another, then is the understanding childed, or brought forth by the Mind pronounced. 13. For the Mind

brings forth all Intellections or Understandings. Good ones w hen it receiveth good Seed from God; and the contrary when it receives them from Devils.

14. For there is no part of the World void of the Devil, which entering in privately, sowed the seed of his own proper operation; and the Mind did make pregnant, or did bring forth that which was sown, Adulteries, Murders, Striking of Parents, Sacrileges, Impieties, Stranglings, throwing down headlong, and all other things which are the works of evil Demons. 15. And the Seeds of God are few but Great, and Fair, and Good Virtue, and Temperance, and Piety.

I6. And the Piety is the Knowledge of God, whom whosoever knoweth being full of all good things, hath Divine Understanding and not like the Many. 17. And therefore they that have that Knowledge neither please the multitude, nor the multitude them, but they seem to be mad, and to move laughter, hated and despised, and many times also murdered.

18. For we have already said, That wickedness must dwell here, being in her own region. 19. For her region is the Earth, and not the World, as some will sometimes say, Blaspheming.

20. But the Godly or God-worshipping Man laying hold on Knowledge, will despise or tread under all these things; for though they be evil to other men, yet to him all things are good. 21. And upon mature consideration, he refers all things to Knowledge, and that which is most to be wondered at, he alone makes evil things good.

22. But I return again to my Discourse of Sense.

23. It is therefore a thing proper to Man, to communicate and conjoin Sense and Understanding. 24. But every man, as I said before, cloth not enjoy Understanding; for one man is material, another essential. 25. And he that is material with wickedness as I said, received from the Devils the Seed of Understanding; but they that are with the Good essentially, are saved with God.

26. For God is the Workman of all things; and when he worketh he useth Nature. 27. He maketh all things good like himsel£ 28. But these things that are made good, are in the use of Operation, unlawful. 29. For the Motion of the World stirring up Generations, makes Qualities, infecting some with evilness, and purifying some with good.

30 And the World, Asclepius, hath a peculiar Sense and Understanding, not like to Man's, nor so various or manifold, but a better and more simple. 31. For this Sense and Understanding of the World is One, in that it makes all things, and unmakes them again into itself; for it is the Organ or Instrument of the Will of God.

32. And it is so organized or framed, and made for an Instrument by God; that receiving all Seeds into itself from God, and keeping them in itself, it maketh all things effectually and dissolving them, reneweth all things. 33. And therefore like a good Husbandman of Life, when things are dissolved or loosened, he affords by the casting of Seed, renovation to all things that grow.

34. There is nothing that it (the World) cloth not beget or bring forth alive; and by its Motion, it makes all things alive. 35. And it is at once, both the Place and the Workman of Life.

36. But the Bodies are from the Matter, in a different manner; for some are of the Earth, some of Water, some of Air, some of Fire, and all are compounded, but some are more compounded, and some are more simple. 37. They that are compounded, are the heavier, and they that are less, are the higher.

38. And the swiftness of the Motion of the World, makes the varieties of the Qualities of Generation, for the spiration or influence, being most frequent, extendeth unto the Bodies qualities with one fulness, which is of Life.

39. Therefore, God is the Father of the World, but the World is the Father of things in the World. 40. And the World is the Son of God, but things in the World are the Sons of the World. 41. And therefore it is well called the World, that is an Ornament, because it adorneth and beautifieth all things with the variety of Generation, and indeficiency of Life, which the unweariedness of Operation, and the swiftness of Necessity with the mingling of Elements, and the order of things done. 42. Therefore it is necessarily and properly called the World.

43. For of all living things, both the Sense and the Understanding, cometh into them from without, inspired by that which compasseth them about, and continueth them. 44. And the World receiving it once from God as soon as it was made, hath it still, What Ever it Once Had.

45. But God is not as it seems to some who Blaspheme through superstition, without Sense, and without Mind, or Understanding.

46. For all things that are, O Asclepius, are in God, and made by him, and depend of him, some working by Bodies, some moving by a Soul-like Essence, some quickening by a Spirit, and some receiving the things that are weary, and all very fitly.

47. Or rather, I say, that he hath them not, but I declare the Truth, He is All Things, not receiving them from without, but exhibiting them outwardly. 48. And this is the Sense and Understanding of God, to move all things always. 49. And there never shall be any time, when any of those things that are, shall fail or be wanting.

50. When I say the things that are, I mean God, for the things that are, God hash; and neither is there anything without him, nor he without anything. 51. These things, O Asclepius, will appear to be true, if thou understand them, but if thou understand them not, incredible.

52. For to understand, is to believe, but not to believe, is not to understand; For my speech or words reach not unto the Truth, but the Mind is great, and being led or conducted for a while by Speech, is able to attain to the Truth. 53. And understanding all things round about, and finding them consonant, and agreeable to those things that were delivered and interpreted by Speech, believeth; and in that good belief, resteth.

54. To them, therefore, that understand the things that have been said of God, they are credible, but to them that understand them not, incredible.

55. And let these and thus many things be spoken concerning Understanding and Sense.

XIV: Operation and Sense

Tat: 1. Thou hast well explained these things, Father: Teach me furthermore these things; for thou sayest, that Science and Art were the Operations of the rational, but now thou sayest that Beasts are unreasonable, and for want of reason, both are and are called Brutes; so that by this Reason, it must needs follow that unreasonable Creatures partake not of Science, or Art, because they come short of Reason.

Hermes: 2. It must needs be so, Son.

Tat: 3. Why then, O Father, do we see some unreasonable living Creatures use both Science and Art? As the pismires treasure up for themselves food against the winter, and Fowls of the Air likewise make them Nests, and four-footed Beasts know their own Dens.

Hermes: 4. These things they do, O Son, not by Science or Art, but by Nature; for Science or Art are things that are taught, but none of these brute Beasts are taught any of these things. 5. But these things being Natural unto them, are wrought by Nature, whereas Art and Science do not happen unto all, but unto some. 6. As men are Musicians, but not all; neither are all Archers or Huntsmen, or the rest, but some of them have learned something by the working of Science or Art. 7. After the same manner also, if some pismires did so, and some not, thou mightest well say, they gather their food according to Science and Art. 8. But seeing they are all led by Nature, to the same thing, even against their wills, it is manifest they do not do it by Science or Art. 9. For Operations, O Tat, being unbodily, are in Bodies, and work by Bodies.

10. Wherefore, O Tat, in as much as they are unbodily, thou must needs say they are immortal. 11. But in as much as they cannot act without Bodies, I say, they are always in a Body. 12. For those things that are to any thing, or for the cause of any thing made subject to Providence or Necessity, cannot possibly remain idle of their own proper Operation. 13. For that which is, shall ever be; for both the Body, and the Life of it, is the same. 14. And by this reason, it follows, that the Bodies also are always, because I affirm: That this corporeity is always by the Act and Operation, or for them. 15. For although earthly bodies be subject to dissolution; yet these bodies must be the Places, and the Organs, and Instruments of Acts or Operations.

16. But Acts or Operations are immortal, and that which is immortal, is always in Act, and therefore also Corporification if it be always. 17. Acts or Operations do follow the Soul, yet come not suddenly or promiscuously, but some of them come together with being made man, being about brutish or unreasonable things. 18. But the purer Operations do insensibly in the change of time, work with the oblique part of the Soul. 19. And these Operations depend upon Bodies, and truly they that are Corporifying come from the Divine Bodies into Mortal ones.

20. But every one of them acteth both about the Body and the Soul, and are present with the Soul, even without the Body. 21. And they are always Acts or Operations, but the Soul is not always in a Mortal Body, for it can be without a Body, but Acts or Operations cannot be without Bodies. 22 This is a sacred speech, Son, the Body cannot Consist without a Soul.

Tat: 23. How meanest thou that, Father?

Hermes: 24. Understand it thus, O Tat, When the Soul is separated from the Body, there remaineth that same Body. 25. And this same Body according to the time of its abode, is actuated or operated in that it is dissolved and becomes invisible. 26. And these things the Body cannot suffer without act or operation, and consequently there remaineth with the Body the same act or operation.

27. This then is the difference between an Immortal Body, and a Mortal one, that the immortal one consists of one Matter, and so doth not the mortal one; and the immortal one doth, but this suffereth.28. And everything that acteth or operateth is stronger, and ruleth; but that which is actuated or operated, is ruled. 29. And that which ruleth, directeth and governeth as free, but the other is ruled, a servant.

30. Acts or Operations do not only actuate or operate living or breathing or insouled Bodies, but also breathless Bodies, or without Souls, Wood, and Stones, and such like, increasing and hearing fruit, ripening, corrupting, rotting, putrifying and breaking, or working such like things, and whatsoever inanimate Bodies can suffer.

31. Act or Operation, O Son, is called, whatsoever is, or is made or done, and there are always many things made, or rather all things. 32 For the World is never widowed or forsaken of any of those things that are, but being always carried or moved in itself, it is in labor to bring forth the things that are, which shall never be left by it to corruption. 33. Let therefore every act or operation be understood to be always immortal, in what manner of Body soever it be.

34. But some Acts or Operations be of Divine, some of corruptible Bodies, some universal, some peculiar, and some of the generals, and

some of the parts of every thing. 35. Divine Acts or Operations therefore there be, and such as work or operate upon their proper Bodies, and these also are perfect, and being upon or in perfect Bodies.

36. Particular are they which work by any of the living Creatures.

37. Proper, be they that work upon any of the things that are.

38. By this Discourse, therefore, O Son, it is gathered that all things are full of Acts or Operations. 39. For if necessarily they be in every Body, and that there be many Bodies in the World, I may very well affirm, that there be many other Acts or Operations. 40. For many times in one Body, there is one, and a second, and a third, besides these universal ones that follow.

41. And universal Operations, I call them that are indeed bodily, and are done by the Senses and Motions. 42. For without these it is impossible that the Body should consist. 43. But other Operations are proper to the Souls of Men, by Arts, Sciences, Studies, and Actions. 44. The Senses also follow these Operations, or rather are the effects or perfections of them.

45. Understand therefore, O Son, the difference of Operations, it is sent from above. 46. But sense being in the Body, and having its essence from it, when it receiveth Act or Operation, manifesteth it, making it as it were corporeal. 47. Therefore, I say, that the Senses are both corporeal and mortal, having so much existence as the Body, for they are born with the Body, and die with it.

48. But mortal things themselves have not Sense, as Not consisting of such an Essence. 49. For Sense can be no other than a corporeal apprehension, either of evil or good that comes to the Body. 50. But to Eternal Bodies there is nothing comes, nothing departs; therefore there is no sense in them.

Tat: 51. Doth the Sense therefore perceive or apprehend in every Body?

Hermes: 52. In every Body, O Son.

Tat: 53. And do the Acts or Operations work in all things?

Hermes: 54. Even in things inanimate, O Son, but there are differences of Senses. 55. For the Senses of things rational, are with Reason; of things unreasonable, Corporeal only, but the Senses of things inanimate are passive only, according to Augmentation and Diminution. 56. But Passion and Sense depend both upon one head, or height, and are gathered together into the same, by Acts or Operations. 57. But in living wights there be two other Operations that follow the Senses and Passions, to wit, Grief and Pleasure.58. And without these, it is impossible that a living wight, especially a reasonable one, should perceive or apprehend. 59. And therefore, I say, that these are the Ideas of Passions that bear rule, especially in reasonable living wights.

60. The Operations work indeed, but the Senses do declare and manifest the Operations, and they being bodily, are moved by the brutish parts of the Soul therefore I say, they are both maleficial or doers of evil. 61. For that which affords the Sense to rejoice with Pleasure is straightway the cause of many evils happening to him

that suffers it.62. But Sorrows gives stronger torments and Anguish, therefore doubtless are they both maleficial.63. The same may be said of the Sense of the Soul.

Tat: 64. Is not the Soul incorporeal, and the Sense a Body, Father? Or is it rather in the Body?

Hermes: 65. If we put it in a Body, O Son, we shall make it like the Soul or the Operations, for these being unbodily, we say are in Bodies. 66. But Sense is neither Operation, nor Soul, nor anything else that belongs to the Body, but as we have said, and therefore it is not incorporeal. 67. And if it be not incorporeal it must needs be a Body; for we always say, that of things that are, some are Bodies and some incorporeal.

XV: Of Truth

1. Of Truth, O Tat, it is not possible that man being an imperfect wight, compounded of imperfect Members, and having his Tabernacle consisting of different and many Bodies, should speak with any confidence. 2. But as far as it is possible, and just, I say, That Truth is only in the Eternal Bodies, whose very Bodies be also true.

3. The Fire is fire itself only, and nothing else; the Earth is earth itself and nothing else; the air is air itself and nothing else; the water, water itself and nothing else.4. But our Bodies consist of all these; for they have of the Fire, they have of the Earth, they have of the Water, and Air, and yet there is neither Fire, nor Earth, nor Water, nor Air, nor anything true.5. And if at the Beginning our Constitution had not Truth, how could men either see the Truth, or speak it, or understand it only, except God would?

6. All things therefore upon Earth, O Tat, are not Truth, but imitations of the Truth, and yet not all things neither, for they are but few that are so. 7. But the other things are Falsehood, and Deceit, O Tat, and Opinions like the Images of the fantasy or appearance. 8. And when the fantasy hath an influence from above, then it is an imitation of Truth, but without that operation from above, it is left a lie. 9. And as an Image shews the Body described, and yet is not the Body of that which is seen, as it seems to be, and it is seen to have eyes, but it sees nothing, and ears, but hears nothing at all; and all other things hath the picture, but they are false, deceiving the eyes of the beholder, whilst they think they see the Truth, and yet they are indeed but lies.

10. As many therefore as see not Falsehood, see the Truth. 11. If therefore we do so understand, and see every one of these things as it is, then we see and understand true things. 12. But if we see or understand any thing besides or otherwise than that which is, we shall neither understand, nor know the Truth.

Tat: 13. Is Truth therefore upon Earth, O Father?

Hermes: 14. Thou cost not miss the mark, O Son. Truth indeed is nowhere at all upon Earth, O Tat, for it cannot be generated or made. 15. But concerning the Truth, it may be that some men, to whom God will give the good seeing Power, may understand it. 16. So that unto the Mind and reason, there is nothing true indeed upon Earth. 17. But unto the True Mind and Reason, all things are fantasies or appearances, and op1nions.

Tat: 18. Must we not therefore call it Truth, to understand and speak the things that are?

Hermes: 19. But there is nothing true upon Earth.

Tat: 20. How then is this true, that we do not know anything true? How can that be done here?

Hermes: 21. O Son, Truth is the most perfect Virtue, and the highest Good itself, not troubled by Matter, not encompassed by a Body, naked, clear, unchangeable, venerable, unalterable Good. 22 But the things that are here, O Son, are visible, incapable of Good, corruptible, passible, dissolvable, changeable, continually altered, and made of another. 23. The things therefore that are not true to themselves, how can they be true? 24. For every thing that is altered, is a lie, not abiding in what it is; but being changed it shows us always, other and other appearances.

Tat: 25. Is not man true, O Father?

Hermes: 26. As far forth as he is a Man, he is not true, Son; for that which is true, hath of itself alone its constitution and remains, and abides according to itself, such as it is. 27. But man consists of many things and doth not abide of himself but is turned and changed, age after age, Idea after Idea, or form after form, and this while he is yet in the Tabernacle. 28. And many have not known their own children after a little while, and many children likewise have not known their own Parents.

29. Is it then possible, O Tat, that he who is so changed, is not to be known, should be true? No, on the contrary, he is Falsehood, being in many Appearances of changes.

30. But do thou understand the true to be that which abides the same, and is Eternal, but man is not ever, therefore not True, but man is a certain Appearance, and Appearance is the highest Lie or Falsehood.

Tat: 31. But these Eternal Bodies, Father, are they not true though they be changed?

Hermes: 32. Everything that is begotten or made, and changed is not true, but being made by our Progenitor, they might have had true Matter. 33. But these also have in themselves, something that is false in regard of their change. 34. For nothing that remains not in itself, is True.

Tat: 35. What shall one say then, Father, that only the Sun which besides the Nature of other things, is not changed, but abides in itself, is Truth?

Hermes: 36. It is Truth, and therefore is he only entrusted with the Workmanship of the World, ruling and making all things whom I do both honor, and adore his Truth; and after the One, and First, I acknowledge him the Workman.

Tat: 37. What therefore doth thou affirm to be the first Truth, O Father?

Hermes: 38. The One and Only, O Tat, that is not of Matter, that is not in a body, that is without Color, without Figure or Shape, Immutable, Unalterable, which always is; but Falsehood, O Son, is corrupted. 39. And corruption hath laid hold upon all things on Earth, and the Providence of the True encompasseth, and will encompass them. 40. For without corruption, there can no Generation consist. 41. For Corruption followeth every Generation, that it may again be generated. 42. For those things that are generated, must of necessity be generated of those things that are corrupted, and the things generated must needs be corrupted, that the Generation of things being, may not stand still or cease. 43. Acknowledge therefore the first Workman by the Generation of things.

44. Consequently the things that are generated of Corruption are false, as being sometimes one thing, sometimes another: For it is impossible they should be made the same things again, and that which is not the same, how is it true? 45. Therefore, O Son, we must call these things fantasies or appearances. 46. And if we will give a

man his right name, we must call him the appearance of Manhood; and a Child, the fantasy or appearance of a Child; an old man, the appearance of an old man; a young man, the appearance of a young man; and a man of ripe age, the appearance of a man of ripe age. 47. For neither is a man, a man; nor a child, a child; nor a young man, a young man; nor an old man, an old man. 48 But the things that pre-exist and that are, being changed are false. 49. These things understand thus, O Son, as these false Operations, having their dependence from above, even of the truth itself.

50. Which being so, I do affirm that Falsehood is the Work of Truth.

XVI: Nothing can Perish

Hermes: 1. We must now speak of the Soul and Body, O Son; after what manner the Soul is Immortal, and what operation that is, which constitutes the Body, and dissolves it. 2. But in none of these is Death (Thanatos,) for it is a conception of a name, which is either an empty word, or else it is wrongly called Death (by the taking away the first letter,) instead of Immortal (Athanatos.) 3. For Death is destruction, but there is nothing in the whole world that is destroyed.

4. For if the World be a second God, and an Immortal living Wight, it is impossible that any part of an Immortal living Wight should die. 5. But all things that are in the World, are members of the World, especially Man, the reasonable living Wight.

6. For the first of all is God, the Eternal and Unmade, and the Workman of all things.

7. The second is the World, made by him, after his own Image and by him holden together, and nourished, and immortalized; and as from its own Father, ever living. 8. So that as Immortal, it is ever living, and ever immortal. 9. For that which is ever living, differs from that which is eternal.

10. For the Eternal was not begotten, or made by another; and if it were begotten or made, yet it was made by itself, not by any other, but it is always made. 11. For the Eternal, as it is Eternal, is the Universe. 12. For the Father himself, is Eternal of himself, but the World was made by the Father, ever living and immortal.

13. And as much Matter as there was laid up by him, the Father made it all into a Body, and swelling it, made it round like a Sphere,

endued it with Quality, being itself immortal, and having Eternal Materiality. 14. The Father being full of Ideas, sowed Qualities in the Sphere, and shut them up, as in a Circle, deliberating to beautify with every Quality, that which should afterwards be made. 15. Then clothing the Universal Body with Immortality, lest the Matter, if it would depart from this Composition, should be dissolved into its own disorder.

16. For when the Matter was incorporeal, O Son, it was disordered, and it hath here the same confusion daily revolved about other little things, endued with Qualities, in point of Augmentation, and Diminution, which men call Death, being indeed a disorder happening about earthly living wights. 17. For the Bodies of Heavenly things have one order, which they have received from the Father at the Beginning, and is by the instauration of each of them, kept indissolveable.

18. But the instauration of earthly Bodies, is their consistence; and their dissolution restores them into indissoluble, that is, Immortal. 19. And so there is made a privation of Sense, but not a destruction of Bodies.

20. Now the third living wight is Man, made after the Image of the World; and having by the Will of the Father, a Mind above other earthly wights. 21. And he hath not only a sympathy with the second God, but also an understanding of the first.

22. For the second God, he apprehends as a Body but the first, he understands as Incorporeal, and the Mind of the Good.

Tat: 23. And doth not this living Wight perish?

Hermes: 24. Speak advisedly, O Son, and learn what God is, what the World, what an Immortal Wight, and what a dissolvable One is. 25. And understand that the World is of God and in God; but Man of the World and in the World.

26. The Beginning, and End, and Consistence of all, is God.

XVII: To be Truly Wise.

Thus speaks Hermes to Asclepius:

1. Because my Son Tat, in thy absence, would needs learn the Nature of the things that are: He would not suffer me to give over (as coming very young to the knowledge of every individual) till I was forced to discourse to him many things at large, that his contemplation might from point to point, be more easy and successful. 2. But to thee I have thought good to write in few words, choosing out the principal heads of the things then spoken, and to interpret them more mystically, because thou hast, both more years, and more knowledge of Nature.

3. All things that appear, were made, and are made. 4. Those things that are made, are not made by themselves, but by another. 5. And there are many things made, but especially all things that appear, and which are different, and not like. 6. If the things that be made and done, be made and done by another, there must be one that must make, and do them; and he unmade, and more ancient than the things that are made.

7. For I affirm the things that are made, to be made by another; and it is impossible, that of the things that are made any should be more ancient than all, but only that which is not made. 8. He is stronger, and One, and only knowing all things indeed, as not having any thing more ancient than himself. 9. For he bears rule, both over multitude, and greatness, and the diversity of the things that are made, and the continuity of the Facture and of the Operation.

10. Moreover, the things that are made, are visible, but he is invisible; and for this cause, he maketh them, that he may be visible; and therefore he makes them always. 11. Thus it is fit to understand

and understanding to admire and admiring to think thy self happy, that knowest thy natural Father.12. For what is sweeter than a Natural Father?

13. Who therefore is this, or how shall we know him? 14. Or is it just to ascribe unto him alone, the Title and Appellation of God, or of the Maker, or of the Father, or of all Three? That of God because of his Power; the Maker because of his Working and Operation; and the Father, because of his Goodness. 15. For Power is different from the things that are made, but Act or Operation, in that all things are made. 16. Wherefore, letting go all much and vain talking, we must understand these two things, That Which is Made, and Him Which is the Maker; for there is nothing in the middle, between these Two, nor is there any third. 17. Therefore understanding All things, remember these Two; and think that these are All things, putting nothing into doubt; neither of the things above, nor of the things below; neither of things changeable, nor things that are in darkness or secret.

18. For All things, are but two Things, That which Maketh, and that which is Made, and the One of them cannot depart, or be divided from the Other. 19. For neither is it possible that the maker should be without the thing made, for either of them is the self-same thing; therefore cannot the One of them be separated from the other, no more than a thing can be separated from itself. 20. For if he that makes be nothing else, but that which makes alone, Simple, Uncompounded, it is of necessity, that he makes the same thing to himself, to whom it is the Generation of him that maketh to be also All that is made.

21. For that which is generated or made, must necessarily be generated or made by another, but without the Maker that which is made, neither is made, nor is; for the one of them without the other, hath lost his proper Nature by the privation of the other. 22. So if these Two be confessed, That which maketh, and that which is made, then they are One in Union, this going before, and that following. 23. And that which goeth before, is, God the Maker, and that which follows is, that which is made, be it what it will.

24. And let no man be afraid because of the variety of things that are made or done, lest he should cast an aspersion of baseness, or infamy upon God, for it is the only Glory of him to do, or make All things. 25. And this making, or facture is as it were the Body of God, and to him that maketh or doth, there is nothing evil, or filthy to be imputed, or There is Nothing thought Evil or Filthy.

26. For these are Passions that follow Generation as Rust doth Copper, or as Excrements do the Body. 27. But neither did the Copper-smith make the Rust, nor the Maker the Filth, nor God the Evilness. 28. But the vicissitude of Generation doth make them, as it were to blossom out; and for this cause did make Change to be, as one should say, The Purgation of Generation. 29. Moreover, is it lawful for the same Painter to make both Heaven, and the Gods, and the Earth, and the Sea, and Men, and brute Beasts, and inanimate Things, and Trees; and is it impossible for God to make these things? O, the great madness, and ignorance of men in things that concern God!

30. For men that think so, suffer that which is most ridiculous of all; for professing to bless and praise God yet in not ascribing to him the making or doing of All things, they know him not. 31. And besides

their not knowing him, they are extremely impious against him, attributing unto him Passions, as Pride, or Oversight, or Weakness, or Ignorance, or Envy. 32. For if he do not make or do all things, he is either proud or not able, or ignorant, or envious, which is impious to affirm.

33. For God hath only one Passion, namely Good and he that is good is neither proud, nor impotent, nor the rest, but God is Good itself. 34. For Good is all power, to do or make all things, and every thing that is made, is made by God, that is by the Good and that can make or do all things. 35. See then how he maketh all things, and how the things are done, that are done, and if thou wilt learn, thou mayest see an Image thereof, very beautiful, and like.

36. Look upon the Husbandman, how he casteth Seeds into the Earth, here Wheat, there Barley, and elsewhere some other Seeds. 37. Look upon the same Man, planting a Vine, or an Apple-Tree, or a Fig-Tree, or some other Tree. 38. So doth God in Heaven sow Immortality, in the Earth Change in the whole Life, and Motion. 39. And these things are not many, but few, and easily numbered for they are all but four, God and Generation, in which are all things.

The Hermetic Arcanum

Anonymous

The Hermetic Arcanum

The secret work of the Hermetic Philosophy

Wherein the secrets of nature and art concerning the matter of the philosophers' stone and the manner of working are explained in an authentic and orderly manner.

The work of an anonymous author, *penes nos unda tagi*.

1. The beginning of this Divine Science is the fear of the Lord and its end is charity and love toward our Neighbor. The all-satisfying Golden Crop is properly devoted to the rearing and endowing of temples and hospices; for whatsoever the Almighty freely bestoweth on us, we should properly offer again to him. So also Countries grievously oppressed may be set free; prisoners unduly held captive may be released, and souls almost starved may be relieved.

2. The light of this knowledge is the gift of God, which by His will He bestoweth upon whom He pleaseth. Let none therefore set himself to the study hereof, until having cleared and purified his heart, he devote himself wholly unto God, and be emptied of all affection and desire unto the impure things of this world.

3. The Science of producing Nature's grand Secret, is a perfect knowledge of universal Nature and of Art concerning the Realm of Metals; the Practice thereof is conversant with finding the principles of Metals by Analysis, and after they have been made much more perfect to conjoin them otherwise than they have been before, that from thence may result a catholic Medicine, most powerful to perfect imperfect Metals, and for restoring sick and decayed bodies, of any sort soever.

4. Those that hold public Honors and Offices or be always busied with private and necessary occupations, let them not strive to attain unto the acme of this Philosophy; for it requireth the whole mans, and being found, it possesseth him, and he being possessed, it debarreth him from all other long and serious employments, for he will esteem other things as strange, and of no value unto him.

5. Let him that is desirous of this Knowledge, clear his mind from all evil passions, especially pride, which is an abomination to Heaven, and is as the gate of Hell; let him be frequent in prayer and charitable; have little to do with the world: abstain from company keeping; enjoy constant tranquility; that the Mind may be able to reason more freely in private and be highly lifted up; for unless it be kindled with a beam of Divine Light, it will not be able to penetrate these hidden mysteries of Truth.

6. The Alchemists who have given their minds to their well-nigh innumerable Sublimations, Distillations, Solutions, Congelations, to manifold Extraction of Spirits and Tinctures, and other Operations more subtle than profitable, and so have distracted themselves by a variety of errors, as so many tormentors, will never be inclined again by their own Genius to the plain way of Nature and light of Truth; from whence their industrious subtilty hath twined them, and by twinings and turnings, as by the Lybian Quicksands, hath drowned their entangled Wits: the only hope of safety for them remaineth in finding out a faithful Guide and Master, who may make the Sun clear and conspicuous unto them and free themselves from darkness.

7. A studious Tyro of a quick wit, constant mind, inflamed with the study of Philosophy, very skilful in natural Philosophy, of a pure heart, complete in manners, mightily devoted to God, though ignorant of practical Chemistry, may with confidence enter into the highway of Nature and peruse the Books of the best Philosophers; let him seek out an ingenious and sedulous Companion for himself, and not despair of obtaining his desire.

8. Let a Student of these secrets carefully beware of reading or keeping company with false Philosophers; for nothing is more

dangerous to a learner of any Science, than the company of an unskilled or deceitful man by whom erroneous principles are stamped as true, whereby a simple and credulous mind is seasoned with false Doctrine.

9. Let a Lover of truth make use of few authors, but of the best note and experience truth; let him suspect things that are quickly understood, especially in Mystical Names and Secret Operations; for truth lies hid in obscurity; for Philosophers never write more deceitfully than when plainly, nor ever more truly than when obscurely.

10. As for the Authors of chiefest note, who have discoursed both acutely and truly of the secrets of Nature and hidden Philosophy, Hermes and Morienus Romanus amongst the Ancients are in my judgment of the highest esteem; amongst the Moderns, Count Trevisan, and Raimundus Lullius are in greatest reverence with me; for what that most acute Doctor hath omitted, none almost hath spoken; let a student therefore peruse his works, yea let him often read over his Former Testament, and Codicil, and accept them as a Legacy of very great worth. To these two volumes let him add both his volumes of Practice, out of which works all things desirable may be collected, especially the truth of the First Matter, of the degrees of Fire, and the Regimen of the Whole, wherein the final Work is finished, and those things which our Ancestors so carefully labored to keep secret. The occult causes of things, and the secret motions of nature are demonstrated nowhere more clearly and faithfully. Concerning the first and mystical Water of the Philosophers he hath set down few things, yet very pithily.

11. As for that Clear Water sought for by many, found by so few, yet obvious and profitable unto all, which is the Basis of the Philosophers' Work, a noble Pole, not more famous for his learning than subtlety of wit, who wrote anonymously, but whose name notwithstanding a double Anagram hath betrayed, hath in his Novum Lumen Chymicum, Parabola and Aenigma, as also in his Tract on Sulphur, spoken largely and freely enough; yea he hath expressed all things concerning it so plainly, that nothing can be more satisfactory to him that desireth knowledge.

12. Philosophers do usually express themselves more pithily in types and enigmatical figures (as by a mute kind of speech) than by words; see for example, Senior's Table, the Allegorical Pictures of Rosarius, the Pictures of Abraham Judaeus in Flamel, and the drawings of Flamel himself; of the later sort, the rare Emblems of the most learned Michael Maierus wherein the mysteries of the Ancients are so fully opened, and as new Perspectives they present antiquated truth, and though designed remote from our age yet are near unto our eyes, and are perfectly to be perceived by us.

13. Whosoever affirmeth that the Philosophers' grand Secret is beyond the powers of Nature and Art, he is blind because he ignores the forces of Sol and Luna.

14. As for the matter of their hidden Stone, Philosophers have written diversely; so that very many disagreeing in Words, do nevertheless very well agree in the Thing; nor doth their different speech argue the science ambiguous or false, since the same thing may be expressed with many tongues, by divers expressions, and by a different character, and also one and many things may be spoken of after diverse manners.

15. Let the studious Reader have a care of the manifold significations of words, for by deceitful windings, and doubtful, yea contrary speeches (as it should seem), Philosophers wrote their mysteries, with a desire of veiling and hiding, yet not of sophisticating or destroying the truth; and though their writings abound with ambiguous and equivocal words; yet about none do they more contend than in hiding their Golden Branch. "Which all the groves with shadows overcast,/ And gloomy valleys hide./ Nor yieldeth it to any Force, /but readily and willingly will follow him, /who knows Dame Venus Birds/ And him to whom of Doves a lucky pair /Sent from above shall hover 'bout his Ear."

16. Whosoever seeketh the Art of perfecting and multiplying imperfect Metals, beyond the nature of Metals, goes in error, for from Metals the Metals are to be derived; even as from Man, Mankind; and from an Ox only, is that species to be obtained.

17. Metals, we must confess, cannot be multiplied by the instinct and labor of Nature only; yet we may affirm that the multiplying virtue is hid in their depths, and manifested itself by the help of Art: In this Work, Nature standeth in need of the aid of Art; and both do make a perfect whole.

18. Perfect Bodies as Sol and Luna are endued with a perfect seed; and therefore under the hard crust of the perfect Metals the Perfect Seed lies hid; and he that knows how to take it out by the Philosophers' Solution, hath entered upon the royal highway; for-
"In Gold the seeds of Gold do lie/
Though buried in Obscurity."

19. Most Philosophers have affirmed that their Kingly Work is wholly composed of Sol and Luna; others have thought good to add Mercury to Sol; some have chosen Sulphur and Mercury; others have attributed no small part in so great a Work to Salt mingled with the other two. The very same men have professed that this Clear Stone is made of one thing only, sometimes of two, or of three, at other times of four, and of five; and yet though writing so variously upon the same subject, they do nevertheless agree in sense and meaning.

20. Now that (abandoning all blinds) we may write candidly and truly, we hold that this entire Work is perfected by two Bodies only; to wit, by Sol and Luna rightly prepared, for this is the mere generation which is by nature, with the help of Art, wherein the union of male and female doth take place, and from thence an offspring far more noble than the parents is brought forth.

21. Now those Bodies must be taken, which are of an unspotted and incorrupt virginity; such as have life and spirit in them; not extinct as those that are handled by the vulgar; for who can expect life from dead things; and those are called impure which have suffered combination; those dead and extinct which (by the enforcement of the chief Tyrant of the world) have poured out their soul with their blood by Martyrdom; flee then a fratricide from which the most imminent danger in the whole Work is threatened.

22. Now Sol is Masculine forasmuch as he sendeth forth active and energizing seed, Luna is Feminine or Negative and she is called the Matrix of Nature, because she receiveth the sperm, and fostereth it by monthly provision, yet doth Luna not altogether want in positive or active virtue.

23. By the name of Luna Philosophers understand not the vulgar Moon, which also may be positive in its operation, and in combining acts a positive part. Let none therefore presume to try the unnatural combination of two positives, neither let him conceive any hope of issue from such association; but he shall join Gabritius to Beia, and offer sister to brother in firm union, that from thence he may receive Sol's noble Son.

24. They that hold Sulphur and Mercury to be the First Matter of the Stone, by the name of Sulphur they understand Sol; by Mercury the Philosophic Luna; so (without dissimulation) good Lullius adviseth his friend, that he attempt not to work without Mercury and Luna for Silver; nor without Mercury and Sol for Gold.

25. Let none therefore be deceived by adding a third to two: for Love admitteth not a third; and wedlock is terminated in the number of two; love further extended is not matrimony.

26. Nevertheless Spiritual love polluteth not any virgin; Beia might therefore without fault (before her betrothal to Gabritius) have felt spiritual love, to the end that she might thereby be made more cheerful, more pure and fitter for union.

27. Procreation is the end of lawful Wedlock. Now that the progeny may be born more vigorous and active, let both the combatants be cleansed from every ill and spot, before they are united in marriage. Let nothing superfluous cleave unto them, because from pure seed comes a purified generation, and so the chaste wedlock of Sol and Luna shall be finished when they shall enter into combination, and be conjoined, and Luna shall receive a soul from her husband by this

union; from this conjunction a most potent King shall arise, whose rather will be Sol and his mother Luna.

28. He that seeks for a physical tincture without Sol and Luna, loseth both his cost and pains: for Sol afforded a most plentiful tincture of redness, and Luna of whiteness, for these two only are called perfect; because they are filled with the substance of purest Sulphur, perfectly clarified by the skill of nature. Let thy Mercury therefore receive a tincture from one or other of these luminaries; for anything must of necessity possess a tincture before it can tinge other bodies.

29. Perfect metals contain in themselves two things which they are able to communicate to the imperfect metals. Tincture and Power of fixation; for pure metals, because they are dyed and fixed with pure Sulphur to wit both white and red, do therefore perfectly tincture and fix, if they be fitly prepared with their proper Sulphur and Arsenic: otherwise they have not strength for multiplying their tincture.

30. Mercury is alone among the imperfect metals, fit to receive the tincture of Sol and Luna in the work of the Philosophers' Stone, and being itself full of tincture can tinge other metals in abundance; yet ought it (before that) to be full of invisible Sulphur, that it may be the more color ed with the visible tincture of perfect bodies, and so repay with sufficient Usury.

31. Now the whole tribe of Philosophers do much assert and work mightily to extract Tincture out of gold: for they believe that Tincture can be separated from Sol, and being separated increases in virtue but:"Vain hope, at last the hungry Plough-man cheats/With empty husks, instead of lusty meats." For it is impossible that Sol's Tincture

can at all be severed from his natural body, since there can be no elementary body made up by nature more perfect than gold, the perfection whereof proceedeth from the strong and inseparable union of pure color ing Sulphur with Mercury; both of them being admirably pre-disposed thereunto by Nature; whose true separation nature denieth unto Art. But if any liquor remaining be extracted (by the violence of fire or waters) from the Sun, it is to be reputed a part of the body made liquid or dissolved by force. For the tincture followeth its body, and is never separated from it. That is a delusion of this Art, which is unknown to many Artificers themselves.

32. Nevertheless it may be granted, that Tincture may be separable from its body, yet (we must confess) it cannot be separated without the corruption of the tincture: as when Artists offer violence to the gold destroying by fire, or use *Aqua Fortis*, thus rather corroding than dissolving. The body therefore if despoiled of its Tincture and Golden Fleece, must needs grow base and as an unprofitable heap turn to the damage of its Artificer, and the Tincture thus corrupted can only have a weaker operation.

33. Let Alchemists in the next place cast their Tincture into Mercury, or into any other imperfect body, and as strongly conjoin both of them as their Art will permit; yet shall they fail of their hopes in two ways. First, because the Tincture will neither penetrate nor color beyond Nature's weight and strength; and therefore no gain will accrue from thence to recompense the expense and countervail the loss of the body spoiled, and thus of no value; so:"Want is poor mortal's wages, when his toil/ Produces only loss of pain and oil." Lastly, that debased Tincture applied to another body will not give that perfect fixation and permanency required to endure a strong trial, and resist searching Saturn.

34. Let them therefore that are desirous of Alchemy, and have hitherto followed impostors and mountebanks, found a retreat, spare no time nor cost, and give their minds to a work truly Philosophical, lest the Phrygians be wise too late, and at length be compelled to cry out with the prophet, "Strangers have devoured his strength."

35. In the Philosophers' work more time and toil than cost is expended: for he that hath convenient matter need be at little expense; besides, those that hunt after great store of money, and place their chief end in wealth, they trust more to their riches than their own art. Let, therefore, the too credulous tyro beware of pilfering pickpockets, for while they promise golden mountains, they lay in wait for gold, they demand bright gold (viz., money beforehand), because they walk in evil and darkness.

36. As those that sail between Scylla and Charybdis are in danger from both sides: unto no less hazard art they subject who pursuing the prize of the Golden fleece are carried between the uncertain Rocks of the Sulphur and Mercury of the Philosophers. The more acute students by their constant reading of grave and credible Authors, and by the radiant sunlight, have attained unto the knowledge of Sulphur but are at a stand at the entrance of their search for the Philosophers' Mercury; for Writers have twisted it with so many windings and meanderings, involved it with so many equivocal names, that it may be sooner met with by the force of the Seeker's intuition, than be found by reason or toil.

37. That Philosophers might the deeper hide their Mercury in darkness, they have made it manifold, and placed their Mercury (yet diversely) in every part and in the forefront of their work, nor will he

attain unto a perfect knowledge thereof, who shall be ignorant of any Part of the Work.

38. Philosophers have acknowledged their Mercury to be threefold; to wit, after the absolute preparation of the First degree, the Philosophical sublimation, for then they call it "Their Mercury," and "Mercury Sublimated."

39. Again, in the Second preparation, that which by Authors is styled the First (because they omit the First) Sol being now made crude again, and resolved into his first matter, is called the Mercury of such like bodies, or the Philosophers' Mercury; then the matter is called Rebis, Chaos, or the Whole World, wherein are all things necessary to the Work, because that only is sufficient to perfect the Stone.

40. Thirdly, the Philosophers do sometimes call Perfect Elixir and Color ing Medicine - Their Mercury, though improperly; for the name of Mercury doth only properly agree with that which is volatile; besides that which is sublimated in every region of the work, they call Mercury: but Elixir - that which is most fixed cannot have the simple name of Mercury ; and therefore they have styled it "Their Mercury" to differentiate it from that which is volatile. A straight may is only laid down for some to find out and discern so many Mercuries of the Philosophers, for those only: " Whom just and mighty Jove/Advanceth by the strength of love;/Or such who brave heroic fire,
Makes from dull Earth to Heaven aspire."

41. The Elixir is called the Philosophers' Mercury for the likeness and great conformity it hath with heavenly Mercury; for to this, being devoid of elementary qualities, heaven is believed to be most

propitious; and that changeable Proteus puts on and increaseth the genius and nature of other Planets, by reason of opposition, conjunction, and aspect. In like manner this uncertain Elixir worketh, for being restricted to no proper quality, it embraceth the quality and disposition of the thing wherewith it is mixed, and wonderfully multiplieth the virtues and qualities thereof.

42. In the Philosophical sublimation or first preparation of Mercury, Herculean labor must be undergone by the workman; for Jason had in vain attempted his expedition to Colchos without Alcides. "One from on high a Golden Fleece displays/ Which shews the Entrance, another says/ How hard a task you'll find." For the entrance is warded by horned beasts which drive away those that approach rashly thereunto, to their great hurt; only the ensigns of Diana and the Doves of Venus are able to assuage their fierceness, if the fates favor the attempt.

43. The Natural quality of Philosophical Earth and the tillage thereof, seems to be touched upon by the poet in this verse: "Let sturdy oxen when the year begins/ Plough up the fertile soil,/For Zephyrus then destroys the sodden clods."

44. He that calleth the Philosophers' Luna or their Mercury, the common Mercury, doth wittingly deceive, or is deceived himself; so the writings of Geber teach us, that the Philosophers' Mercury is Argent vive, yet not of the common sort, but extracted out of it by the Philosophers' skill.

45. The Philosophers' Mercury is not Argent vive in its proper nature, nor in its whole substance, but is only the middle and pure substance thereof, which thence hath taken its origin and has been

made by it. This opinion of the grand Philosophers is founded on experience.

46. The Philosophers' Mercury hath divers names, sometimes it is called Earth; sometimes Water, when viewed from a diverse aspect; because it naturally ariseth from them both. The earth is subtle, white and sulphurous, in which the elements are fixed and the philosophical gold is sown; the water is the water of life, burning, permanent, most clear, called the water of gold and silver; but this Mercury, because it hath in it Sulphur of its own, which is multiplied by art, deserves to be called the Sulphur of Argent vive. Last of all, the most precious substance is Venus, the ancient Hermaphrodite, glorious in its double sex.

47. This Argent vive is partly natural, partly unnatural; its intrinsic and occult part hath its root in nature, and this cannot be drawn forth unless it be by some precedent cleansing, and industrious sublimation; its extrinsic part is preternatural and accidental. Separate, therefore, the clean from the unclean, the substance from the accidents, and make that which is hid, manifest, by the course of nature; otherwise you make no further progress, for this is the foundation of the whole work and of nature.

48. That dry and most precious liquor doth constitute the radical moisture of metals wherefore by some of the ancients it is called Glass; for glass is extracted out of the radical moisture closely inherent in ashes which offer resistance, except to the hottest flame notwithstanding our inmost or central Mercury discovers itself by the most gentle and kindly (though a little more tedious) fire of nature.

49. Some have sought for the latent Philosophical earth by Calcination, others by Sublimation; many among glass, and some few between vitriol and salt, even as among their natural vessels; others enjoin you to sublime it out of lime and glass. But we have learned of the Prophet that "In the beginning God created the Heaven and the Earth, and the Earth was without form and void, and darkness was upon the face of the Deep, and the spirit of God moved upon the Waters, and God said, Let there be Light, and there was Light; and God saw the Light that it was good, and he divided the light from the darkness, etc." Joseph's blessing spoken of by the same Prophet will be sufficient to a wise man. "Blessed of the Lord be his Land, for the Apples of Heaven, for the dew, and for the Deep that liveth Beneath: for the Apples of fruit both of sun and moon, for the top of the ancient mountains, for the Apples of the everlasting hills, etc.," pray the Lord from the bottom of thy heart (my son) that he would bestow upon Thee a portion of this blessed earth.

50. Argent vive is so defiled by original sin, that it floweth with a double infection; the first it hath contracted from the polluted Earth, which hath mixed itself therewith in the generation of Argent vive, and by congelation hath cleaved thereunto; the second borders upon the dropsy and is the corruption of intercutal Water, proceeding from thick and impure water; mixed with the clear, which nature was not able to squeeze out and separate by constriction; but because it is extrinsic; it flies off with a gentle heat. The Mercury's leprosy infesting the body, is not of its root and substance, but accidental, and therefore separable from it; the earthly part is wiped off by a warm wet Bath and the Laver of nature; the watery part is taken away by a dry bath with that gentle fire suitable to generation. And thus by a threefold washing and cleansing the Dragon putteth off his old scales and ugly skin is renewed in beauty.

51. The Philosophical sublimation of Mercury is completed by two processes; namely by removing things superfluous from it, and by introducing things which are wanting. In superfluities are the external accidents, which in the dark sphere of Saturn do make cloudy glittering Jupiter. Separate therefore the leaden color of Saturn which cometh up out of the Water until Jupiter's purple Star smile upon thee. Add hereunto the Sulphur of nature, whose grain and Ferment it hath in itself, so much as sufficeth it; but see that it be sufficient for other things also. Multiply therefore that invisible Sulphur of the Philosophers until the Virgin's s milk come forth: and so the First Gate is opened unto thee.

52. The entrance of the Philosophers' garden is kept by the Hesperian Dragon, which being put aside, a Fountain of the dearest water proceeding from a sevenfold spring floweth forth on every side of the entrance of the garden; wherein make the Dragon drink thrice the magical number of Seven, until having drunk he put off his hideous garments; then may the divine powers of light-bringing Venus and horned Diana, be propitious unto thee.

53. Three kinds of most beautiful flowers are to be sought, and may he found in this Garden of the wise: Damask-color ed Violets, the milk-white Lily, and the purple and immortal flower of love, the Amaranth. Not far from that fountain at the entrance, fresh Violets do first salute thee, which being watered by streams from the great golden river, they put on the most delicate color of the dark Sapphire; then Sol will give thee a sign. Thou shall not sever such precious flowers from their roots until thou make the Stone; for the fresh ones cropped off have more juice and tincture; and then pick them carefully with a gentle and discreet hand; if the Fates frown not, this will easily follow, and one White flower being plucked, the

other Golden one will not be wanting; let the Lily and the Amaranth succeed with still greater care and longer labor.

54. Philosophers have their sea also, wherein small fishes plump and shining with silver scales are generated; which he that shall entangle, and take by a fine and small net shall be accounted a most expert fisherman.

55. The Philosophers' Stone is found in the oldest mountains, and flows from everlasting brooks; those mountains are of silver, and the brooks are even of gold: from thence gold and silver and all the treasures of Kings are produced.

56. Whosoever is minded to obtain the Philosophers' Stone, let him resolve to take a long peregrination, for it is necessary that he go to see both the Indies, that from thence he may bring the most precious gems and the purest gold.

57. Philosophers extract their stone out of seven stones, the two chief whereof are of a diverse nature and efficacy; the one infuseth invisible Sulphur, the other spiritual Mercury; that one induceth heat and dryness, and this one cold and moisture: thus by their help, the strength of the elements is multiplied in the Stone; the former is found in the Eastern coast, the latter in the Western: both of them have the power of color ing and multiplying, and unless the Stone shall take its first Tincture from them it will neither color nor multiply.

58. Recipe then the Winged Virgin very well washed and cleansed, impregnated by the spiritual seed of the first male, and fecundated in the permanent glory of her untouched virginity, she will be

discovered by her cheeks dyed with a blushing color; join her to the second, by whose seed she shall conceive again and shall in time bring forth a reverend off-spring of double sex, from whence an immortal Race of most potent Kings shall gloriously arise.

59. Keep up and couple the Eagle and Lion well cleansed in their transparent cloister, the entry door being shut and watched lest their breath go out, or the air without do privily get in. The Eagle shall snap up and devour the Lion in this combination; afterwards being affected with a long sleep, and a dropsy occasioned by a foul stomach, she shall be changed by a wonderful metamorphosis into a coal black Crow, which shall begin to fly with wings stretched out, and by its flight shall bring down mater from the clouds, until being often moistened, he put off his wings of his own accord, and falling down again he be changed into a most White Swan. Those that are ignorant of the causes of things may wonder with astonishment when they consider that the world is nothing but a continual Metamorphosis; they may marvel that the seeds of things perfectly digested should end in greatest whiteness. Let the Philosopher imitate Nature in his work.

60. Nature proceedeth thus in making and perfecting her works, that from an inchoate generation it may bring a thing by divers means, as it were by degrees, to the ultimate term of perfection: she therefore attaineth her end by little and little, not by leaps; confining and including her work between two extremes; distinct and severed as by spaces. The practice of Philosophy, which is the imitator of Nature, ought not to decline from the way and example of Nature in its working and direction to find out its happy stone, for whatsoever is without the bounds of Nature is either in error or is near one.

61. The extremes of the Stone are natural Argent vive and perfect Elixir: the middle parts which lie between, by help whereof the work goes on, are of three sorts; for they either belong unto matter, or operations, or demonstrative signs: the whole work is perfected by these extremes and means.

62. The material means of the Stone are of divers kinds, for some are extracted out of others successively: The first are Mercury Philosophically sublimated, and perfect metals, which although the be extreme in the work of nature, yet in the Philosophical work they supply the place of means: of the former the seconds are produced; namely the four elements, which again are circulated and fixed: of the seconds, the third is produced, to wit, Sulphur, the multiplication hereof doth terminate the first work: the fourth and last means are leaven or ointments weighed with the mixture of the things aforesaid, successively produced in the work of the Elixir. By the right ordering of the things aforesaid, the perfect Elixir is finished, which is the last term of the whole work, wherein the Philosophers' Stone resteth as in its centre, the multiplication whereof is nothing else than a short repetition of the previous operations.

63. The operative means (which are also called the Keys of the Work) are four: the first is Solution or Liquefaction; the second is Ablution; the third Reduction; the fourth Fixation. By Liquefaction bodies return into their first form, things concocted are made raw again and the combination between the position and negative is effected, from whence the Crow is generated lastly the Stone is divided into four confused elements, which happeneth by the retrogradation of the Luminaries. The Ablution teacheth how to make the Crow white, and to create the Jupiter of Saturn, which is done by the conversion of the Body into Spirit. The Office of Reduction is to restore the soul

to the stone exanimated, and to nourish it with dew and spiritual milk, until it shall attain unto perfect strength. In both these latter operations the Dragon rageth against himself, and by devouring his tail, doth wholly exhaust himself, and at length is turned into the Stone. Lastly, the operation of the Fixation fixeth both the White and the Red Sulphurs upon their fixed body, by the mediation of the spiritual tincture; it decocteth the Leaven or Ferment by degrees ripeneth things unripe, and sweeteneth the bitter. In fine by penetrating and tincturing the flowing Elixir it generateth, perfecteth, and lastly, raiseth it up to the height of sublimity.

64. The Means or demonstrative signs are Color s successively and orderly affecting the matter and its affections and demonstrative passions, whereof there are three special ones (as critical) to be noted; to these some add a Fourth. The first is black, which is called the Crow's head, because of its extreme blackness whose crepusculum Sheweth the beginning of the action of the fire of nature and solution, and the blackest midnight sheweth the perfection of liquefaction, and confusion of the elements. Then the grain putrefies and is corrupted, that it may be the more apt for generation. The white color succeedeth the black wherein is given the perfection of the first degree, and of the White Sulphur. This is called the blessed stone; this Earth is white and foliated, wherein Philosophers do sow their gold. The third is Orange color , which is produced in the passage of the white to the red, as the middle and being mixed of both is as the dawn with his saffron hair, a forerunner of the Sun. The fourth color is Ruddy and Sanguine, which is extracted from the white fire only. Now because whiteness is easily altered by another color before day it quickly faileth of its candor. But the deep redness of the Sun perfecteth the work of Sulphur, which is called the Sperm of the male, the fire of the Stone,

the King's Crown, and the Son of Sol, wherein the first labor of the workman resteth.

65. Besides these decretory signs which firmly inhere in the matter, and shew its essential mutations, almost infinite color s appear, and shew themselves in vapors, as the Rainbow in the clouds, which quickly pass away and are expelled by those that succeed, more affecting the air than the earth: the operator must have a gentle care of them, because they are not permanent, and proceed not from the intrinsic disposition of the matter, but from the fire painting and fashioning everything after its pleasure, or casually by heat in slight moisture.

66. Of the strange colors, some appearing out of time, give an ill omen to the work: such as the blackness renewed; for the Crow's young ones having once left their nest are never to be suffered to return. Too hasty Redness; for this once, and in the end only, gives a certain hope of the harvest; if therefore the matter become red too soon it is an argument of the greatest aridity, not without great danger, which can only be averted by Heaven alone forthwith bestowing a shower upon it.

67. The Stone is exalted by successive digestions, as by degrees, and at length attaineth to perfection. Now four Digestions agreeable to the four abovesaid Operations or Governments do complete the whole work, the author whereof is the fire, which makes the difference between them.

68. The first digestion operateth the solution of the Body, whereby comes the first conjunction of male and female, the commixtion of both seeds, putrefactium, the resolution of the elements into

homogeneous water, the eclipse of the Sun and Moon in the head of the Dragon, and lastly it bringeth back the whole World into its ancient Chaos, and dark abyss. This first digestion is as in the stomach, of a melon color and weak, more fit for corruption than generation.

69. In the second digestion the Spirit of the Lord walketh upon the waters; the light begins to appear, and a separation of waters from the waters occurs; Sol and Luna are renewed; the elements are extracted out of the chaos, that being perfectly mixed in Spirit they may constitute a new world; a new Heaven and new Earth are made; and lastly all bodies become spiritual. The Crow's young ones changing their feathers begin to pass into Doves; the Eagle and Lion embrace one another in an eternal League of amity. And this generation of the World is made by the fiery Spirit descending in the form of Water, and wiping away Original sin; for the Philosophers' Water is Fire, which is moved by the exciting heat of a Bath. But see that the separation of Waters be done in Weight and Measure, lest those things that remain under Heaven be drowned under the Earth, or those things that are snatched up above the Heaven, be too much destitute of aridity. Here let slight moisture leave a barren Soil.

70. The third digestion of the newly generated Earth drinketh up the dewy Milk, and all the spiritual virtues of the quintessence, and fasteneth the quickening Soul to the body by the Spirit's mediation. Then the Earth layeth up a great Treasure in itself, and is made like the coruscating Moon, afterwards like to the ruddy Sun; the former is called the Earth of the Moon, the latter the Earth of the Sun; for both of them are beget of the copulation of them both; neither of them any longer feareth the pains of the Fire, because both want all spots; for they have been often cleanseth from sin by fire, and have

suffered great Martyrdom, until all the Elements are turned downward.

71. The Fourth digestion consummateth all the Mysteries of the World, and the Earth being turned into most excellent leaven, it leaveneth all imperfect bodies because it hath before passed into the heavenly nature of quintessence. The virtue thereof flowing from the Spirit of the Universe is a present Panacea and universal medicine for all the diseases of all creatures. The digestions of the first work being repeated will open to thee the Philosophers secret Furnace. Be right in thy works, that thou mayest find God favourable otherwise the ploughing of the Earth will be in vain; Nor "Will the expected Harvest e'er requite/ The greedy husbandman."

72. The whole Progress of the Philosophers' work is nothing but Solution and Congelation; the Solution of the body, and Congelation of the Spirit; nevertheless there is but one operation of both: the fixed and volatile are perfectly mixed and united in the Spirit! Which cannot be done unless the fixed body be first made soluble and volatile. By reduction is the volatile body fixed into a permanent body, and volatile nature doth at last change into a fixed one, as the fixed nature had before passed into volatile. Now so long as the Natures were confused in the Spirit, that mixed spirit keeps a middle Nature between Body and Spirit, Fixed and Volatile.

73. The generation of the Stone is made after the pattern of the Creation of the World; for it is necessary, that it have its Chaos and First matter, wherein the confused Elements do fluctuate, until they be separated by the fiery Spirit; they being separated, the Light Elements are carried upwards, and the heavy ones downwards: the light arising, darkness retreats: the waters are gathered into one

place and the dry land appears. At length the two great Luminaries arise, and mineral, vegetable and animal are produced in the Philosophers' Earth.

74. God created Adam out of the mud of the Earth, wherein were inherent the virtues of all the Elements, of the Earth and Water especially, which do more constitute the sensible and corporeal heap: Into this Mass God breathed the breath of Life, and enlivened it with the Sun of the Holy Spirit. He gave Eve for a Wife to Adam, and blessing them he gave unto them a Precept and the Faculty of multiplication. The generation of the Philosophers Stone, is not unlike the Creation of Adam, for the Mud was made of a terrestrial and ponderous Body dissolved by Water, which deserved the excellent name of Terra Adamica, wherein all the virtues and qualities of the Elements are placed. At length the heavenly Soul is infused thereinto by the medium of the Quintessence and Solar influx, and by the Benediction and Dew of Heaven; the virtue of multiplying ad infinitum by the intervening copulation of both sexes is given it.

75. The chief secret of this work consisteth in the manner of working, which is wholly employed about the Elements: for the matter of the Stone passeth from one Nature into another, the Elements are successively extracted, and by turns obtain dominion; everything is agitated by the circles of humidum and siccum, until all things be turned downwards, and there rest.

76. In the work of the Stone the other Elements are circulated in the figure of Water, for the Earth is resolved into Water, wherein are the rest of the Elements; the Water is Sublimated into Vapor, Vapor retreats into Water, and so by an unwearied circle, is the Water

moved, until it abide fixed downwards; now that being fixed, all the elements are fixed. Thus into it they are resolved, by it they are extracted, with it they live and die; the Earth is the Tomb, and last end of all.

77. The order of Nature requireth that every generation begin from humidum and in humidum. In the Philosophers' Work, Nature is to be reduced into order, that so the matter of the Stone which is terrestrial, compact and dry, in the first place may be dissolved and flow into the Element of Water next unto it, and then Saturn will be generated of Sol.

78. The Air succeeds the Water, drawn about by seven circles or revolutions, which is wheeled about with so many circles and reductions, until it be fixed downwards, and Saturn being expelled, Jupiter may receive the Sceptre and Government of the Kingdom, by whose coming the Philosophers' Infant is formed, nourished in the womb, and at length is born; resembling the splendor of Luna in her beautiful and Serene countenance.

79. The Fire executes the courses of the Nature of the Elements, extreme Fire assisting it; of the hidden is made the manifest; the Saffron dyeth the Lily; Redness possesseth the cheeks of the blushing Child now made stronger. A Crown is prepared for him against the time of his Reign. This is the consummation of the first work, and the perfect rotation of the Elements the sign whereof is, when they are all terminated in Siccum, and the body void of Spirit lieth down, wanting pulse, and motion; and thus all the Elements are finally resolved into Terra.

80. Fire placed in the Stone is Nature's Prince, Sol's Son and Vicar, moving and digesting matter and perfecting all things therein, if it shall attain its liberty, for it lieth weak under a hard bark; procure therefore its freedom that it may succour thee freely; but beware that thou urge it not above measure, for being impatient of tyranny it may become a fugitive, no hope of return being left unto thee; call it back therefore by courteous words, and keep it prudently.

81. The first mover of nature is External Fire, the Moderator of Internal Fire, and of the whole Work; Let the Philosopher therefore very well understand the government thereof, and observe its degrees and points; for from thence the welfare or ruin of the work dependeth. Thus Art helpeth Nature, and the Philosopher is the Minister of both.

82. By these two Instruments of Art and Nature the Stone lifteth itself up from Earth to Heaven with great ingenuity, and slideth from Heaven to Earth, because the Earth is its Nurse, and being carried in the womb of the wind, it receiveth the force of the Superiors and Inferiors.

83. The Circulation of the Elements is performed by a double Whorl, by the greater or extended and the less or contracted. The Whorl extended fixeth all the Elements of the Earth, and its circle is not finished unless the work of Sulphur be perfected. The revolution of the minor Whorl is terminated by the extraction and preparation of every Element. Now in this Whorl there are three Circles placed, which always and variously move the Matter, by an Erratic and Intricate Motion, and do often (seven times at least) drive about every Element, in order succeeding one another, and so agreeable, that if one shall be wanting the labor of the rest is made void. These

Circulations are Nature's Instruments, whereby the Elements are prepared. Let the Philosopher therefore consider the progress of Nature in the Physical Tract, more fully described for this very end.

84. Every Circle hath its proper Motion, for all the Motions of the Circles are conversant about the subject of Humidum and Siccum, and are so concatenated that they produce the one operation, and one only consent of Nature: two of them are opposite, both in respect of their causes and the effects; for one moveth upwards, drying by heat; another downwards, moistening by cold; a third carrying the form of rest and sleep by digesting, induceth the cessation of both in greatest moderation.

85. Of the three Circles, the first is Evacuation, the labor of which is in extracting the superfluous Humidum and also in separating the pure, clean and subtle, from the gross and terrestrial dregs. Now the greatest danger is found in the motion of this Circle, because it hath to do with things Spiritual and makes Nature plentiful.

86. Two things are chiefly to be taken heed of in moving this Circle; first, that it be not moved too intensely; the other, that it be not moved for too long a time. Motion accelerated raiseth confusion in the matter, so that the gross, impure and undigested part may fly out together with the pure and subtle, and the Body undissolved be mixed with the Spirit, together with that which is dissolved. With this precipitated motion the Heavenly and Terrestrial Natures are confounded, and the Spirit of the Quintessence, corrupted by the admixture of Earth is made dull and invalid. By too long a motion the Earth is too much evacuated of its Spirit, and is made so languishing, dry and destitute of Spirit, that it cannot easily be

restored and recalled to its Temperament. Either error burneth up the Tincture, or turneth it into flight.

87. The Second Circle is Restoration; whose office is to restore strength to the gasping and debilitated body by Potion. The former Circle was the Organ of sweat and labor, but this of restoration and consolation. The action of this is employed in the grinding and mollifying the Earth (Potter-like), that it may be the better mixed.

88. The motion of this Circle must be lighter than that of the former, especially in the beginning of its Revolution, lest the Crow's young ones be drowned in nest by a large flood, and the growing world be drowned by a deluge. This is the Weigher and Assayer of Measures, for it distributeth Water by Geometrical Precepts. There is usually no greater Secret found in the whole practice of the Work than the firm and justly weighed Motion of this Circle; for it informeth the Philosophers' infant and inspireth Soul and Life into him.

89. The Laws of this Circle's motions are, that it run about gently: and by little and little, and sparingly let forth itself, lest that by making haste it fail from its measure, and the Fire inherent be overwhelmed with the Waters, the Architect of the Work grow dull, or also be extinguished: that meat and drink be administered by turns, to the end there may be a better Digestion made, and the best temperament of Humidum, and Siccum; for the indissoluble colligation of them both is the End and Scope of the Work. Furthermore see that you add so much by Watering, as shall be found wanting in assaying, that Restoration may restore so much of the lost strength by corroborating, as Evacuation hath taken away by debilitating.

90. Digestion, the last Circle, acteth with silent and insensible Motion; and therefore it is said by Philosophers, that it is made in a secret furnace; it decocteth the Nutriment received, and converteth it into the Homogeneous parts of the body. Moreover, it is called Putrefaction; because as meat is corrupted in the Stomach before it passeth into Blood and similar parts; so this operation breaketh the Aliment with a concocting and Stomach heat and in a manner makes it to putrefy that it may be the better Fixed, and changed from a Mercurial into a Sulphurous Nature. Again, it is called Inhumation, because by it the Spirit is inhumated, as a dead man buried in the ground. But because it goeth most slowly, it therefore needeth a longer time. The two former Circles do labor especially in dissolving, this in congealing although all of them work in both ways.

91. The Laws of this Circle are, that it be moved by the Feverish and most gentle heat of Dung, lest that the things volatile fly out, and the Spirit be troubled at the time of its strictest Conjunction with the Body, for then the business is perfected in the greatest tranquillity and ease; therefore we must especially beware lest the Earth be moved by any Winds or Showers. Lastly, as this third Circle may always succeed the second straightways and in due order, as the second the first: so by interrupted works and by course those three erratic Circles do complete one entire circulation, which often reiterated doth at length turn all things into Earth, and makes similarity between opposites.

92. Nature useth Fire, so also doth Art after its example, as an Instrument and Mallet in cutting out its works. In both operations therefore Fire is Master and Perfector. Wherefore the knowledge of Fire is most necessary for a Philosopher, without which as another

Ixion (condemned to labor in vain) he shall turn about the Whorl of Nature to no purpose.

93. The name Fire is Equivocal amongst Philosophers; for sometimes it is used by Metonymy for heat; and so there be as many fires as heats. In the Generation of Metals and Vegetables Nature acknowledgeth a Three-fold Fire; to wit, Celestial, Terrestrial and Innate. The First flows from Sol as its Fountain into the Bosom of the Earth; it stirreth up Fumes, or Mercurial and Sulphurous vapors, of which the Metals are created, and mixeth itself amongst them; it stirreth up that torpid fire which is placed in the seeds of Vegetables, and addeth fresh sparks unto it, as a spur to vegetation. The Second lurketh in the bowels of the Earth, by the Impulse and action whereof the Subterraneous vapors are driven upwards as through pores and pipes, and thrusts outwards from the Centre towards the surface of the Earth, both for the composition of Metals, where the Earth swelleth up, as also for the production of Vegetables, by putrefying their seeds, by softening and preparing them for generation. The third Fire, viz., Innate is also indeed Solar; it is generated of a vapid smoke of Metals, and also being infused with the monthly provision grows together with the humid matter, and is retained as in a Prison; or more truly, as form is conjoined with the mixed body; it firmly inhereth in the seeds of Vegetables, until being solicited by the point of its Father's rays it be called out, then Motion intrinsically moveth and informeth the matter, and becomes the Molder and Dispenser of the whole Mixture. In the generation of Animals, Celestial Fire doth insensibly co-operate with the Animal, for it is the first Agent in Nature; for the heat of the female answereth to Terrestrial Fire; when the Seed putrefies, this warmth prepareth it. For truly the Fire is implanted in the Seed; then the Son of Sol disposeth of the matter, and being disposed, he informeth it.

94. Philosophers have observed a three-fold Fire in the matter of their work, Natural, Unnatural, and Contra-Natural. The Natural they call the Fiery Celestial Spirit Innate, kept in the profundity of matter, and most strictly bound unto it, which by the sluggish strength of metal grows dull, until being stirred up and freed by the Philosophers' discretion and external heat, it shall have obtained a faculty of moving its body dissolved, and so it may inform its humid matter, by Un-folding Penetration, Dilatation and Congelation. In every mixed body Natural Fire is the Principle of Heat and Motion. Unnatural Fire they name that which being procured and coming from without is introduced into the matter artificially; that it may increase and multiply the strength of the natural heat. The Fire Contrary to Nature they call that which putrefieth the Compositum, and corrupteth the temperament of Nature. It is imperfect, because being too weak for generation, it is not carried beyond the bounds of corruption: such is the Fire or heat of the menstruum: yet it hath the name improperly of Fire against Nature, because in a manner it is according to Nature, for although it destroys the specific form, and corrupteth the matter, yet it disposeth it for reproduction.

95. It is more credible nevertheless that the corrupting Fire, called Fire against Nature, is not different from the Innate, but the first degree of it, for the order of nature requireth, that Corruption should precede Generation: the fire therefore that is innate, agreeable to the Law of Nature, performeth both, by exciting both successively in the matter: the first of corruption more gentle stirred up by feeble heat to mollify and prepare the body: the other of generation more forcible, moved by a more vehement heat, to animate and fully inform the Elementary body disposed of by the former. A double Motion doth therefore proceed from a double degree of heat of the same fire; neither is it to be accounted a double Fire, for far better may the

name of "Fire contrary to Nature" be given to violent and destructive fire.

96. Unnatural Fire is converted into Natural or Innate Fire by successive degrees of Digestion, and increaseth and multiplieth it. Now the whole secret consisteth in the multiplication of Natural Fire, which of itself is not able to Work above its proper strength, nor communicate a perfect Tincture to imperfect Bodies; for although it be sufficient to itself, yet hath it not any further power; but being multiplied by the unnatural, which most aboundeth with the virtue of multiplying doth act far more powerfully, and reacheth itself beyond the bounds of Nature-color ing strange and imperfect bodies, and perfecting them, because of its plentiful Tincture, and the abstruse Treasure of multiplied Fire.

97. Philosophers call their Water, Fire, because it is most hot, and indued with a Fiery Spirit; again Water is called Fire by them, because it burneth the bodies of perfect Metals more than common fire doth for it perfectly dissolveth them, whereas they resist our Fire, and will not suffer themselves to be dissolved by it; for this cause it is also called Burning Water. Now that Fire of Tincture is hid in the belly of the Water and manifests itself by a double effect, viz., of the body's Solution and Multiplication.

98. Nature useth a double Fire in the Work of generation, Intrinsic and Extrinsic; the former being placed in the seeds and mixtures of things, is hid in their Centre; and as a principle of Motion and Life doth move and quicken the body. But the latter, Extrinsic, whether it be poured down from Heaven or Earth, raiseth the former, as drowned with sleep, and compels it to action; for the vital sparks

implanted in the seeds stand in need of an external motor, that they may be moved and act.

99. It is even so in the Philosophers' work; for the matter of the Stone possesseth his Interior Fire, which is partly Innate, partly also is added by the Philosophers Art, for those are united and come inward together, because they are homogeneous: the internal standeth in need of the external, which the Philosopher administereth according to the Precepts of Art and Nature; this compelleth the former to move. These Fires are as two Wheels, whereof the hidden one being moved by the visible one, it is moved sooner or later; and thus Art helpeth Nature.

100. The Internal Fire is the middle agent between the Motor and the Matter; whence it is, that as it is moved by that, it moveth this; and if so be it shall be driven intensely or remissly, it will work after the same manner in the matter. The Information of the whole Work dependeth of the measure of External Fire.

101. He that is ignorant of the degrees and points of external Fire, let him not start upon the Philosophical Work; for he will never obtain light out of darkness, unless the heats pass through their middle stages, like the Elements, whose Extremes are not converted, but only their Means.

102. Because the whole work consisteth in Separation and perfect Preparation of the Four Elements, therefore so many grades of Fire are necessary there unto; for every Element is extracted by the degree of Fire proper to it.

103. The four grades of Heat are called the heat of the Water Bath, the heat of Ashes, of Coals, and of Flame, which is also called "Optetic:" every grade hath its degrees, two at least, sometimes three; for heat is to be moved slowly and by degrees, whether it be increased or decreased; so that Matter, after Nature's example, may go on by degrees and willingly unto formation and completion; for nothing is so strange to Nature as that which is violent. Let the Philosopher propound for his consideration the gentle access and recess of the Sun, whose Light and Lamp bestoweth its heat to the things of the world, according to the times and Laws of the Universe, and so bestoweth a certain temperament upon them.

104. The first degree of the Bath of Heat is called the heat of a Fever; the second, of Dung. The first degree of the second grade is the simple heat of Ashes, the second is the heat of Sand. Now the degrees of Fire, Coals and Flame want a proper Name, but they are distinguished by the operation of the intellect, according to their intensity.

105. Three Grades only of Fire are sometimes found amongst Philosophers, viz., the Water Bath, of Ashes and of Flame: which latter comprehendeth the Fire of Coals and of Flame: the Heat of Dung is sometimes distinguished from the Heat of the Bath in degree. Thus for the most part Authors do involve the light in darkness, by the various expressions of the Philosophers' Fire; for the knowledge thereof is accounted amongst their chief secrets.

106. In the White Work, because three Elements only are extracted, Three degrees of Fire do suffice; the last, to wit the "Optetic," is reserved for the Fourth Element, which finisheth the Red Work. By the first degree the eclipse of Sol and Luna is made; by the second

the light of Luna begins to be restored; by the third Luna attaineth unto the fulness of her splendor; and by the fourth Sol is exalted into the highest apex of his glory. Now in every part the Fire is administered according to the rules of Geometry; so that the Agent may answer to the disposition of the Patient, and their strength be equally poised betwixt themselves.

107. Philosophers have very much insisted upon secrecy in regard to their Fire; they scarce have been bold to describe it but shew it rather by a description of its qualities and properties, than by its name: as that it is called Airy Fire, Vaporous, Humid and Dry, Clear or Star-like; because it may easily by degrees be increased or remitted as the Artificer pleaseth. He that desireth more of the knowledge of Fire may be satisfied by the Works of Lullius, who hath opened the Secrets of Practice to worthy minds candidly.

108. Of the conflict of the Eagle and the Lion also they write diversely, because the Lion is the strongest animal, and therefore it is necessary that more Eagles act together (three at least, or more, even to ten) to conquer him: the fewer they are, the greater the contention, and the slower the Victory; but the more Eagles, the shorter the Battle, and the plundering of the Lion will more readily follow. The happier number of seven Eagles may be taken out of Lullius, or of nine out of Senior.

109. The Vessel wherein Philosophers decoct their work is twofold; the one of Nature, the other of Art; the Vessel of Nature which is also called the Vessel of Philosophy is the Earth of the Stone, or the Female or Matrix, whereinto the sperm of the Male is received putrefies, and is prepared for generation; the Vessel of Nature is of three sorts, for the secret is decocted in a threefold Vessel.

110. The First Vessel is made of a transparent Stone, or of a stony Glass, the form thereof some Philosophers have hid by a certain Enigmatic description; sometimes affirming that it is compounded of two pieces, to wit, an Alembic and a Bolt-head; sometimes of three at other times of the two former with the addition of a Cover.

111. Many have feigned the multiply of such like Vessels to be necessary to the Philosophical Work, calling them by divers names with a desire of hiding the secret by a diversity of operations; for they called it Dissolvent of solutions; Putrefactory for putrefaction; Distillatory for distillation; Sublimatory for sublimation; Calcinatory for calcination etc.

112. But all deceit being removed we may speak sincerely, one only Vessel of Art sufficeth to terminate the Work of either Sulphur; and another for the Work of the Elixir; for the diversity of digestions requireth not the change of Vessels; yea we must have a care lest the Vessel be changed or opened before the First work be ended.

113. You shall choose a form of glass Vessel round in the bottom (or cucurbit), or at least oval, the neck a hand's breadth long or more, large enough with a straight mouth made like a Pitcher or Jug, continuous and unbroken and equally thick in every part, that it may resist a long, and sometimes an acute Fire The cucurbit is called a Blind-head because its eye is blinded with the Hermetic seal, lest anything from without should enter in, or the Spirit steal out.

114. The second Vessel of Art may be of Wood, of the trunk of an Oak, cut into two hollow Hemispheres, wherein the Philosophers' Egg may be cherished till it be hatched; of which see the Fountain of Trevisan.

115. The third Vessel Practitioners have called their Furnace, which keeps the other Vessels with the matter and the whole work: this also Philosophers have endeavoured to hide amongst their secrets.

116. The Furnace which is the Keeper of Secrets, is called Athanor, from the immortal Fire, which it always preserveth; for although it afford unto the Work continual Fire, yet sometimes unequally, which reason requireth to be administered more or less according to the quantity of matter, and the capacity of the Furnace.

117. The matter of the Furnace is made of Brick, or of daubed Earth, or of Potter's clay well beaten and prepared with horse dung, mixed with hair, so that it may cohere the firmer, and may not be cracked by long heating; let the walls be three or four fingers thick, to the end that the furnace may be the better able to keep in the heat and withstand it.

118. Let the form of the Furnace be round, the inward altitude of two feet or thereabouts, in the midst whereof an Iron or Brazen plate must be set, of a round Figure, about the thickness of a Penknife's back, in a manner possessing the interior latitude of the Furnace, but a little narrower than it, lest it touch the walls; it must lean upon three or four props of Iron fixed to the walls, and let it be full of holes, that the heat may be the more easily carried upwards by them, and between the sides of the Furnace and the Plate. Below the Plate let there be a little door left, and another above in the walls of the Furnace, that by the Lower the Fire may be put in, and by the higher the temperament of the heat may be sensibly perceived; at the opposite part whereof let there be a little window of the Figure of a Rhomboid fortified with glass, that the light over against it may shew the color s to the eye. Upon the middle of the aforesaid plate,

let the Tripod of secrets be placed with a double Vessel. Lastly, let the Furnace be very well covered with a shell or covering agreeable unto it, and take care that the little doors be always closely shut, lest the heat escape.

119. Thus thou hast all things necessary to the First Work, the end whereof is the generation of two sorts of Sulphur; the composition and perfection of both may be thus finished.

The Practice of the Sulphur.

Take a Red Dragon, courageous, warlike, to whom no natural strength is wanting; and afterwards seven or nine noble Eagles (Virgins), whose eyes will not wax dull by the rays of the Sun: cast the Birds with the Beast into a clear Prison and strongly shut them up; under this let a Bath be placed, that they may be incensed to fight by the warmth, in a short time they will enter into a long and harsh contention, until at length about the 45th day or the 50th the Eagles begin to prey upon and tear the beast to pieces, which dying will infect the whole Prison with its black and direful poison, whereby the Eagles being wounded, they will also be constrained to give up the ghost. From the putrefaction of the dead Carcasses a Crow will be generated, which by little and little will put forth its head, and the Heat being somewhat increased it will forthwith stretch forth its wings and begin to fly; but seeking chinks from the Winds and Clouds, it will long hover about; take heed that it find not any chinks. At length being made white by a gentle and long Rain, and with the dew of Heaven it will be changed into a White Swan, but the new born Crow is a sign of the departed Dragon. In making the Crow White, extract the Elements, and distil them according to the order prescribed, until they be fixed in their Earth, and end in Snowlike and most subtle dust, which being finished thou shalt enjoy thy first desire, the White Work.

120. If thou intendest to proceed further to the Red, add the Element of Fire, which is not needed for the White Work: the Vessel therefore being fixed, and the Fire strengthened by little and little through its grades, force the matter until the occult begin to be made manifest, the sign whereof will be the Orange color arising: raise the Fire to the Fourth degree by its degrees, until by the help of Vulcan, purple Roses be generated from the Lily, and lastly the Amaranth dyed with the dark Redness of blood: but thou mayest not cease to bring out Fire by Fire, until thou shalt behold the matter terminated in most Red ashes, imperceptible to the touch. This Red Stone may rear up thy mind to greater things, by the blessing and assistance of the holy Trinity.

121. They that think they have brought their work to an end by perfect Sulphur, not knowing Nature or Art, and to have fulfilled the Precepts of the secret are much deceived, and will try Projection in vain; for the Praxis of the Stone is perfected by a double Work; the First is the creation of the Sulphur; the Second is the making of the Elixir.

122. The aforesaid Philosophers' Sulphur is most subtle Earth, most hot and dry, in the belly whereof the Fire of Nature abundantly multiplied is hidden. Therefore it deserveth the name of the Fire of the Stone, for it hath in itself the virtue of opening and penetrating the bodies of Metals, and of turning them into its own temperament and producing its like, wherefore it is called a Father and Masculine seed.

123. That we may leave nothing untouched, let the Students in Philosophy know that from that first Sulphur, a second is generated which may be multiplied ad infinitum: let the wise man, after he hath got the everlasting mineral of that Heavenly Fire, keep it diligently. Now of what matter Sulphur is generated, of the same it is multiplied, a small portion of the first being added, yet as in the Balance. The rest, a tyro may see in Lullius, it may suffice only to point to this.

124. The Elixir is compounded of a threefold matter, namely, of Metallic Water or Mercury sublimated as before; of Leaven White or Red, according to the intention of the Operator; and of the Second Sulphur, all by Weight.

125. There are Five proper and necessary qualities in the perfect Elixir, that it be fusible, permanent, penetrating, tincturing, and multiplying; it borroweth its tincture and fixation from the Leaven; its penetration from the Sulphur; its fusion from Argent vive, which is the medium of conjoining Tinctures; to wit of the Ferment and Sulphur; and its multiplicative virtue from the Spirit infused into the Quintessence.

126. Two perfect Metals give a perfect Tincture, because they are dyed with the pure Sulphur of Nature, and therefore no Ferment of Metals may be sought except these two bodies; therefore dye thy Elixir White and Red with Luna and Sol; Mercury first of all receives their Tincture, and having received it, doth communicate it to others.

127. In compounding the Elixir take heed you change not or mix any thing with the Ferments, for either Elixir must have its proper Ferment, and desireth its proper Elements; for it is provided by

Nature that the two Luminaries have their different Sulphurs and distinct tinctures.

128. The Second work is concocted as the First, in the same or a like Vessel, the same Furnace, and by the same degrees of fire, but is perfected in a shorter time.

129. There are three humours in the Stone, which are to be extracted successively; namely, Watery, Airy, and Radical; and therefore all the labor and care of the Workman is employed about the humour, neither is any other Element in the Work of the Stone circulated beside the humid one. For it is necessary, in the first place, that the Earth be resolved and melted into humour. Now the Radical humour of all things, accounted Fire, is most tenacious, because it is tied to the Centre of Nature, from which it is not easily separated; extract, therefore, these three humours slowly and successively; dissolving and congealing them by their Whorls, for by the multiplied alternative reiteration of Solution and Congelation the Whorl is extended and the whole work finished.

130. The Elixir's perfection consisteth in the strict Union and indissoluble Matrimony of Siccum and Humidum, so that they may not be separated, but the Siccum may flow with moderate heat into the Humidum, abiding every pressure of Fire. The sign of perfection is that if a very little of it be cast in above the Iron or Brazen Plate while very hot, it flow forthwith without smoke.

Let three weights of Red Earth or of Red Ferment, and a double weight of Water and Air well ground up be mixed together. Let an Amalgama be made like Butter, or Metalline Paste, so that the Earth being mollified maybe insensible to the touch. Add one weight and a half of Fire; let these be transferred to the Vessel and exposed to a Fire of the first degree; most closely sealed; afterwards let the Elements be extracted out of their degrees of Fire in their order, which being turned downwards with a gentle motion they may be fixed in their Earth, so as nothing Volatile may be raised up from thence; the matter at length shall be terminated in a Stone, Illuminated, Red and Diaphanous; a part whereof take at pleasure, and having cast it into a Crucible with a little Fire by drops give it to drink its Red Oil and incerate it, until it be quite melted, and do flow without smoke. Nor mayest thou fear its flight, for the Earth being mollified with the sweetness of the Potion will retain it, having received it, within its bowels: then take the Elixir thus perfected into thine own power and keep it carefully. In God rejoice, and be silent.

132. The order and method of composing and perfecting the white Elixir is the same, so that thou usest the white Elements only in the composition thereof ; but the body of it brought to the term of decoction will end in the plate; white, splendid, and crystal-like, which incerated with its White Oil will be fused. Cast one weight of either Elixir, upon ten times its weight of Argent-vive well washed and thou wilt admire its effect with astonishment.

133. Because in the Elixir the strength of Natural Fire is most abundantly multiplied by the Spirit infused into the Quintessence, and the depraved accidents of bodies, which beset their purity and the true light of Nature with darkness, are taken away by long and manifold sublimations and digestions; therefore Fiery Nature freed from its Fetters and fortified with the aid of Heavenly strength, works most powerfully, being included in this our Fifth Element: let it not therefore be a wonder, if it obtain strength not only to perfect imperfect things, but also to multiply its force and power. Now the

Fountain of Multiplication is in the Prince of the Luminaries, who by the infinite multiplication of his beams begetteth all things in this our Orb, and multiplieth things generated by infusing a multiplicative virtue into the seeds of things

134. The way of multiplying the Elixir is threefold: By the first: Mingle one weight of Red Elixir, with nine times its weight of Red Water, and dissolve it into Water in a Vessel suitable for Solution; the matter being well dissolved and united coagulate it by decoction with a gentle Fire, until it be made strong into a Ruby or Red Lamel, which afterwards incerate with its Red Oil, after the manner prescribed until it melt and flow; so shalt thou have a medicine ten times more powerful than the first. The business is easily finished in a short time.

135. By the Second manner. What Portion thou pleasest of thy Elixir mixed with its Water, the weights being observed; seal it very well in the Vessel of Reduction, dissolve it in a Bath, by inhumation; being dissolved, distil it separating the Elements by their proper degrees of fire, and fixing them downwards, as was done in the first and second work, until it become a Stone; lastly, incerate it and Project it. This is the longer, but yet the richer way, for the virtue of the Elixir is increased even an hundred fold; for by how much the more subtle it is made by reiterated operations, so much more both of superior and inferior strength it retaineth, and more powerfully operateth.

136. Lastly, take one Ounce of the said Elixir multiplied in virtue and project it upon an hundred of purified Mercury, and in a little time the Mercury made hot amongst burning Coals will be converted into pure Elixir; whereof if thou castest every ounce upon another hundred of the like Mercury, Sol will shine most purely to thine

eyes. The multiplication of White Elixir may be made in the same way. Study the virtues of this Medicine to cure all kinds of diseases, and to preserve good health, as also other uses thereof, out of the Writings of Arnold of Villa Nova, Lullius and of other Philosophers.

137. The Significator of the Philosopher will instruct him concerning the Times of the Stone, for the first Work "ad Album" must be terminated in the House of Luna; the Second, in the second House of Mercury. The first Work "ad Rubeum," will end in the Second House of Venus, and the last in the other Regal Throne of Jupiter, from whence our most Potent King shall receive a Crown decked with most precious Rubies: "Thus doth the winding of the circling Year/ Trace its own Foot-steps, and the same appear."

138. A Three-Headed Dragon keepeth this Golden Fleece; the first Head proceedeth from the Waters, the second from the Earth, the third from the Air; it is necessary that these three heads do end in One most Potent, which will devour all the other Dragons; then a way is laid open for thee to the Golden Fleece. Farewell! diligent Reader; in Reading these things invoke the Spirit of Eternal Light ; Speak little, Meditate much, and Judge aright.

The Times of the Stone.

The interpretation of The Philosophers' Significator. To every Planet two Houses were assigned by the Ancients, Sol and Luna excepted; whereof the planet Saturn hath his two houses adjoining. Philosophers in handling their Philosophical work, begin their years in Winter, to wit; the Sun being in Capricorn, which is the former House of Saturn; and so come towards the right hand. In the Second place the other House of Saturn is found in Aquarius, at which time Saturn, i.e., the Blackness of the work of the Magistery begins after the forty-fifth or fiftieth day. Sol coming into Pisces the work is black, blacker than black, and the head of the Crow begins to appear. The third month being ended, and Sol entering into Aries, the sublimation or separation of the Elements begin. Those which follow unto Cancer make the Work White, Cancer addeth the greatest whiteness and splendor, and doth perfectly fill up all the days of the Stone, or white Sulphur, or the Lunar work of Sulphur; Luna sitting and reigning gloriously in her House, In Leo, the Regal Mansion of the Sun, the Solar work begins, which in Libra is terminated into a Ruby Stone or perfect Sulphur. The two signs Scorpio and Sagittarius which remain are required for the completing of the Elixir. And thus the Philosophers' admirable offspring taketh its beginning in the Reign of Saturn, and its end and perfection in the Dominion of Jupiter.

Like nothing that has ever been before!

Covenstead Press, purveyors of fine Esoterica, presents this, the first in the Magician's Library series of book compilations. The works here are presented in their original forms, lovingly reset and reprinted. While some other presses present some of these same works, our editions aren't cheap photocopies but lovingly compiled new editions, their contents chosen by 21st century practitioners of the arts portrayed within.

Look for a new volume, and a new magus, every fall!

Covenstead Press
Buffalo, New York
CovensteadPress.com

Covenstead Press is a publishing co-op focused on the esoteric and the magical. We publish new works, reprints, esoteric journals and much, much more. We do not work with a stable of authors, publishing agents or any of the other tactics of the large New Age presses, and are always open to new submissions. Visit our website for more information today!